European Football in Black and White

European Football in Black and White

Tackling Racism in Football

CHRISTOS KASSIMERIS

LEXINGTON BOOKS

A division of
ROWMAN & LITTLEFIELD PUBLISHERS, INC.
Lanham • Boulder • New York • Toronto • Plymouth, UK

LEXINGTON BOOKS

A division of Rowman & Littlefield Publishers, Inc.
A wholly owned subsidiary of The Rowman & Littlefield Publishing Group, Inc.
4501 Forbes Boulevard, Suite 200
Lanham, MD 20706

Estover Road
Plymouth PL6 7PY
United Kingdom

British Library Cataloguing in Publication Information Available

Library of Congress Cataloging-in-Publication Data

Kassimeris, Christos, 1974–
  European football in black and white : tackling racism in football / Christos Kassimeris.
     p. cm.
  Includes bibliographical references and index.
  ISBN-13: 978-0-7391-1959-4 (cloth : alk. paper)
  ISBN-10: 0-7391-1959-1 (cloth : alk. paper)
  ISBN-13: 978-0-7391-1960-0 (pbk. : alk. paper)
  ISBN-10: 0-7391-1960-5 (pbk. : alk. paper)
  1. Racism in sports—Europe. 2. Mass media and sports—Europe. 3. Soccer—
Europe—Public opinion. 4. Public opinion—Europe. I. Title.
  GV706.32.K37 2007
  796.334'630941—dc22   2007033189

Printed in the United States of America

To Lina

Contents

Acknowledgements

This book is a tiny contribution to the campaign against racism in football. For the support, kindness, and professionalism I would like to thank Delia Fischer (Media Officer Marketing Communication, FIFA); Federico Addiechi (Manager Corporate Social Responsibility Department, FIFA); Jérôme Champagne (Delegate of the President for Special Affairs, FIFA); Rob Faulkner (Head of UEFA Media Services, UEFA); Gasser Patrick (Manager Corporate Social Responsibility, UEFA); Martin Spitzl (Deutscher Fußball-Bund); Barbara Moschini (Press Office, Federazione Italiana Giuoco Calcio); Colleen Macauley (Community Relations Officer, Irish Football Association); Tracey Bates (Customer Relations, English Football Association); Raffaele Poli (Centre International d'Etude du Sport); Carine Bakken (Information Service, Commission for Racial Equality); Mark Etherton (Home Affairs Committee, House of Commons); Hayley Meachin (Communications Manager, Sporting Equals); Kurt Wachter (FARE); Heidi Thaler (FARE); Ashley Green (Progetto Ultrá); Zoobia Aslam (Show Racism the Red Card—Scotland); Amrik Singh (Kick It Out); Gavin Sutherland (Project Worker, Show Racism the Red Card); Gerd Dembowski (Flutlicht); Ruth Johnson (Resources and Information Worker, Football Unites Racism Divides Educational Trust); Rafal Pankowski (Never Again Association); Athos Papachristoforou and Efthymios Agathokleous (Marketing Managers Apollon Football Club); Jad Zoghbi (LICRA Sport). Special thanks to Cyprus College for providing me with the necessary funding to purchase all the books used for the completion of this book. Last, but certainly not least, I wish to thank my wife, Lina, for her endless patience and constant support during the countless hours dedicated to reading and writing about football.

Chapter One

Introduction

Scores of books have been published on football, simply reflecting the game's vast popularity. As it happens, most delve into the past of the game and assess the history of a multitude of clubs, famous football players (and not just for their technical ability), competitions at club and national level, and the premier football governing bodies. Not all publications, however, glorify the beautiful game, taking into account the number of studies that deviate from the more captivating aspects of football to devote themselves to other issues, equally 'colorful,' such as football-related scandals. *Calciopoli*, for example, demonstrated the degree of corruption in Italian football and was allocated a prestigious post in national media, as the 2006 World Cup unfolded in Germany at the same time. Yet other books have the unenviable task of exploring the causes of football's supreme tribulations, namely hooliganism and racism, against all backgrounds and in all forms. Racism in European football commands attention not merely because it discolors the principles and spirit of the popular game; it also challenges the notions of integration and cultural diversity—both central to the proper development of football, community cohesion and, of course, the European Union.

It is somewhat difficult to approach the concept of 'racism,' as well as to produce a concrete definition. There is no doubt that the subject under examination is, indeed, controversial and complex in nature. Anthropologists, political scientists, sociologists and psychologists, have all addressed the issue of racism from different perspectives, thus delivering contrasting conclusions, even though the point of departure of their research is, seemingly, identical. Despite certain difficulties in providing an accurate definition of racism, nevertheless, it is understood that modern-day racism is probably poles apart from the appalling phenomenon that marked European societies until some hundred years ago. In earlier times, racism was largely associated to biological differences, in an unsophisticated manner, such as the color of skin. However, from the hideous period of slavery, through the era of colonialism (Nazism included), to the celebration of the 50th anniversary of the European Union, a variety of perceptions has been attributed to racism. The degradation and anguish of black people due to their perceived inferiority among all human races, until considered human

1

enough to abolish the slave trade, stemmed from the racial superiority of their white 'masters' and, gradually, evolved into ideas linked to intellectual superiority. Despite the fact that no science can nowadays credit these utterly unethical and unsubstantiated views, society seems to maintain them and has even developed novel expressions of racial discrimination pertaining to cultural, economic, political and social divisions. In this respect, a definition of 'racism' today may also encompass impressions of ethnicity, religion and cultural background, particularly, in the post-9/11 period.

Naturally, equality and cultural diversity, as regards integration policies, are central to the aspirations of the European Union, an ardent supporter of supranationalism, since the apparent divisions that have long characterized Europe often demonstrated the denominator of conflicts. The fall of communism in Central and Eastern Europe, however, coupled with the revival of extreme forms of nationalism throughout the continent, have altered the status quo in Europe and could, perhaps, demoralize an already diverse population. The emergence of fascist formations, some organized in political parties that witnessed relative electoral success, certainly constitutes a grave concern to long-established democratic practices in Europe, not to mention the sudden increase in racially aggravated violent incidents. More often than not, the people that usually fall victims to racial discrimination are members of ethnic minority groups. In fact, the European Commission's Directorate—General Employment, Social Affairs and Equal Opportunities, published a report in January 2007, *Discrimination in the European Union*, which revealed that people are far more likely to be discriminated against because of their ethnic origins, as opposed to issues concerning disability, sexual orientation, age, gender or religion.

Religion is yet another factor that accounts for divisions in European societies. Apart from the more traditional religious divisions between Catholicism and Protestantism or the schism that separated the Eastern Orthodox Church from the Roman Catholic Church, the persecution of Jews has surely marked contemporary European history as well. Key to understanding the prevalence of anti-Semitism is the association of Jews to the crucifixion of Jesus Christ, the Son of God. Anti-Semitism, still present today among neo-Nazi groups in particular, currently relishes the company of anti-Islamism or else the end result of Islamophobia. Although anti-Islamism is more often treated as a consequence of atrocities that took place on 11 September, its roots can be traced back to medieval times, when the Moors and the Ottoman Turks threatened Europe by occupying the Iberian and Balkan Peninsulas respectively. The superficial risk to Christianity exempted, Islam is occasionally understood to pose a serious threat to modernization, taking into account the impact of international terrorism. The latter has also deeply affected immigration policies in a number of European countries and the prospects of integration. Yet this is only one dimension of racism and xenophobia in Europe, even though it expands over issues that question the loyalty of people from this background to their host nation and the granting of civil rights.

Today, as Europe is concerned with the rise of extreme-right groups and ethnocentric attitudes, a probable characteristic of the continent's diversity, racism has largely contributed to delinquency in both society and football matches. Football does not generate anti-social behavior, let alone racist sentiments; however, because of the game's popularity, football has often been used as a powerful vehicle to emphasize discrimination within society as a whole. To this end, football stadiums have been converted into political arenas for fans willing to exploit the sport's ability to unite, at least people of one mind, in order to underline social divisions. Racism has become a considerable force that has caused, as occasion served, serious disturbances during football matches across Europe, whereas certain clubs seem to attract an inherently racist support, even though the number of non-white football players has increased dramatically. At this point, it is also important to note that participation from ethnic minority communities remains marginal, despite the appeal of the game the world over. Regrettably, the fact that racist chanting has become almost as widespread as in the 1970s and 1980s, while support for national teams has reached levels of extreme 'patriotism,' possibly accounts for the lack of interest of individuals from minority background. The role of extreme right groups should not be underestimated either, as football grounds provide unique opportunities for the dissemination of racist material, the expression of radical views and the recruitment of new members. All in all, the politicization of football and the footballization of politics are obviously intertwined phenomena, given that the popular game has often been exploited as a substitute for politics whenever necessary to convey powerful messages to society as a whole. In addition, while the European Union strives to overcome national differences, football offers a civilized approach for European nations to settle their differences. As it happens, football stadiums have, indeed, witnessed racist incidents, nevertheless, their very cause lies predominantly in European society. Even so, it is imperative to assess the nature and scope of discrimination in football by focusing exclusively on issues relevant to ethnicity, religion and race. In this respect, this study provides a detailed overview of racism and ethno-national tensions across the European domain in an attempt to illustrate the degree of racial segregation that characterizes the continent.

To this end, chapter 1 produces a brief historical account of the development of football, as well as evidence of earlier versions of 'ball games.' The evolution of football is anything but monotonous, at least, considering the number of countries the popular game achieved in enchanting around the world. Yet this chapter intends to portray football as an immigrant, since the king of sports was not always welcomed with pleasure and warmth, nor was it accessible to all, and present data that both validate the game's rapid expansion and stress its exceptional ability to magnetize people from distinct cultural, economic, political and social backgrounds. Certainly, due reference is also made to the premier football governing bodies, namely the Fédération Internationale de Football Association (FIFA) and the Union of European Football Associations (UEFA), and the early European football competitions at club and national level. Evidently, both FIFA and UEFA were instrumental in supporting and further improving the game.

Chapter 2 demonstrates, at first, the degree of humiliation suffered by football under fascist and communist regimes. The two extremes of the political spectrum manipulated the game of football to safeguard their interests and reinforce a unique sense of collective identity. Sadly, the impact of both fascism and communism on football, particularly the former, has not faded away. Fans inclined to the extreme right continue to dominate the terraces of football stadiums that are home to clubs with a fascist history and a matching political orientation. Furthermore, it appears that nationalism and national identity are intricately related to football in some countries, given the level of politicization that the popular game has had to endure for certain subnational groups to emphasize their distinct background and cultural heritage. In the same context, sectarianism has the capacity to divide football clubs and fans, just as it has separated societies, therefore, attaching a new meaning to discrimination in football. Anti-Semitism, too, has exploited the appeal of the beautiful game, usually targeting football clubs with a seemingly Jewish past. All things considered, extreme forms of nationalism have materialized during football matches, often dictating the composition of a given team or the culture of football fans. Subsequently, the Bosman case and the influx of foreign players in European football leagues only complicated the already awkward relationship between football and nationalism. The ethno-national divisions exemplified, our attention is then directed to the very core of the matter.

The next two chapters concentrate exclusively on racial discrimination in football at all levels and underline the deep-rooted stereotypes that persist in the game. Chapter 3 addresses the issue of racism across Europe and brings to light a number of disturbing incidents that have scarred continental football, not to mention the extent to which they have undermined the integrity of the game. In the final section of the same chapter, the performance of foreign football players is assessed, in an attempt to vindicate their overall contribution to football. The following chapter is devoted on racism in English football, given that England's football governing bodies were, most probably, the first to combat racial discrimination effectively. The apparent lack of participation from ethnic minority communities is discussed at length, together with the profile of English fans and the impact of football-related legislation, as regards the campaign against racism. The section devoted to the number of arrests related to racist incidents during football matches is key to understanding that racism among segments of fans that support certain clubs is, indeed, a recurring phenomenon. Finally, chapter 4 produces an analysis of the role of both the English Football Association and several Premier League clubs, in terms of eliminating racism from football.

Likewise, chapter 5 explores the potential of creating a racism-free environment in football stadiums across Europe, by examining the work of both FIFA and UEFA in connection with racial discrimination in football. Evidently, football's two premier governing bodies have long declared their genuine commitment to eradicating racism and penalizing offenders appropriately, including football clubs and players that fail to conform to the game's spirit. Naturally, the highly praised contribution of relevant anti-racism organizations, such as the Football Against Racism in Europe network, Kick It Out, Progetto Ultrà and Bündnis Aktiver Fussballfans, is central to the subject of examination. These pioneering organizations have already witnessed considerable success, given the effectiveness of their anti-racism campaigns and their educational nature, as they often employ innovative strategies to highlight the problem of racism in football and combat it in effect. Apart from exemplifying the work of anti-racism organizations, this chapter also makes reference to football-related projects that aim at promoting integration and community cohesion through sport.

Finally, chapter 6 highlights the impact of the European Union in addressing effectively the issue of racial discrimination. The subject matter of this chapter would necessitate a series of volumes on European Union and national legislation; however, due to obvious limitations a more conservative approach was adopted. The purpose of this chapter is to produce evidence regarding the presence of political formations inclined to the extreme right and their impact on political discourse. The magnitude of racial discrimination in Europe has already caused much anxiety to European Union circles, particularly to the European Commission, the European Parliament and other agencies, all dedicated to the successful elimination of this extremist phenomenon. In this respect, the assessment of both European Union and national antidiscrimination legislation is imperative. To this end, this chapter explores reports that have been largely commissioned by European Union institutions and relevant bodies, in order to illustrate the endeavors of the European Union in a more comprehensive manner. As one might expect, the final section of this chapter concerns the overall contribution of the European Union in ridding football of racism.

All in all, the present study should appeal to general readers, professionals working in NGOs, predominantly in the football industry, and to academics and students with an interest in social science, humanities and, in particular, courses related to sport and law. While the present study is by no means intended for courses in any case related to English literature, nonetheless, it is necessary to define the two words/colors that set out part of our title. The Oxford English Dictionary dictates that the adjective 'white,' under different conditions, could be ascribed to anyone or anything that is: morally or spiritually pure, innocent, harmless, beneficent, free from malignity or evil intent, propitious, favorable, auspicious, fortunate, happy, precious, beloved and plausible. On the other hand, the adjective 'black' may imply: dirty, foul, deadly, disastrous, sinister, sad, atrocious, iniquitous, horribly wicked, dismal, gloomy, disgrace, censure, threatening, anger, frowning, sorrow and melancholy. Further interpretations of the two adjectives pertain to color of skin and ethnic background. As far as football is concerned, the popular game requires no formal introduction. Yet as a final remark, it is important to note—as the reader has already discovered by now—that 'football' was preferred over 'soccer,' since the former is more widely used in the European version of the game. Quite the opposite, in the United States football is, normally, associated with American Football—you guessed right, it is that *other* game played, predominantly, by hands.

Chapter Two

Football as a migrant

Thousands of followers congregate every weekend consistently and with immense enthusiasm to attend a ritual that fascinates a worldwide audience and yet the venue is no church, mosque, synagogue or any sort of temple, but an ordinary stadium. Perhaps, no faith is as widely recognized as football is, since the popular game enjoys enormous support across all social classes, religious convictions, political beliefs, cultures and nations. Besides, as with conventional religious duties, football too necessitates commitment and sacrifice. In every single football match there will be times when the ball is beyond the reach of any one of the twenty-two players involved, more often than not the end result of a long ball or an awkward kick; nevertheless, there will be at least one footballer striving to claim the ball for his team, even though the player, just like the commentator, the spectators and TV viewers alike, are all aware that the ball will most probably end up outside the football field. In essence, the ball often performs the ungraceful task of an ordinary magnet, though with unrivalled glamour, as it has the capacity to attract the attention of all pertinent actors with excess elegance. Football is a game that requires team spirit and joint effort from all players and, therefore, the successful assimilation of a team's players is exceptionally meaningful, as well as a critical precondition. However, this sense of belonging is not exclusive to footballers. Unlike other aspects of life, where failure may deter one from further pursuing his goals, football-related disappointment never prevents fans from entering their club's football ground to watch the team they support with such fervor score goals. The game of football is spontaneous enough to turn heroes into villains within minutes and so unpredictable that, occasionally, 'David' beats 'Goliath.' Suppose you are a Danish international who has just completed a long, stressful, football season enjoying your well deserved summer holidays at a remote tourist resort, when you receive an unexpected invitation to join your national team with the purpose of representing your country at the European Championship and, beyond any player's wildest imagination, succeed in winning the competition. That was precisely the turn of events, only weeks before the opening game of EURO 1992 kicked off, when Denmark was asked to replace war-torn Yugoslavia. Football's rare simplicity

not only magnetizes players and supporters, it is a universal language that tran-
scends traditional linguistic barriers, thus allowing the sport to thrive in any environment, weather permitting. No wonder why all football aficionados have the
game at heart.

HISTORY OF FOOTBALL

Considering that football is, indeed, the king of sports, it is only natural that
many nations and civilizations contend for the precious crown. Evidence suggests that various forms of 'football' were played around the world thousands of
years ago, long before England invented soccer and succeeded in setting up the
first football association. In the Americas, ball games first appeared among
tribes of the Amazon around 1500 BC. When Europeans discovered the New
World, they stumbled upon an extraordinary sporting culture as *pasuckquakko-
howog* was played in North America, *pilimatun* in Chile and *tchoekah* in Pata-
gonia. However, China claims a longer football tradition considering that ball
games were played during the Neolithic Age using stone balls, followed by *cuju*
during the Han Dynasty. In Europe, the earliest civilizations of the ancient
Greeks and Romans developed *episcyros* and *harpastum* respectively, while
similar games existed in the British Isles as pastime and northern France, where
the Gauls associated sport-like rituals to religious ceremonies dedicated to the
worship of sun. Furthermore, the Celtic people played the game of *cad*, peasants
in France had *soule* and Florence, later on, gave birth to *calcio*.

The appeal to the public of the football-like games that were played at the
British Isles and Ireland during the Middle Ages were, occasionally, so violent
and disruptive that authorities were forced to ban the game frequently between
the fourteenth and seventeenth centuries. Despite the oppression that football
suffered at the hands of the occasional British monarch the game never disappeared. Contemporary football has its origins in nineteenth century England,
where the game was played at public schools, however, the popular ball game
had two versions, as one adaptation of the game allowed handling too, other
than merely kicking a ball around. The term 'football,' in the modern sense,
prevailed when a few students from Cambridge University—graduates of
schools like Eton, Harrow, Winchester and Shrewsbury, where the game was
only played by feet—laid down rules and set up the first ever Football Association in 1863. Hence, football or else soccer—an offshoot of association—was
born, while those that played the game by using their hands too founded in 1871
the Rugby Football Union. Naturally, the first football club, Sheffield, was
founded in England as early as 1857 by a few friends who played eleven-a-side
matches, whereas the English language nearly reached official status, taking into
account that football's terminology contains terms such as 'corner,' 'penalty'
and 'foul,' which are still used the world over.[1] As football marked a new depar-

ture in Britain's popular culture, it was time for the game to take its course, travel to distant places, blend with native customs and, eventually, settle in foreign countries. Football was destined to conquer the world.

FOOTBALL IN EUROPE

As the geographic location of England dictates, the first fortunate, if not privileged, nations to welcome football were European. England's influence was strong in the Netherlands, ever since English textile workers introduced the game to the Dutch, considering that some clubs retain their English names today—Be Quick in Gronigen and Go Ahead in Deventer. It is noteworthy that the names of some clubs, such as Ajax and Hercules, have their origins in classical Greece, founded, as it happens, by students of Greek history. The first Dutch football club, Haarlemse, was founded in 1879 by a Dutchman called Pim Mulier who studied in England, while the Dutch Football Association was formed in 1889. It was Belgium, however, the first continental country that was introduced to football. The game witnessed rapid expansion as it was, principally, played in British schools in Antwerp, Bruges and Brussels from the early 1860s and, later on, promoted further by British students as well as engineering and textile workers. Belgium's first club, Bruges, was founded in 1891 and the national league kicked off in 1896. France's first football club was Le Havre, established by sailors from Britain, as the game was initially introduced to the west coast, due to the proximity to England's shores. The French Football Federation was set up in 1919, though five organizations claimed this role until they were unified. Similar patterns apply in Central Europe as football in Germany was heavily influenced by the local British population and visiting students. Even though football did not resemble Germany's dominant sport, gymnastics, Anglo-American FC was established in 1881 (renamed Hamburg in 1897) and Hertha Berlin in 1892, with the first recorded game between German teams involving the aforementioned clubs in 1896. The German Football Association was established in 1900 and the national league kicked off in 1902. Austria's first two clubs, First Vienna and the Vienna Cricket and Football Club, were founded by local English expatriates, while John Gramlick set up the Challenge Cup—a competition among clubs of the Austro-Hungarian Empire—and Mark Nicholson was deeply involved in setting up the Austrian Football Association. Switzerland's first club was St Gallen, formed in 1879, followed by Grasshoppers Zurich in 1886. Grasshoppers was founded by Englishmen that supported Blackburn Rovers, hence the blue-and-white strips. In Bohemia, today's Czech Republic, Athletic Club King's Vineyard—renamed to Sparta Prague soon after—and Slavia Prague were established in 1892 and 1893 respectively, while a Prague League was set up in 1896. The fact that Bohemia was part of the Austro-Hungarian Empire accounts for its football league being somewhat limited to Prague. In Scandinavia, football first appeared in Denmark in 1876, when Kjobenhavns Boldklub, the continent's first club outside Britain, was founded by Englishmen in Copenhagen, followed by the Danish Football Association in 1889 and the commencement of the league in 1915.

Obviously, Mediterranean countries could not afford to be left behind the kind of 'modernization' that football entailed. In Italy, Genoa Cricket and Football Club became the first football club when it was formed in 1893 by British sailors and tradesmen. James Richardson Spensely is considered as the founder of the club that was made up by English players, as no Italians were allowed before 1897. The Italian Football Association was founded in 1898. During the same year, Athletic Bilbao was the product of cooperation between English and Basques. The impact of the English proved strong once more, as the club played in red-and-white strips after Sunderland. However, Spain's first football club is Recreativo Huelva, an all-Spanish side founded as early as 1889, although the Real Federacion Espanola de Futbol was formed in 1913, under the presidency of King Alfonso XIII. In neighboring Portugal, Lisbon was founded in 1875 by British sailors, while Boavista's Footballers—today known as Boavista—was founded by British entrepreneurs and Portuguese textile workers in 1903. As for Greece, English bankers set up the first club in Athens. The club was initially called Panhellenic, but its name changed to Panathinaikos in 1908. Another football team that shared, to an extent, the history of Grasshoppers Zurich was Orekhovo Sports Club. Orekhovo was founded in 1887 by Clement and Harry Charnock, two English brothers involved in the textile business who also supported Blackburn Rovers. Nowadays, the club is known as Dinamo Moscow, renamed after the Russian Revolution of 1917, and continues to play in Blackburn's blue-and-white colors. However, it appears that football was more widely played in 1890 among Englishmen in St. Petersburg. Sweden and Norway's football were also influenced by the British in the late nineteenth century.

FOOTBALL AROUND THE WORLD

A similar pattern characterized football's induction to Latin American countries. As in Europe, British commerce produced the necessary grounds considering that in Brazil and Chile the game was originally played by British sailors. As a matter of fact, Britain's role was of paramount significance as the clubs that made up the Chilean Football Association, for example, which was formed in 1895, all had British origins. In Argentina, the local British population founded teams that maintain their English names, such as Newell's Old Boys (formed by students of an English teacher), Rosario Central (named after the local train station) and River Plate. Furthermore, English was the main language of the Argentinean Football Association until 1934, when it was replaced by the Spanish language. British railway workers in Uruguay set up Penarol in 1891, whereas their arch rivals, Nacional, were founded in 1899 by local students to honor their Hispanic heritage. Manifestly, the impact Britain had on Latin American football can only be fully appreciated when taking into account the roots of the age-old football rivalry between Argentina and Uruguay. Upon close examination, it seems that the two nations developed a relationship full of antagonism ever since the two national associations were invited to compete on a yearly basis for the Lipton Cup, which was named after and sponsored by a Scottish tea magnate named Sir Thomas Lipton. Elsewhere around the world, Canadians were introduced to football by Scottish immigrants soon after the game was codified. The Canadians soon endorsed the game and when a select team of top Canadian footballers toured Britain in 1888, they drew 1–1 with Glasgow Rangers and managed to win a good number of matches against decent British opposition. Nevertheless, Canadian sport's culture was dominated by U.S. sports such as ice hockey. Later on, football reached the shores of Africa, through European colonists during the 1920s and 1930s, where the game witnessed extreme popularity among the indigenous peoples. Apparently, football meant so much to the Africans that the attempts of the Europeans to take administrative control of the game were strongly resisted. In South Africa, however, the whites took control as soon as apartheid was brought about. Unlike Africa, football in Australia, initially, met the resistance of local games like Aussie Rules; however, the game was revived when immigrants from Europe arrived before the outbreak of the Second World War and, particularly, after the end of it.

FOOTBALL RIVALRIES

Beyond any shadow of doubt, Britain deserves much credit for developing and organizing a game that the whole world received with considerable gusto. Whether it was tradesmen or students, sailors or immigrants, there was always something British to accompany the game as it embarked on its long journey around the world. Upon reaching its destination, different people from all sorts of backgrounds soon learned to love the game and chose to support a club for a multitude of reasons. Roma, for example, represent the capital, while their arch-rivals and neighboring Lazio attract support from the nearby rural area. Genoa and Inter Milan represent urban areas, whereas their local rivals, Sampdoria and AC Milan respectively, stand for the industrial regions. Right-wing oriented clubs like Sevilla and Hamburg SV are strongly opposed by left-wing Real Betis and St Pauli. Regional rivalries come to life during matches between Newcastle United and Sunderland, Brescia vs. Verona, Benfica vs. Porto and Feyernoord vs. Ajax. Longstanding social inequalities, or else the struggle involving the poor and the rich, are embodied during matches between Flamengo and Fluminense or Cruzeiro and Atletico Mineiro in Brazil, Cerro Porteno and Olimpia in Paraguay, Gimnasia y Esgrima and Estudiantes, Colon vs. Union and

Rosario Central vs. Newell's Old Boys in Argentina. Israel's football league is divided between leftist Hapoel and nationalist Maccabi teams. In Turkey, Galatasaray represent the upper class, Fenerbahce the middle class and Besiktas the lower class, whereas, in Greece, AEK Athens are perceived as a leftist club, Panathinaikos are known as the Generals' team and Olympiakos Piraeus represent the working class. From a different perspective, Schalke 04, Fiorentina, Auxerre and Tottenham Hotspur may be popular teams; however, they usually strive to match the financial might and overall success of Bayern Munich, AC Milan, Paris Saint-Germain and Arsenal. Likewise, clubs such as Torino, Manchester City, and 1860 Munich enjoy sizeable local support, unlike their rivals Juventus, Manchester United and Bayern Munich, clubs of gigantic proportions that attract less local support but have a more broad appeal on national and international level.

Nationalism, too, is often reflected during football games as in the matches of Barcelona or Athletic Bilbao against Real Madrid and the North vs. South rivalry in Italy. Certainly, there are also the more 'traditional' football rivalries between rival nations such as England and Scotland, Holland and Germany, Greece and Turkey, Bulgaria and Romania, Argentina and either Brazil or Uruguay (the choice is yours) or the United States and almost every single Latin American country. Israel's case is also quite revealing, as its national team and clubs take part in European competitions to avoid tension with local Arab nations. More profoundly, a football match between Dinamo Zagreb from Croatia and the Serbian Red Star Belgrade seems to have triggered the war in former Yugoslavia, similar to the small-scale war between El Salvador and Honduras. Last, but certainly not least, religion too has the potential to deeply affect football in divided societies such as Scotland, Northern Ireland, Belgium (between Protestants and Catholics), the Middle East (between Jews and Arabs) and the Asian subcontinent (among Hindus, Muslims and Christians).

All in all, football matches between either national sides or clubs from different regions and countries offer nothing less than the festive, peaceful, atmosphere that the games promises to deliver to its dedicated fans, even though supporters may sometimes prove bad tempered. For the record, the first official international match took place in 1904 between France and Belgium. When England faced Scotland in Glasgow on 30 November 1872, the English Football Association had no other association to play against. On that occasion, Scotland was represented by its oldest club, Queen's Park, as the Scottish Football Association was founded in 1873, thus we may dismiss that fixture as the first ever international match. It was, however, the first time that foreign sides met on a football pitch.

FÉDÉRATION INTERNATIONALE DE FOOTBALL ASSOCIATION

All things considered, the successful migration of football and its swift development deemed necessary that football be organized at an international level in order to facilitate the proper regulation and administration of the game. The *Fédération Internationale de Football Association* (FIFA) was founded on 21 May 1904 by Belgium, Denmark, France, the Netherlands, Spain, Sweden and Switzerland. The English Football Association joined the year after, together with Austria, Germany, Hungary and Italy, followed later on by the first non-European nations. Argentina and Chile joined in 1912, South Africa in 1910 and the United States in 1913. Given that not all European countries had a national football association in place when FIFA was established Real Madrid represented Spain, whereas in 1905 Slavia Prague joined FIFA representing Czechoslovakia. As a newly-established organization, FIFA came across all sorts of difficulties such as the issue of professionalism, as well as the organization's own ambition to inaugurate an international tournament—the World Cup.

Nonetheless, the degree of controversy that surrounded the term 'country' marked FIFA's early years and affected severely the prospects for membership of a number of candidate associations. More precisely, problems arose when Bohemia applied for membership with FIFA, but was rejected by the Austrian Football Association as Bohemia was perceived as part of Austria's territory, while Ireland, Scotland and Wales also met the strong opposition of Austria and Germany when the former expressed the desire to join FIFA. In that case, the Austrian and German Football Associations considered the United Kingdom—of which the three British nations were part—as a single football entity that was adequately represented by the English Football Association. In fact, Austria and Germany stressed that should Ireland, Scotland and Wales join FIFA, so would the thirty-eight provinces that comprised the two Central European countries. Eventually, the three British nations joined in 1912, after FIFA underlined the long existence of the Irish, Scottish and Welsh Football Associations. Britain's rivalry with Germany resumed following the end of the First World War, when the British nations took the decision to leave FIFA altogether in 1920 since their request to expel Germany from the organization for having initiated WWI was not satisfied, but rejoined football's international governing body in 1923. Evidently, FIFA desperately sought to become detached from political issues and inter-state disputes, however, it seems that national interests dominated the organization's relations with the national football associations. Hence the decision to move from Paris to Zurich in 1932, as Switzerland was a neutral country that clearly better reflected FIFA's ideals and values.

The game of football was in a precarious condition during the war as national league competitions were virtually abandoned, but the Europeans' need to distance themselves from the misery caused by the war gave football the opportunity to excel as it suddenly became an ideal pastime. What's more, when workers in some European countries won the eight-hour workday in 1919, attendance at matches increased rapidly, often reaching more than fifty thousand, while the number of clubs and players also grew dramatically. Actually, the popularity of football increased further following the end of the Second World

War and, as soon as peace and stability were restored, the Europeans had to ready themselves for the greatest spectacle ever.

FOOTBALL COMPETITIONS

Despite the kind of football rivalries that reflect social, political, economic, nationalistic and religious divisions, the sheer competitive nature of the game itself suggested that true sporting rivalries would emanate from a competition where only one club could prevail as the dominant side. In Europe, the first continental competition was the European Cup. As the year 1954 drew to its close, Gabriel Hanot, a journalist for L'Equipe, proposed the setting up of a competition where the champions of European countries could take part in a pan-European league. True to their character, the majority of Europe's top clubs openly declared their enthusiasm over the prospect of contesting for the ultimate prize and supported the idea of a competition, but thought that a league would require a lot of fixtures and was thus considered a strenuous task. Instead, they favored a cup competition. Given the clubs' eagerness, L'Equipe invited, in January 1955, eighteen clubs to enter the first competition. However, not all contestants were champions, as some clubs were preferred over the actual winners of their domestic league because of their massive appeal to fans, though from the next competition onwards only the legitimate champions would contest for the title.

Although the degree of success of this novel competition was intrinsically linked to match attendance, the clubs' performance and attractiveness overall, there was one significant ingredient that was missing from the recipe. It was imperative that an independent body be in charge for the organization of the competition, mediation between clubs and the implementation of all appropriate policies and regulations. That organization was the Union of European Football Associations (UEFA) which, although established a year earlier, had a rather ambiguous role in European football. Clearly, the European Cup gave a fresh impetus to UEFA. Just as the European Cup soon became Europe's leading football competition, UEFA would gain unparalleled prestige in continental football. It is noteworthy that, following FIFA's rationale, UEFA, too, moved their headquarters from France to Switzerland in 1960. In the context of the Cold War, Switzerland's geographic location, ideological neutrality, political stability and economic prosperity made the Central European country all the more appealing. Switzerland, in other words, offered the ideal environment for UEFA to maintain their impartiality between the two halves of Europe.

Anyway, during the same year that the European Cup took shape, the Inter-Cities Fair Cup was established. It was renamed the UEFA Cup in 1971 and was, at first, open to clubs coming from cities that had hosted trade fairs. The success of these two competitions, in particular the European Cup, prompted

UEFA to set up a third competition. The European Cup-Winners' Cup commenced in 1960 and was open to clubs that had won their domestic cup competition. As it happens, the European Cup-Winners' Cup was yet another football competition that witnessed considerable success. The impact of all three competitions and their contribution to European football was fundamental, when taking into consideration the fact that they enabled UEFA to promote further interaction among Europe's premier football clubs and, of course, greater mobility throughout the continent. In the meantime, the secretary of the French Football Federation, Henri Delaunay, proposed in the mid-1950s the founding of a competition that would encompass, in a sense, all regional tournaments such as the British Home Championship, the Mitropa Cup and the Nordic Cup, where the various European football associations would field their national sides to play one another. The competition, in its early stages, included home and away matches, whereas the semi-finals and final took place in one single country. Of the thirty-three European national football associations, only seventeen countries entered a competition that was called the European Nations Cup, since the British nations, Italy, Sweden and West Germany, among others, decided to abstain due to the perceived purposelessness of a continental tournament.

As a result, for the European Nations Cup, today's European Championship, to become the continent's premier football competition, a preliminary round was necessary in order to reduce the number of contending nations to sixteen. Therefore, on 5 April 1958, Czechoslovakia beat the Republic of Ireland and paved the way to the first ever pan-European tournament. At times, the European Championship has caused great excitement, since the so-called 'underdogs' have managed to disturb the waters by winning the competition more than once, as in the case of Denmark and, more recently, Greece. In fact, the participation of Greece during the European Championship of 2004 in Portugal and, ultimately, her amazing triumph inspired two researchers from the Football Governance Research Centre to produce a paper on the performance of the winning team. In their concluding remarks, they argued that "Greece's success came down to tactics, confirming the importance of good management combined with team morale and cohesion."[2] While 'good management' is a crucial component of every successful project, 'team morale and cohesion' emphasize football's spirit. In this respect, it is the good qualities of football that are called into question, given that the beautiful game today needs to rid itself of an ever-present plague that answers to the name of racial discrimination.

CONCLUSION

There is no doubt that the game of football deservedly became the world's most celebrated sport. From the ancient times and the early civilizations of Asia,

Europe and South America, through the stagnation of the Middle Ages, to the more advanced society of contemporary England, football games never failed to stir up unique emotions and fill people with enthusiasm. Most certainly, the success of football's long-lasting journey around the world may well be ascribed to the spherical shape of the ball that utilized the human body's flexibility well, enough to allow greater movement and spectacular actions. Consequently, once football was properly redeveloped, Britain introduced the game—perhaps from a sense of duty—to a whole host of nations worldwide, just like all goods that freely circulated within her vast Empire, thus assigning football cosmopolitan overtones.

The multicultural background of football is certainly much related to the fact that mobility, at the time, was not as disturbing an issue as migration seems today. Immigrants arriving on board of trains and ships were a usual phenomenon, during a period when labor was much needed, and coupled with the expansion of trade and the need to maintain links with foreign markets the game's journey around the world was definitely made much easier. This brief historical account certainly fails to describe the magnitude of the game. In fact, the history of football warrants a book, at least, of the size and length of Goldblatt's *The Ball is Round, A Global History of Football*, nevertheless, it is important to note, again, that football was introduced by foreigners to their host countries. The very same foreigners that taught natives how to play the game by setting up football teams and leagues, found themselves before long excluded from clubs, banned from the game and subjected to horrific abuse.

As soon as football was taught to all those that ignored the virtues of the game, the next logical step was to form unofficial teams that were transformed into proper football clubs and, then, set up the relevant national associations in a timely fashion. When FIFA was established, all national football associations rushed to join the game's international governing body, probably, in an attempt to receive recognition, as well as to lend their much needed support to an organization that was in its infancy. Football spread quickly and came into being in substantial, if not majestic, proportions, particularly in Europe. Even during war times, football never ceased to console the tormented Europeans, considering that the game was even played at the Front among soldiers. Inevitably, the three leading club competitions, at European level, and the European Championship that sprang in the mid-1950s and early 1960s witnessed enormous success.

Actually, football showed incredible resolve throughout the Great War, yet peace and stability in Europe was a fanciful dream, since the popular game still had to endure ruthless fascist regimes in Germany, Italy and Spain, the Second World War and, eventually, the ideological division of the continent during the Cold War era. These issues are discussed at length in the following chapter, since extreme forms of nationalism are often the cause of racism and, therefore, central to our examination.

Notes

1. Richard Giulianotti, *Football: A Sociology of the Global Game* (Polity Press, 1999), 9.

2. Fiona Carmichael and Dennis Thomas, "Does the Best Team Win? An Analysis of Team Performances at EURO 2004," Research Paper No. 2, Football Governance Research Centre, Birkbeck, University of London (2005).

Chapter Three

Nation-building and football

Sport has the capacity to reinforce national identity and football, in particular, "has provided the most important setting within popular culture in which symbols and discourses of national identity may be displayed and mediated through mass communication."[1] The history of football dictates that when Britain introduced the game to mainland Europe, the process of nation-building was already on course throughout the continent and, as games between national teams were dominated by national anthems and flags, football helped produce a distinct sense of national identity and solidarity. During the first half of the 20th century, football parted with entertainment, suppressed the invariability of conventional emblems and promoted an assumed identity. For example, the majority of Europe's national football associations decided almost chauvinistically to translate 'football' into their language after the Great War, France and Russia exempted, opting for either a phonetic translation as in Spain (*Fútbol*) and Portugal (*Futebol*) or a literal translation as in Germany (*Fußball*), Croatia (*Nogomet*), Hungary (*Labdarugas*) and Greece (*ποδόσφαιρο*). In addition, the fascist regimes of Germany, Italy and Spain in West Europe and the more concentrated approach of the communist countries in East Europe, transformed football into a propaganda symbol and adapted the popular game to the party machine with the intention to propel extreme forms of nationalism. Reinforcing national sentiments, however, was certainly not football's only virtue. Football also emphasized the essence of communities, provincialism too, as clubs often represented a particular urban or rural area, a distinct section of the population and even the much narrower dimension of a city or, at least, part of it.

FASCIST LEADERS PLAYING FOOTBALL

Italy
There is no doubt that both Catholicism and socialism failed to exploit the game's appeal in Italy.[2] Nationalism, on the other hand, was far more successful.

When Italy played her first international football match against France in May 1910, the players took to the field in white, merely, because of how costly colored outfits were. However, ever since January 1911 the team's appearance changed to blue, *azzurro* in Italian, in honor of Italy's royal family. Previously, in yet another attempt to reinforce national identity, the Italian authorities decided in 1908 to ban football clubs that included foreigners in their rosters from playing in the national league and 'relegated' them, instead, to a competition exclusively designed for all such clubs. The decision was overturned the year after, since Italy's leading football teams decided to abstain. Nationalism, nevertheless, remained strong and, having realized football's potential, the Italian's changed the name of the popular game to the more Florentine *calcio* and that of the *Federazione Italiana Football* to *Federazione Italiana del Giuoco del Calcio* (FIGC) in 1909. The process of football's Italianization was completed when Benito Mussolini's regime forced clubs to modify, in a sense, their original names. Hence, AC Milan became Milano and Internazionale, also known as Inter Milan, was renamed Ambrosiana, after the patron Saint of Milan, as its initial name was, apparently, related to the communist '*Internationale*.' In fact, when some players of AC Milan opposed the heavy concentration of Italian players in the team, they left the club and formed Internazionale, a club that had a cosmopolitan mentality and was, therefore, far more open to foreigners.

Once the regime brought football under its control, it succeeded in further strengthening its grip when the Viareggio Charter of 1926 came into effect. The Charter dictated the game's new regulations, which endorsed professionalism, banned foreigners, again, and set up national leagues—the Serie A and Serie B—that commenced in the 1929–1930 season. By 1928, only a year before the newly-established national leagues came into being, football was limited to Italian nationals, since foreign players were considered untalented and lacking the necessary qualities. Later on, as in Nazi Germany and occupied Austria, Jews were banned in 1938 from football in Italy, including a successful Hungarian Jew coach named Arpad Weisz. Obviously, the regime sacrificed nationalism in the name of racism, given the overtones of xenophobia that often characterized it, keeping in mind that the only 'foreigners' that were allowed in the game happened to be offspring of first-generation expatriot Italians from Latin America, usually Argentina and Uruguay. Mauro Camoranesi, who currently plays his football for Juventus, was the sixteenth player of Italian and Argentine origin that was called up to represent Italy, standing thirty-fifth on the list of 'foreigners' of Italian descent that played for the country in the past. The epitome of Italy's xenophobic attitude, nonetheless, is more accurately described in the regime's decision to translate all football terminology from English to Italian.

Considering that Mussolini's apparatus intended to strengthen the Italians' national identity, local rivalries among football clubs were strongly dissuaded and impressive stadiums were built, fit for the regime's propaganda machine, such as those in Bologna, Florence, Turin and Rome. It is important to note that the Stadio Mussolini, in Turin, was built in 1931 within six months, whereas the Littorialle, in Bologna, truly was a remarkable piece of architecture, taking into account its enormous size, the extraordinary Marathon Tower and the beautifully crafted statue of Mussolini on horseback. Of course, these magnificent stadiums deserved highly competitive teams, capable of winning trophies and spreading the message of fascism across the nation. Bologna, for example, was financed by the local authorities and, indeed, became quite successful at both national and European level, given the triumphs in the *Coppa d'Europa* in 1932 and 1934, before claiming the Paris Exhibition tournament trophy in 1937, with the regime relishing the club's achievements, popularity and fame. Bologna was, undisputedly, the regime's most suitable ambassador in Europe. In the domestic scene, Bologna won five domestic titles between 1929 and 1941, the same period when Leandro Arpinati, a Bologna-based Fascist, headed the FIGC. The Giovanni Berta stadium in Florence, named after a navy officer who fought during the Adriatic campaign and was made a martyr following his death at the hands of communists, served the regime's propaganda as AC Fiorentina was yet another club that had strong links with the local fascist authorities. Palestra Gimnastica Libertas and Club Sportivo di Firenze were fierce rivals that dominated the local sport culture of Florence, until the promotion of the former to the top division when the two merged to create AC Fiorentina. Roma, created in 1926 by a local fascist named Italo Foschi, shares a similar history as three Rome clubs (L'Alba, La Fortitudo and La Roman) were fused into one, whereas Lazio decided against the merger. For the record, even though Mussolini was considered a fan of Lazio, it is not certain whether the political orientation of Lazio's fans today is anyway related. As it happens, Lazio's fascist elements occupy a section of the ground that is called 'black curve,' *curva in nero,* a color that goes well with the dark face of fascism.

The regime's contribution to the popular game was further celebrated as footballers were asked to give the Roman Salute—clearly a fascist gesture— before football games kicked off, whereas a small fascist symbol also appeared on Italy's national team shirts. Within a few years, the regime was rewarded for its drastic intervention in football, as Italy's clubs and national team dominated Europe. Italy won the 1934 World Cup at home, the 1936 Olympic football tournament in Berlin and the 1938 World Cup in France. It is noteworthy that the campaign concerning the promotion of the 1934 World Cup in Italy included posters that featured Hercules with a foot on a ball and his right arm outstretched in the fashion of a fascist salute. With no doubt, the 1934 World Cup provided Italy's regime with an excellent opportunity to demonstrate the merits of fascism. While Mussolini's attitude during the first ever international football competition was more than just imposing, but still decent, as UEFA's archive indicates that "The Italian dictator's passion for football may have had something to do with a number of questionable refereeing decisions which seemed to go in the home side's favour,"[3] Italy's powerful leader exceeded expectations on the eve of the 1938 World Cup final, when he sent a telegram to the national team that read 'Win or die.'[4] Mussolini was even more successful in projecting Italy's ambition for territorial expansion and regional domination through football, given that her national team often played in international friendly matches against Central European nations, states of the former German and Austro-Hungarian Empires, since that area was central to the geopolitical interests of Fascist Italy.

Spain

Francisco Franco's Spain had striking similarities with Mussolini's Italy, particularly, considering what football had to endure in order to satisfy the dictator's ambitions. Just as Barcelona and Athletic Bilbao were synonymous to separatism during the civil war, Espanyol and Osasuna represented centralization. The degree of militarization of the Spanish society deeply characterized Spain's football given that Atlético de Madrid became known as Atlético Aviación, while the Spanish Football Federation was regulated by military personnel and football players were required to give the fascist salute before kickoff, sing the *Cara dell Sol*, a fascist anthem, and chant '*Arriba España! Viva Franco*.' By 1941 the names of all football clubs were Hispanicized after a directive of the Home Office Department for Press and Propaganda (*Delegacion Nacional de Prensa y Propaganda*) was put into effect and, thus, Football Club Barcelona became Club de Futbol de Barcelona, Athletic Bilbao changed to Atletico Bilbao and Sporting Gijon was renamed to Deportivo Gijon. Still, people in Catalonia and the Basque country resisted Franco's oppression by refusing to give the fascist salute, singing their own anthems and waving their flags. In 1943 the national association did not even hesitate to change the name of the domestic cup competition from *Copa del Rey*, the King's Cup, to *Generalisimo's Cup*, to emphasize Franco's prominence.

Given Spain's relative domestic instability and isolation, Franco intended to promote his own sense of Spanish identity and distract the public's attention by bombarding his people with extensive coverage of football matches. His idea proved disastrous because all he achieved was to put great emphasis on Spain's regional rivalries, although the team selected to propel the nation's identity was unusually successful. Just as the Spanish cup changed its naming to reflect the country's new political reality and abandoned its royal connotations to serve the military's cause, the club that King Alfonso III himself had baptized by awarding them the title 'Royal,' *Real* in Spanish, became Franco's favored football team. The president of Real Madrid, Santiago Bernabeu, maintained good relations with Franco's regime, even though the club was inclined to the Republicans before the Spanish civil war. When Bernabeu became president, his predecessor, Rafael Sanchez Guerra, was exiled and Vice President Gonzalo Aguirre and Treasurer Valero Rivera were both murdered. Franco and Bernabeu's ambitions almost coincided as both aimed at centralizing power in Madrid, in political and football terms respectively. Hence, Real Madrid's success during the second half of the 1950s elevated the club to ambassador-like status and their triumphs became the regime's ultimate message to its people and the rest of the world. Real Madrid was Spain's symbol for nationalism and, more accurately, centralized power, still in use today when either Barcelona or Real Sociedad play host to the club from the capital.

Key to the victorious campaign of Real Madrid, at home and abroad, was an Argentine player who earned his fame for his extraordinary style on the pitch. Alfredo Di Stefano's incredible performance was, admittedly, instrumental to Real Madrid's triumphs. However, his transfer to the Bernabeu was surrounded by much controversy, taking into consideration the fact that the first Spanish club to set their sight on Di Stefano was Barcelona. The Catalans were almost certain they had secured his signature, until Real Madrid realized the player's potential and decided to become involved. As neither of the two clubs was willing to give up on the player, Spain's football governing body proposed a bizarre settlement to a problem that clearly defied solution. Oddly enough, Di Stefano would offer his services to both clubs by spending every other season playing for them over a period of four years. Eventually, Barcelona felt dishonored and conceded an own goal by allowing the charismatic football player to move to Real Madrid. Di Stefano's affair certainly highlighted the degree of competition between the two clubs, taking into account that the transfer of football players was not as commonplace a practice as nowadays.

Much unlike Benito Mussolini, the Spanish dictator failed dreadfully to make good use of football's potential to attract huge crowds, as the sport was fairly unsuccessful during Franco's years, with the notable exception of Real Madrid. Even though the General's regime witnessed the construction of two of the world's better known stadiums by any standards, namely, Barcelona's Nou Camp and the Santiago Bernabeu of Real Madrid, both renowned for their enormous size, regional divisions never produced the necessary grounds to solidify the Spaniards' national identity *en masse*. To the game's misfortune, the stadium of Real Betis was transformed to a parking space for military vehicles, whereas Sevilla's facilities served the cause of Franco's local administration. On the whole, the regime's oppressive measures, intended to thwart all separatist aspirations, obviously proved futile, given Franco's ethnocentric, Castilian rather, approach to the issue of national identity. Most certainly, Franco's failure to promote a Spanish identity materialized in the 1960s and 1970s when the colors of Athletic Bilbao and Real Sociedad were substituted by the red-green-and-white of the Basque flag, *ikurrina*, and the language of the Basques, *Euskera*, was spoken widely in their stadiums. In Catalonia, Barcelona's football ground was one of the few public places available where the Catalan language, long banned by Franco's faithful, was used more freely, while the red-and-blue colors of Barcelona stood for the red-and-yellow of Catalonia's flag. The near historical decision of Barcelona to illustrate Catalonia's colors and the cross of its patron, *St Jordi*, on the club's badge is anything but a coincidence. On the contrary, it was a clear statement of Barcelona's 'national' identity and commitment to the struggle against the establishment. Barcelona, eventually, changed their name back to the Catalan version in the 1974–1975 season, just before Franco's death in November 1975. To demonstrate Barcelona's resilience to Franco's regime, Manuel Vazquez Montalban published a novel, *Offside*, which described the club as 'the epic weapon of a country without a state . . . El Barca's victories were like those of Athens over Sparta.'[5] In the same way as Athenian democracy confronted Sparta's military machine, the election of Barcelona's presidents was a clear statement of resistance towards an oppressive regime.

Portugal — Greece
The association of the popular game with European, Mediterranean more accurately, dictatorial regimes is not exclusive to Italy and Spain. Southern Europe witnessed the rise and fall of the Portuguese and Greek dictatorships, with both having played some part in the development of football and, most importantly, the exploitation of the game's appeal to maintain their stay in power. In the case of Portugal, relative success in the 1966 World Cup, when the Iberian nation made its first appearance, finishing third after losing only to England in the semi-finals, prolonged Salazar's regime for a few years. The Portuguese regime seemed to favor Benfica in the domestic scene and its contribution to football included the construction of Estadio da Luz in Lisbon. Much later, while dictatorial regimes continued to rule Spain and Portugal, another club that was sponsored by an equally ruthless regime took European football by surprise. The Greek side Panathinaikos achieved in reaching the 1971 final of the European Cup, Europe's prestigious football competition, during the Greek dictatorship. Amidst allegations of match fixing, the club was coached by the legendary Ferenc Puskas, frankly a coach too good for the standards of Greek football at the time, and triumphed over Everton and Red Star on their way to Wembley Stadium.

Germany — Austria
Football was introduced to Germany at the end of the 19th century as a native game that the indigenous population of the region played during the Middle Ages, since her modern inhabitants simply disapproved anything that England stood for. A few decades later, German nationalization was brought back to life, this time as the principal feature of the Nazi party's policies. As Nazism revived the ethnocentric aspirations of the German people, a reinforced sense of national identity was deemed necessary. The utterly unethical decision to ban Jews from the public sphere, including sports, demonstrated the Nazis' determination to cleanse the nation and restore its prestige. When the education minister, Bern-

hard Rust, ordered their expulsion on 2 June 1933, the new leadership sought to place the Jewish population on the fringe of society—just like those inclined to the Left—and thus, eliminate the regime's political rivals. Two months earlier, the German Football Association made an audacious statement in *kicker*, a sports magazine founded by a Jew named Walther Bensemann, which encouraged prejudice among its affiliated clubs at the expense of their Jewish members. While some clubs like FV Karlsruhe, 1. FC Nürnberg and Eintracht Frankfurt rushed to implement the 'recommendations' of their national football association and rid themselves of Jews, Bayern Munich never failed to challenge the regime and declare their support to Kurt Landauer, the club's former Jewish president. Not surprisingly, Munich's resistance was the main reason why their local rivals, 1860 Munich, were favored by the Nazis. On the whole, German football and the national association, in particular, contributed with effect to Adolph Hitler's stay in power.

Another consequence of the regime's shameful conduct was that club members had to prove their Aryan origins, whereas youngsters were forced to join the Hitler Youth, ultimately bringing the people's game under the severe control of the National Socialist Workers Party of Germany (NSDAP). Nazi officials also aimed at replacing old football clubs with new ones, in order to underline the change of the political environment. For example, VfL Bochum emerged in 1938, following the merging of three teams, however, the regime's ambition remained largely unfulfilled due to the outbreak of the Second World War. Before the war, Nazi Germany took part in the 1934 World Cup and served their propaganda well, as the regime joined forces with fascist Italy. Considering Germany's withdrawal from the League of Nations in 1933, participation in international events was vital and, therefore, football replaced the more conventional embassies—when representing the country abroad—and served her superiority complex by winning games. Apart from a memorable defeat in Stockholm, the German national team succeeded in defeating all of its opponents for more than a decade, by scoring plenty of goals in every football match. The friendly football match between Germany and England, in particular, commands our attention, not so much for the score line or the performance of the two teams. On 14 May 1938, in the Olympic Stadium of Berlin, the football players of England's national team gave the fascist salute, a sad incident that certainly scarred the country's contemporary football history. Arguably, the decision of the English Football Association to play Germany was a clear gesture of support towards Nazi Germany's leadership. Quite the opposite, when Spain played Germany at home in 1936, there was a lot of confusion before the match started, "as both sides argued over whether 'Deutschland über Alles' would be played and whether the Germans would salute."[6]

After Nazism took over Austria, football was, more often than not, played in concentration camps once the Jewish community was subjected to similar abusive policies. As in neighboring Germany, Jews were excluded from all activities anyhow related to sport, including sports journalism, with Maccabi Vienna the only oasis where football players of Jewish origin could be found. Discrimination, at the expense of Austria's Jewish population and, therefore, football, persisted as FK Austria—a club known for their connections to the local Jewish community—was renamed FK Osterreich and Hakoah Vienna, a Jewish club, was banned. Regrettably, when Hakoah was dismantled, an early part of Austria's official football history was erased, given that the club had been crowned champions of the first ever professional league in 1925. Evidently, the game was suffocated, since Hakoah was not the only team that vanished. The majority of small football clubs ceased to exist and new football talents became a rarity, taking into account that a great deal of emphasis was put on race, football training resembled military exercise and young males were recruited by the Hitler Youth. Astoundingly, some welcomed these radical changes, such as Wiener Sportklub, a club with a nationalist past, and SK Rapid and WAC, which appointed Nazi officials to their management so to make possible the use of young players for key matches and even postpone their military service. As Nazism tightened its control of football, the foreign names of more clubs were translated in German, players that served the military had to wear the insignia of their branch or service, swastikas were displayed in all football grounds and every footballer had to give the 'German sports salute' before and after the games.

Germany's division, following the end of World War II and the implementation of the Yalta Agreement, accounts for football's lethargic development in the country. In West Germany, the first football league, Bundesliga, had to wait until 1963, whereas in the German Democratic Republic the game was clearly oppressed. Still, West Germany produced some fine players whose reputation was highlighted by utilizing their national identity with effect, as Franz Beckenbauer was *Der Kaiser*, while Karl-Heinz Rummenigge was known as *Der Blonde Bomber*. Although East German football produced some fine players, like Andreas Thom, Ulf Kirsten, Matthias Sammer and Thomas Doll, as well as talented youngsters such as Jörg Heinrich, Carsten Jancker, Thomas Linke, Alexander Zickler and Jens Jeremies, to name a few, success was conspicuous by its absence. Only three East German clubs ever reached a European final—all in the Cup-Winners' Cup, the weakest of the three European competitions—winning just one, when Magdeburg defeated AC Milan in 1974. Likewise, the national team never qualified for the European Championship, though it managed a single appearance in the World Cup. It seems that political issues account for the disastrous performance of the German Democratic Republic's football representatives on the pitch, as the leadership manipulated football in a manner similar to the Nazis. The communist regime did not hesitate to relocate or rename teams and even encouraged the transfer of great players to the bigger teams, without the consent of their own clubs, since Manfred Ewald, head of the

Gymnastics and Sport Union (DTSB), believed in the so-called 'concentration performance.'[7]

FOOTBALL BEHIND THE IRON CURTAIN

The ugly face of communism dictated that football clubs be related to the party's structure and relevant worker organizations, which aimed to project the supremacy of communism over capitalism through success at international and European competitions for clubs and country. Political interference in the organization and selection of the national team was commonplace in communist Europe; however, the countries' national sides were the sole beneficiaries of this practice, though with limited success on the pitch, as there was no issue whether clubs or country came first when football clubs were asked to make players available for the national team. For example, when Dynamo Kiev won the European Cup-Winners' Cup in 1975, the authorities selected the club's players as the Soviet Union XI for two consecutive years, but were largely unsuccessful as the number of games played at both national and club level affected the performance of the footballers. All in all, East European nations reached the World Cup final on four occasions, twice in the name of both Czechoslovakia and Hungary, the European Championship final five times, winning the competition twice, and managed seven gold and six silver medals in Olympic football tournaments. Success was central to the objectives of the communist regimes, but rarely experienced. To this extent, the Soviet Union did not take part in the World Cup until 1958, due to a lack of confidence in performing with effect at international level. If truth be told, CDSA—initially known as CDKA, later renamed to CSKA Moscow—was the Soviet Union's greatest club in the 1940s, but when they suffered two defeats during a three-match tour of Czechoslovakia in 1947, the Soviet authorities imposed a two-year ban on matches that involved foreign clubs and nations. When the Soviets made an attempt to recover their prestige, the 1952 Olympic football tournament proved a disaster. The Soviet Union expected nothing but success, as the national team largely comprised CDSA players. In the first round of the competition, Stalin's Soviet Union met the Yugoslav Federation of Tito. Given Tito's ambiguous ideological stance in relation to the Soviet Union, it was imperative that the Yugoslav national team was defeated. However, Yugoslavia emerged victorious, as they beat the mighty Soviet Union by three goals to one, and CDSA was all of a sudden wiped out from the football map as a consequence of harming the interests of the Soviet Union.

Football players in communist countries were not considered professionals, since they were usually paid by the organization that funded the club and registered its members as employees. In Czechoslovakia, for example, Banik Ostrava and Plastika Nitra were sponsored by the miners' trade union and a plastics' factory respectively, whereas a coal mining company and a locomotive manufacturer supported Hungary's Tatabanya and Raba Gyor. In the Soviet Union, Lokomotiv Moscow was funded by the rail workers' union and Torpedo Moscow by workers that manufactured cars. The more 'privileged' clubs, however, were either funded by the army or sponsored by the security services. Furthermore, the transfer of football players from the communist bloc to West European clubs was generally prohibited, unless the player in question was of thirty years and had represented his country, until Gorbachev reversed the policy to keep pace with glasnost. Despite communism's shady side, East European regimes, in an attempt to offer more employment opportunities and a football feast to their public or, perhaps, for propaganda purposes, had a fundamental role in the construction of huge stadiums, such as Budapest's Nepstadion (seventy-two thousand capacity), Sofia's Vasilij Levski Stadion (fifty-five thousand), Bucharest's 23 August Stadionul (sixty-five thousand), Chorzow's Slaski Stadion (seventy thousand), Moscow's Centralny (formerly Lenin) Stadion (one hundred thousand), Kiev (one hundred thousand) and Tbilisi (seventy-four thousand). These stadiums were capable of accommodating large crowds and, as in fascist Italy, football during the communist era became an important tool in promoting national identity, since support for the national team or the state-sponsored clubs was interpreted as support to the regime. In addition, football seemed to reflect key values of communism such as teamwork. It is anything but a coincidence that not many individual football heroes existed at the time, as the team was always given priority. Hungary's national football team was renowned for its unique style of play and success in the first half of the 1950s. Ferenc Puskas once said "We were the forerunners for 'Total Football.' When we attacked, we all attacked and when we defended it was the same," though the team's coach, Guzstav Sebes, preferred to describe it as 'socialist football.'[8]

East Europe's powerhouses were funded, and often fabricated, by the army, as was the case of CSKA Moscow, Dukla Prague (originally ATK), Steaua Bucharest (formerly CCA), CSKA Sofia (initially CDNA) and Red Star Belgrade, and were automatically 'promoted' to the national league's top division. These clubs were particularly successful, since the army provided them with young and talented players enrolled for military service. Sure enough, the army's clubs amassed an impressive number of trophies by occupying top spot in the national league so frequently that, eventually, ridiculed the standards of domestic competition. As a matter of fact, CSKA Sofia were crowned champions a record twenty-seven times, Red Star Belgrade sixteen times, Steaua Bucharest fourteen, Honved Budapest twelve and Dukla Prague eleven times. In the case of Dukla and Honved, their players were guaranteed a career in football as soon as they gained promotion to the army's higher ranks, since they would, then, be eligible to remain at the club the moment they fulfilled their military duty. To fully appreciate the military's impact on football, it is only necessary to mention that the club once known as Kispest was renamed Honved, which stands for 'Defenders of the Motherland.' The army, nevertheless, was not supportive to all. In Yugoslavia, the army suppressed the Serb Orthodox Church, thus inspiring in the 1980s supporters of Red Star Belgrade to display icons of saints during football matches. However, following the demise of the Soviet Union and the collapse of communism throughout Eastern Europe, of all clubs sponsored by the army only Partizan in Serbia, CSKA in Bulgaria and Steaua Bucharest in Romania continued to receive wide support. In contrast, Dukla Prague, a club that failed to attract popular support during communism despite its success, was twice relegated to the third division by the mid-1990s. From this aspect, Dukla was certainly unsuccessful, particularly, when taking into account that their neighbors, Viktoria Zizkov, played before much larger crowds, though in leagues as low as the third and fourth divisions.

An alternative to the army-funded clubs, were teams sponsored by the secret services or else the Interior Ministry. The clubs that they supported were the Dynamo, or Dinamo, clubs in Bucharest, Dresden, Kiev, Moscow, Prague, Sofia, Tbilisi, Tirana and Zagreb. Similar to the clubs supported by the army, the Dynamo clubs were also incredibly successful. The club in Tirana won the domestic league on fourteen occasions, Bucharest thirteen times, Kiev twelve, Moscow eleven and Dresden eight. Dynamo Kiev relished the support of Volodymyr Scherbytskyi, leader of the Ukrainian Communist Party, and became a national symbol, a club capable of beating their powerful opponents from Moscow, as other Ukrainian clubs were forced to provide them with their most gifted players. Likewise, in East Germany, the secret police, *Stasi*, and the regime influenced the development of football heavily. The quality players somehow always ended up playing for Dynamo Berlin, which, coincidentally, was Erich Mielke's favorite team. Mielke, other than Minister of State Security, was also heading the Dynamo Sports Association that represented the State Security and Interior Ministries and, acting in this capacity, ordered Dynamo Dresden in 1954 to relocate to Berlin and, naturally, change their name to fit the new environment. Dynamo Berlin's story is striking as the club was simply created in the absence of a strong, successful, team in Berlin. With such considerable support, it is not surprising that the club became a symbol of success, winning the league a record ten times between 1979 and 1988. Other clubs humiliated in a similar manner included Empor Lauter, which moved to Rostock and became, first, Empor Rostock and, then, Hansa Rostock; Vorwarts Berlin, a club forced to move to Frankfurt; and Oder, which shared Dresden's destiny and followed them to Berlin. MTK (their name changed from Textiles to Bástya to Voros Lobogo—'Red Banner'—and back to MTK from 1950 to 1957) was also supported by the secret police in Hungary. Ferencvaros, on the other hand, are known as the bitter enemies of MTK that opposed the communist regime, priding themselves on their fans' participation in the 1956 Uprising. Similarly, Spartak Moscow, named after Spartacus, a Thracian (Eastern Greece) slave who led a rebellion against the Roman forces, opposed the regime and was the only club of the capital that was not sponsored in any way by the Soviet authorities.

In other Eastern European countries, during the 1950s and 1960s, quite a few clubs had to change their names and meet the new political reality as well, nevertheless, their fans continued to chant the original names of their beloved teams during football matches. Levski Sofia, named after a Bulgarian hero who fought the Turks, became Dynamo Sofia from 1949 to 1956. In Czechoslovakia, Bohemians Prague became Spartak Stalingrad (1951–1961), Slavia Prague changed to Dynamo Prague (1953–1965) and Sparta Prague was renamed Spartak Sokolovo (1953–1965). Eventually, football clubs in Czechoslovakia reverted to their original names after the 1965 'Prague spring.' Hungarian clubs' names changed in 1956 with the October uprising, as Polish clubs led by example between 1950 and 1956. However, the fall of communism in Eastern Europe signaled the transformation of football, once again, as it was necessary to rid the game of its murky past. The army club Honved in Budapest replaced the soldier on their badge with a lion and were renamed Kispest-Honved, whereas, in Bulgaria, Trakia Plovdiv reverted to Boten Plovdiv—their original name since 1912. In the newly established Czech Republic, Ruda Hvezda (Red Star) Cheb became Union Cheb and Dynamo Tbilisi became Liberiya Tbilisi in Georgia. Some football clubs even changed names to match that of their new sponsors such as Body Brno, formerly Zbrojovka, in the Czech Republic and Dunaujvaros, originally Dunafeer, in Hungary. Moreover, political interference in Bulgarian football became evident when in the 1968–1969 season the government ordered a number of clubs to merge. Of the six merges, two occurred at the expense of the capital's clubs, where Levski and Spartak joined forces and Slavia merged with Lokomotiv. While the second merger lasted only until 1971, due to opposition from the two rivals' fans, Levski had to await the revolution of 1989 before gaining 'independence.' Romania's F Colt and Victoria Bucharest, two clubs associated with the notorious Ceausescu family, were remarkably successful until the violent downfall of the country's regime when they were both vigorously relegated.

The politicization of football in East Europe during the communist era is irrefutable. Nonetheless, this practice was not exclusive to communist regimes. Stanley Rous, president of the *Fédération Internationale de Football Association* (FIFA), believed that politics should be kept out of sport, but insisted in 1973 that the World Cup qualifier between the Soviet Union and Chile be played in Santiago. The Soviets were not prepared to play in the National Stadium, however, given that a number of political prisoners had suffered at the hands of Chile's cruel right-wing military regime there. When the Soviet officials requested that the game be played on neutral grounds, Rous refused and the superpower was left with no alternatives other than withdraw. Likewise, the dawn of the postcommunist era found East European nations in turmoil, due to their mixed populations. Intercommunal tension was often expressed during football matches in Romania, given that some clubs were widely supported by the Hungarian minority, and in Czechoslovakia, when Czech and Slovak teams played one another. Similar neighborly rivalries revived in matches between Bulgaria, on one hand, and Romania and Yugoslavia on the other, but the matches that really attracted large crowds were those between any of the above and Russia. Obviously, four decades of Soviet domination still commanded attention. It is noteworthy that the peaceful partition of Czechoslovakia in 1993 was fully completed once the 1994 World Cup in the United States drew to a close. The country that once comprised two distinct ethnic groups stood united on one last occasion as the Representatives of Czechs and Slovaks played their football at the highest competitive level.

NATIONALISM

Balkans

In 1969, the infamous "Futbol War" took place after a violent World Cup qualifying match triggered El Salvador's invasion of Honduras.[9] Some twenty years later, it was Europe's turn to stage a 'football war.' As already noted, the army in Yugoslavia suppressed all forms of Serb identity, including the Orthodox Church, because of the perceived threat to the unity of the federation and its opposition to communist ideology. In the late 1980s, those fears materialized when Red Star fans demanded secession, thus causing tension during football matches. Zelijko Raznatovic, also known as Arkan, was asked to restrain Red Star's hooligans, but when war broke out in Yugoslavia Raznatovic became leader of the Tigers—a group of Red Star fanatics trained to kill in the name of Serbia—and took part in the first Serb offensive of 1991. The atrocities in Yugoslavia begun on 13 May 1990, when Dinamo Zagreb hosted Red Star Belgrade in a match that was abandoned due to violent clashes between Croat and Serb fans. Today, a statue of soldiers outside the football ground of Dynamo Zagreb, or rather Croatia Zagreb to keep up with the changes, stands as a constant reminder of the hostilities that divided the people of former Yugoslavia, with an inscription that reads "To the fans of this club, who started the war with Serbia at this ground on May 13, 1990."[10] It is quite likely that the next meeting between Red Star and Dinamo Zagreb supporters took place on the battlefield, as some Croat fighters were hard-core fans of Dinamo that belonged to a group known as the Bad Blue Boys. Another section of Dinamo Zagreb's fans, nevertheless, gave up supporting their club, when the Croatian President, Franjo Tudman, abused his authority and decided to alter Dinamo's name for the more politically correct Croatia. Elsewhere in the Balkans, Bosnia-Hercegovina's football clubs were ethnically separated, following the end of the war, into Bosniak, Croat and Serb leagues until 1998, when the top Bosniak and Croatian clubs competed for the Bosnian championship. Two years later, a single Bosniak-Croat league was set up, which Serb clubs decided to join in 2002. Today, Bosnia's football association (NSBiH) is probably the country's only true national body. Naturally, the bitter memories of the war continued to dominate football matches between the once warring nations. For example, when Croatia hosted the Serb national team during a European Championship qualifier, some Croatian fans displayed an enormous banner that read 'Vukovar 91,' a message reminiscent of violence.

Belgium

Football in Belgium was predominantly played and, later on, organized by the local French elite. Thus, when the *Union Belge des Societes de Football Association* (UBSFA) was set up in 1912, French became the official language of Belgium's football governing body, barely acknowledging the Flemish dimension when the relevant translation (*Belgische Voetbalbond*) was incorporated the year after. The ethnic division of Belgium was reflected in football and was unmistakably highlighted in a 1906 document of the national football association that made reference to all member clubs. According to the relevant list, which enclosed fifty-three football clubs, only one had a Flemish name, Atheneum Voetbal Vereeniging from Brussels (*Voetbal Vereeniging* is Flemish for 'football club'). The document also recorded the presence of three Anglicized clubs that included Antwerp, the country's oldest football club. The fact that the founding members opted for 'Antwerp' as the club's name, rather than the French *Anvers* or the Flemish *Antwerpen*, even though the club comes from Flanders, is open to interpretation. The remaining clubs all had French names, as in the case of Antwerp's Club Sportif Anversois and Union Sportive Roularienne from Flanders, a club that adopted the French name of the city, Roulers, instead of the Flemish Roselare. On the whole, eighteen clubs from Flanders had French names. Although the number of clubs with Flemish names increased to eleven by 1914, they retained their 'minority' status in a total of 107 clubs, thus emphasizing that football was almost exclusive to the francophone community, just as all referees were French speaking. Even when football attracted a wider, than ever before, support from the working-class right after the Great War, the elitist approach to football prevailed as the national association was renamed *Union Royale Belge des Societes de Football Association* in 1920, clearly reinforcing the political dimension of the game in Belgium. The Flemish community responded vigorously and established in 1930 the Flemish Football Association, *Vlaamsche Voetbalbond*, as well as a separate football league. However, *Vlaamsche Voetbalbond* never received the necessary recognition of the Belgian Football Association or FIFA that would facilitate its proper operation, considering that its affiliated clubs were refrained from playing against clubs that were members of the official Belgian association or foreign opposition that belonged to other official national football associations. In a desperate attempt to satisfy its need for legitimacy, the Flemish Football Association established close relations with a Flemish separatist party called *Vlaamsch National Verbond*, which advocated secession for Flanders and unification with the Netherlands. On the contrary, the politicization of the Flemish Football Association brought about its downfall in 1944, when it was revealed that certain members of the *Vlaamsch National Verbond* cooperated with the Nazis during Belgium's occupation. During World War II, the Nazi regime followed the so-called policy of 'Flamenpolitik,' which clearly favored the Flemish community because of the linguistic similarities to the German language, thus encouraging the hard-core Flemish nationalists to team up with the occupation forces. Furthermore, the impact of Catholicism during the 1930s and early 1940s facilitated the promotion of Flemish identity, which was considerably strengthened in 1932 with the enactment of a law that formally recognized Flemish as the official language of Flanders, Wallonia as French-speaking and Brussels as bilingual. Despite the obvious divisions that characterize society in Belgium, the national team relishes support from both ethnic communities. Quite the opposite, the separation between Flemings and Walloons is manifest at club level, as Bruges and Standard Liege, respectively, are considered their most prominent representatives, even though these divisions are, occasionally, enhanced by the disproportional selection of players from the two communities to represent country in international football matches.

Cyprus

The civil war in Greece had a severe impact on Cyprus too, dividing the East Mediterranean island into Right and Left-wing supporters. This political division affected the world of sport, as clubs demanded that leftist elements denied their political ideology officially by signing a written statement, thus preceding, in a sense, McCarthyism, by a few years. Some refused to subject to the fascist conduct of the governing bodies and were expelled from football clubs and prohibited from training. Subsequently, these players formed Alki Larnaca, Nea Salamina, Omonia and Orfeas. These four clubs together with AMOL Limassol and Asteras Morphou set up the Cyprus Amateur Football Federation, as well as a separate football league in 1948. Alki Larnaca was the answer to right-wing EPA Larnaca, just as Nea Salamina was supposed to counter-balance the political effect of Anorthosis Ammohostos, whereas in the case of Omonia, the club was formed by players that came from the ranks of APOEL, all taking part in a, seemingly, leftist league until 1953. The semiotics of Cypriot football reveals that the game was vastly politicized, considering that Anorthosis' banner displays a phoenix and that APOEL stands for Athletic Football Club of Greeks in Nicosia. On the other hand, more likely the left one, Omonia's opposition to the political division of Cyprus was accurately illustrated in both the name of the club, 'concord,' and its logo, a shamrock, given that green is the color of hope. Eventually, four years after the Greek civil war came to an end, the Cyprus Football

Association merged with the Cyprus Amateur Football Federation on 19 September 1953.

Still, football was a long way from attaining maturity, since colonialism was yet another external factor that affected the game's development in Cyprus. As it happens, by 1956 the British had put into effect a number of oppressive measures to thwart the Cypriots' demands for independence, therefore, forcing football supporters away from the game. When the colonial authorities decided to tighten up on domestic violence, any sort of gathering that had the potential of turning into a political rally and cause tension was deemed undesirable and thus, prohibited. As a matter of fact, a decree issued by the colonial office dictated that football stadiums in the capital, Nicosia, remained closed for an indefinite period of time, or else until stability was restored, prompting the Cyprus Football Association to restructure the national league and operate two separate competitions. The Nicosia clubs exempted, football matches took place among clubs located in coastal cities, hence the so-called 'coastal' league, or clubs from the mainland. In the end, football was spared the humiliation when the two competitions merged into one and Nicosia clubs were again eligible to take part in the national league after only six games into the season.

Out of habit, perhaps, there was no end to football's misfortunes, despite Cyprus gaining independence in 1960. The Greek-Cypriots' desire to achieve union with Greece was in some measure facilitated by the participation of the winner of Cyprus' domestic football competition in the Greek national league. While Olympiakos Nicosia became in 1967 the first Cypriot club to 'qualify' for the Greek championship, APOEL completed an extremely embarrassing experience for the Cypriot clubs in the 1973–1974 season, since all clubs performed rather poorly and ended up on the wrong side of the table on all but one occasion, finishing eighteenth four times, seventeenth twice and thirteenth once in a league of eighteen clubs. It is important to note that during the exact same period Greece was under military rule and that the dictators shared the ambitions of the Greek-Cypriot people. In fact, some hold the Greek dictatorship responsible for the under-performance of the Cypriot clubs, as the regime despised clubs inclined to the left-wing. For example, when Omonia played Panathinaikos in Athens during the 1972–1973 season, the club from Cyprus lost the game by four goals to two after giving away a 2–0 lead, allegedly, due to questionable refereeing. Anyway, one would assume that having survived such unfavorable conditions within a space of a decade, football would follow its own course undisturbed. Yet the 1974 Turkish invasion of Cyprus brought about the de facto partition of the island, not to mention the official segregation of the two ethnic communities between Greeks and Turkish Cypriots, and, therefore, another football governing body was soon established. Nevertheless, the Cyprus Turkish Football Federation, *Kibris Turk Futbol Federasyoni*, in the occupied areas, is certainly not part of football's international family or a FIFA member, unlike the official Cyprus Football Association that represents the Greek-Cypriot community.

France

In France, regional diversity is largely reflected in football, given that a number of clubs, for example, FC Nantes Atlantique, CS Sedan Ardennes, Montpellier Herault SC, FC Girondins de Bordeaux and AS Nancy Lorraine, clearly indicate their geographical background. This sense of localism becomes all the more evident when taking into account that all football stadiums, with the exception of Auxerre, are owned by the local authorities, which sponsor the clubs financially. This sort of involvement of the public sector in football also promotes a sense of community and draws the citizens' attention to local politics. To this end, it is not surprising that Paris Saint-Germain was founded in 1970 to emphasize Parisian identity, since the club that had part in this business, Racing Club de Paris, disappeared to the lower national divisions by the mid-1960s. However, when France met football, society was divided between the Republican left and the Catholic right, or else between State and Church, thus halting the game's proper development to a great extent. At the time, divisions existed within French sport too, as four different governing bodies claimed control over football, with only two focusing on the game alone, *Union des societes francaises de France* and *Ligue de football association*. The lack of maturity that characterized these bodies could prove costly for football, particularly, since the game witnessed great success and popularity from the outset. Hence, the *Comite francais interfederal* was set up to regulate the conduct of all four federations and prepare the grounds for the French Football Federation, which came to being in 1919. Given that political and social divisions manipulated the game, football was denied the 'nation-building' status that it was certainly attributed elsewhere in Europe.

On the contrary, "France's formation as a modern nation-state was a century too early for football to have been a tool for forging an initial shared national identity."[11] As a result, football's constructive features were put aside until 1938, when France hosted the World Cup, as the popular game achieved in promoting a distinct sense of collective national identity. The game's connection with the nation was also enhanced when it became customary that the President of the Republic attended the final of the French Cup, shake hands with the players before kickoff and present the trophy to the club that emerged victorious. Even though football contributed fairly little to French nationalism, at least during the early stages of the game's development, French officials, driven by an imperialistic stance, turned their attention to supranational structures, like FIFA and UEFA (Union of European Football Associations), and were instrumental in setting up competitions such as the World Cup and the European Championship at national level, as well as the European competitions at club level. From an ethnocentric viewpoint, the awkward role of football in France is underlined today by the fact that many football terms somehow retain their English origins.

Italy
Italian society is divided in both political and geographic terms, thus separating the left-wing AC Milan and Bologna from the right-wing Internazionale and Verona, as well as Atalanta in northern Italy from Napoli in the south, as dictated by the *mezzogiorno* line. These rivalries reflect the identity of different *ultras*—groups of hard-core fans typically mistaken for hooligans—that occupy a particular stand on the terraces, usually located behind the goal, known as the *curva*. Naturally, it is the rhetoric of the *ultras* that is central to our subject; however, the *curva* too commands attention. It appears that the *curva* possesses just about nationalistic features and, therefore, the need to preserve its integrity and deter likely intruders is compelling. Consequently, some *ultras* often express antisocial views redolent of racist and xenophobic content. When a large number of immigrants arrived in the late 1980s, xenophobic parties like the *Lega Nord*, Northern League, jumped at the opportunity to serve their unethical cause by promoting a sense of intolerance towards foreigners that was reproduced without restraint in football stadiums through racist chants, Nazi symbols and anti-Semitism.

However, long before the first waves of immigrants reached the shores of Italy, it was predominantly southern Italians that were racially abused during football matches. It was a usual phenomenon to insult the dignity of those Italians coming from the less privileged, poorer, part of Italy, by calling them *Negro di Merda*, black shit, because of south Italy's relative proximity to Africa. As a response, clubs like Napoli displayed the American Confederate army's flag to accentuate their southern identity, as well as sardonic banners that read 'Welcome to Africa.' Sadly, these divisions were also reflected in matches during the 1990 World Cup finals in Italy, when segments of Napoli fans preferred to support Argentina over the Italian national team, as the South American nation featured Diego Maradona, the rising star of the club from Naples. Likewise, northern Italians strongly opposed Argentina, while a section of supporters known for their racist views did not hesitate to cheer on Cameroon, rather than support say other European nations, out of sheer chauvinism. What matters, nevertheless, is the fact that some of these racist elements are oftentimes recruited by movements similar to those that established the *ultras* during the 1970s, stimulated by the political divisions of the time. For example, the Italian Social Movement, an extreme right-wing party, was fundamental in organizing the *ultras* of Internazionale and Lazio. More recently, parties and movements of the same posture have been involved in recruiting new members inside football stadiums. Indeed, a number of Parliamentary Members that belonged to the National Alliance, an extreme right party, actually came from the ranks of Verona's *ultras*, whereas at local government level, the 1993 administrative elections witnessed the appointment of certain representatives that were among Roma and Lazio's fans. The politicization of football in Italy is unquestionable, particularly, considering Silvio Berlusconi's impressive record in both football and politics. The fact that the name of his political party, *Forza Italia*, is a widely used football chant is no accident either. Apparently, Berlusconi's club, AC Milan, was instrumental in his election as Italy's Prime Minister. Berlusconi, perhaps, was the first to achieve in reversing the 'politicization of football' practice to a successful 'footballization of politics' strategy during his term in office.

Spain

Spain is characterized by a lack of collective identity, due to the apparent existence of separate 'nations.' National sentiment may be expressed through football, but in the case of Spain the popular game seems to emphasize regional, cultural and linguistic differences. Hence, the national team often fails to attract the attention of the Spanish and it is often questionable whether the selection of players is representative enough. For example, when Javier Clemente, of Basque origin, was in charge of the Spanish national team (1992–1998), he often selected quite a few Basque players, thus rousing suspicion. Other factors that have undermined the authenticity of the Spanish national team also pertain to regionalism. Football clubs like Barcelona in Catalonia and the Basque Athletic de Bilbao and Real Sociedad have always sought to promote a distinct identity. The Basque country, actually, has been represented by an all-Basque team in a number of international friendly matches, the first in 1979, while an all-Catalan team played a friendly game against Bulgaria in 1998. Moreover, all Spanish football clubs have a particular song, or hymn, that reflects their history and culture, with club colors being a mirror image of the city's emblem, the *escudo*. In fact, club colors, for this reason, are of fundamental semiotic value as illustrated in the case of Real Betis, which play in the green-and-white stripes of Andalusia, Las Palmas sport the yellow-and-blue of the Canary Isles and Celta de Vigo the blue-and-white of Galicia. As a consequence, when Spain hosted the 1982 World Cup, Catalans and Basques did not match the profile of the national team's ardent supporters, which prompted the Spanish Football Federation to have the team play, apart from the capital, in different venues across the country to raise support. Usually, the Spanish national team plays its football in southern Spain, as it enjoys far more support, but mostly in Madrid, which could be considered as a sign of centralization.

Being an integral part of Catalonia's dominant club does not simply signify an illustrious career in football; it is above all an extraordinary experience. Johan Cruyff attests our line of reasoning both as a cherished Barcelona player from 1973 to 1978 and as a successful coach from 1988 to 1996. The legendary Dutchman was genuinely committed to the club's objectives and values, embraced the local culture and, therefore, was deemed Catalan enough, unlike Bernard Schuster and Luis Figo, since both footballers disgraced Barcelona the moment they stepped onto the pitch of Santiago Bernabeu to play for fierce rivals Real Madrid. Obviously, not all deserve the Catalans' warm welcome and approval. When Louis van Gaal succeeded Cruyff as new manager of Barcelona in 1997, his apparent obsession of purchasing fellow Dutch players, as well as a number of other non-Catalans, encouraged fans to oppose his transfer policy criteria and stress the essence of the club's identity and culture. However, fans of Barcelona, mostly revere the club's colors, rather than the players that come and go on a regular basis. This unusual sense of respect is also reflected in the board's decision to refrain from the club wearing advertising.

This long-standing tradition came to an end on September 2006, after Barcelona signed an agreement with UNICEF that will see them wearing the organization's logo for the next five years. Unlike common commercial sponsorship deals, however, it is UNICEF that will be receiving financial support, not Barcelona. This distinctive phenomenon certainly does not frustrate either club or fans, since it serves the cause of the children's charity. Anyway, the badge of Barcelona is a clear reminder of the club's background. The original emblem displayed the cross of *St. Jordi*, St. George, and the colors of the Catalan flag, the *senyera*. The modern day emblem includes Barcelona's initials, FCB, in a manner that exemplifies the relationship between club and city, if not Catalonia, as Barcelona present themselves as *the* Catalan team, succinctly referred to as *mes que un club*, 'more than a club.' The club's cosmopolitan roots are still opposed by local rivals Espanyol, originally known as Sociedad Espanola de Football, thus underlining their Spanish identity. Despite Espanyol's relations to Franco's regime, the club is today divided between fans inclined to fascism and a section of supporters that promote their Catalan identity. While the hard-core Brigadas Blanquizules, blue-and-white brigades, display Spanish flags and chant 'Viva Espana,' the more Catalan fans respond with jeers and wave the Catalan flag instead. It is noteworthy that in 1994 the club changed its name from the Castilian Espanol to the Catalan Espanyol, to stress their identity more accurately.

The case of Basque clubs is even more peculiar. Basque clubs are unique in that they limit their transfer options to Basque players only, though their approach varies from club to club. Athletic de Bilbao's strict policy of excluding non-Basque players is much related to Basque nationalism and the political beliefs that characterize the Basque country in general, though they also reflect their founder's, Sabino de Arana y Goira, xenophobia too. Athletic de Bilbao, founded in 1898, adopted their Basque-only policy in 1919 and, as a result, they only recruit players that were born in the Basque country, offspring of Basques. However, Athletic de Bilbao's association with nationalism is far more explicit than its non-Basque policy reveals. The club has been closely related to the Basque Nationalist Party (Partido Nacionalista Vasca—PNV), since the president of the first legitimate Basque government of 1936, Jose Antonio Aguirre, was formerly playing his football for Bilbao. Similar, perhaps, to how secret societies operate, ever since Aguirre's presidency, all presidents of the club have been members of the Partido Nacionalista Vasca. Real Sociedad, on the other hand, was established in 1909, a whole decade before Athletic de Bilbao adopted their rather discriminatory policy, but had a different approach to the issue of employing non-Basque players, as anyone born in the Basque country—including the offspring of immigrants—was eligible to play for the team. It is important to note that 'immigrants' were supposed to be all non-Basque Spanish citizens that relocated to the Basque country, primarily, when 'foreign' labor was much needed. To that extent, Bilbao's strict policy towards immigrants is definitely confusing, considering that the latter were welcomed exactly because they were necessary, but were at the same time resented and discouraged from playing the popular game. Apart from the differences in relation to the players that composed their teams, Athletic de Bilbao and Real Sociedad developed an unusual rivalry that was based on the fact that Athletic de Bilbao was perceived more appropriate to promote the Basques' cause for being central to Basque nationalist politics. If anything, the anthems of both clubs make good use of the Basque language, but Athletic de Bilbao's is more elaborate, thus revealing a more intimate relation to Basque history and nationalism. Nevertheless, in the 1960s the two Basque clubs improved relations and formed a common front to oppose Franco's regime more effectively. Ever since, there have been some stories about members of the PNV penetrating the clubs to project the party's objectives, in regard to regional autonomy, while members of the clubs' boards were often strong supporters of the Basque separatist group known as *Euzkadi ta Askatasuna* (ETA).

Beyond any shadow of doubt, the most extreme form of regionalism in Spanish football was witnessed when Deportivo La Coruna from Galicia threatened to leave the *Primera Liga* in 1995 and, instead, join the Portuguese League. Obviously, the fans' conduct could not possibly escape these historical, regional, rivalries. Due to the country's fascist past, neo-Nazi groups have emerged in Spanish football, such as the *Ultrasur* of Real Madrid and *Frente Atletico* of Atlético de Madrid, which promote extreme nationalism, racism and xenophobia. Other groups, like the *Ultras Mujica* of Real Sociedad, *Herri Norte* of Athletic Bilbao and *Boixos Nois* of Barcelona, are believed to have established connections with extreme separatist movements and often take part in nationalist demonstrations. The *Ultrasur*, on the other hand, oppose separatism, take great pride in the fascist history of the country and dominate that part of the stadium that was traditionally occupied by Franco's supporters in the past.

United Kingdom

Britain's ethnic divisions are more prevalent, perhaps, than any other European country, not so much for the omnipresent cultural differences, as for the geographical distinction and political autonomy of the four nations that comprise the

British state. Undoubtedly, a football team representing Britain as a whole would be far stronger than England, Northern Ireland, Scotland and Wales' national team yet, due to nationalist aspirations, they appear divided and thus, considerably weaker at international level. Unlike football, the spirit of the Olympic Games dictates that all British nations are represented in one single team, only to be separated again for the purpose of competitive rugby. The case of Ireland, taking into consideration Northern Ireland as well as the Republic of Ireland, is more perplexing, since the Irish appear united in international rugby competitions, but field different national teams in football tournaments. In this respect, national identity in Britain is of paramount significance, as one can be English, Irish (from Northern Ireland), Scottish or Welsh and, at the same time, British, but, in football, the opposite does not apply. Evidently, when England hosted the 1966 World Cup, supporters were waving the British flag, but when England won the 2003 World Rugby Cup, the flag of St. George was more widely used. Although the sense of belonging is fundamental in British football, nevertheless, it is not limited to national teams. At local level, the 'City' and 'United' clubs emphasize citizenship and community values, while others indicate mobility such as 'Wanderers,' 'Rangers' and 'Rovers.' In Britain, the capacity of football to unite is certainly undermined by nationalism, though it never fails to unify each and every nation when playing one another.

The account of England's poor performances at international level, with the notable exception of 1966 when they hosted and won the World Cup, are typically chronicled with bitterness for having disappointed their fans and damaged the prestige of the nation. Sadly, when the nation's pride calls for defending, extreme nationalism is echoed through the acts of hooligans, as in February 1995, when a football match between the Republic of Ireland and England in Dublin was marred by violence. Patriotic fervor, or else 'Englishness,' was traditionally personified by a muscular and aggressive animal, thus fitting perfectly well the stereotype of a football thug. The bulldog was England's official mascot during the 1982 World Cup in Spain, however, the National Front, an extreme right party, also sported the powerful animal to advance an acute sense of nationalism infested with racism and xenophobia. The press, too, may have played a role in the conduct of England's supporters, as foreign opposition is often ridiculed and ascribed features that allude to inferiority, weakness and poor quality. Exactly forty years after celebrating the first and only trophy at international level, England played hosts to European nations as the continent's premier football competition unfurled. During the European Championship, the English national football team was followed everywhere by supporters singing the 'Three Lions' anthem. Evidently, both the song's title and its lyrics were associated to England's football history. By 1996, England had replaced the bulldog with the more 'royal' lion. From the times of Richard the Lionhearted, through England's first international game (when the nation's badge sported the three lions), to EURO 1996, the king of beasts has linked England's imperial past to modern football. Another element of England supporters' conduct was their rekindled interest in the nation's flag of St. George, thus replacing the Union Jack. Concerning the song's contents, the part stressing that 'football is coming home' symbolized England's contribution to world sports with the organization of football and the origins of the popular game, thus making it an English game. It is not surprising that England first joined the World Cup in 1950, as they objected FIFA's authority and questioned the substance of other national football associations.

Although the Irish Football Association has a long history, founded in 1880, football in Ireland was widely played in the northern part of the island that, eventually, was brought under British control in 1921. Evidently, Gaelic games dominated Irish sports culture, but when the Republic of Ireland was established, originally Irish Free State, an independent football identity was developed when its national team took part in international competitions like the Paris Olympics of 1924 and the 1934 World Cup. Following its independence, as one might expect, the Republic of Ireland set up the Football Association of Ireland in Dublin. Similar divisions are reflected in Scottish football. For example, the Scottish Football Association was founded in 1873 in Glasgow, rather than the English-dominated capital of Edinburgh. In Scotland, football rivalries revolve around ethnic and religious issues, and concern, primarily, Glasgow Rangers and Celtic. Impressive as it is, the two clubs have won ninety league titles and fifty-seven FA cups between them. However, except for the family problems, the Scottish also developed an awkward relation with their neighbors. Evidently, the Scottish footballers that decided to pursue a career in England were called 'Anglos' and had few opportunities to represent Scotland. It appears that the rivalry between these two nations has political implications as well, given that Scottishness is commonly defined as anti-Englishness. In 1977, after a football match in London between England and Scotland, Scottish supporters removed little parts of Wembley's pitch and sung 'give us an assembly and we'll give you back Wembley.'[12] The situation in Wales is also complicated, as a number of clubs have undermined the status of the Welsh Football Association. As a matter of fact, Cardiff City, Wrexham and Swansea City realized the financial benefits that stem from taking part in English leagues and made an unusual agreement with the Welsh football governing body, which stipulates that all three are represented in the national football league by their reserves. There were other clubs that shared the dreams of the three apostates, but decided to play in the Welsh national league dreading the national association's retribution. Newport AFC, for example, decided to play in the English Beazer Homes league and, consequently, the club was banned from Wales and had to cover a distance of eighty miles to play their home fixtures.

FOOTBALL vs. RELIGION

Anti-Semitism

As the history of football indicates, clubs and players have suffered at the hands of anti-Semites. In the 1920s, Jewish clubs emerged in most Central European capitals and major cities, principally, in Berlin, Budapest, Innsbruck, Liz and Vienna. These early representatives of Zionism never failed to emphasize their origins by displaying King David's star and the blue-and-white colors of Israel. Their names, meticulously selected, promoted Jewish nationalism, as Hagibor, 'The Hero,' Bar Kochba, named after a revolutionary who fought the Romans, and Hakoah, 'The Strength,' were clubs that obviously took great pride in their past and defied anti-Semitism. Discrimination against the Jews was growing stronger in Europe, and, even though the most prominent Jewish clubs, such as Hakoah, represented Zionism with success, the outbreak of the Second World War brought about an abrupt end to their aspirations. Jewish football clubs faded away almost at the same time when the persecution of the Jews begun, as football was displaced by the atrocities of the Holocaust.

However, anti-Semitism in football is not a thing of the past, as certain European clubs are still haunted by their history. Austria Vienna, Bayern Munich and AS Roma, for example, are nowadays considered as 'Jewish' clubs, merely, because some of their early supporters and benefactors had Jewish origins. MTK, originally known as Hungaria, was founded by Jewish businessmen in 1888 and maintain their Jewish identity to this day, which certainly constitutes the main reason of their rivalry with Ferencvaros and the racial abuse they suffer. For obvious reasons, Hungaria was disbanded during the Second World War and was reestablished after the end of it as MTK so to prevent the ill-treatment of their members. Ajax is another football club with a Jewish past, often the target of abuse from fans of Feyenoord, that have developed an exceptional style to oppose anti-Semitism. Ajax supporters, including the hard-core 'f-side,' proclaim their Jewish identity ingeniously, as they unfurl Israeli flags during football matches. In fact, the club's disposition is much related to the fans' inventive response to anti-Semitism, with an ever-increasing number of Ajax supporters conceding their Jewish identity. As it happens, the Jewish community of Amsterdam, prior to the Second World War, was located near the stadium of Ajax, thus the awkward association of Ajax to Jewry. Today, the chief representative of Jewish football in Amsterdam answers to the name of WV-HEDW, formed after the merging of Wilhelmina Vooruit, Hortus and Eendracht Doet Winnen. Elsewhere in Europe, Jewish clubs existed in Belgium, Czechoslovakia, Denmark, England (Wingate and Finchley won the London Cup in 1995), Finland, France, Romania, the Soviet Union (Makabi Vilnius in 1992 won the cup competition), Sweden, Switzerland and the former Yugoslavia. Nevertheless, the vast majority of football clubs with Jewish background were concentrated in Germany, the Netherlands and Poland, but their activities were terminated with the outbreak of World War II.

Northern Ireland

For years, the situation in Northern Ireland was quite tensed. Belfast Celtic was a club that enjoyed wide support from the Catholic community and, as such, when they played either Linfield or Glentoran, clubs with Protestant supporters, serious crowd violence ensued. In fact, during a game between Belfast Celtic and Linfield at Windsor Park in 1948, riotous fans assaulted Belfast Celtic's players, thus forcing the club to withdraw from the league and join that of the Republic of Ireland. Derry City, from Londonderry, was successful in attracting support from both religious communities, but instability in the area forced them to follow Belfast Celtic's example. Religion in Northern Ireland has long scarred the beautiful game and although the criteria for selecting the players to represent the country are not dictated by religion, tension between the two communities forced the national team to play its home games on the British mainland from 1972 to 1978. However, Linfield seems to have copied Rangers' policy against signing Catholic players, from the 1950s to mid-1980s, but their case never made the headlines outside Northern Ireland, until related evidence was brought forward in 1992 thanks to the Irish National Caucus, an Irish-American pressure group committed to anti-discrimination and social inclusion in the area. Glentoran is another club that enjoys considerable support from the Protestant community, but the fact that it has Catholic supporters too gives them the opportunity to differentiate by criticizing Linfield for sectarianism. In any case, the response of clubs to sectarianism simply reflects the fact that even though "large numbers of Catholics play and watch football in the north of Ireland, the dominant character of the game at the senior level has tended to be both Protestant and unionist."[13] Moreover, support for Celtic or Rangers is a clear indication of religious identity and when Scotland's premier clubs meet, tension rises between the divided communities of the island. To this end, the 'Football for All' scheme in Northern Ireland aims at tackling sectarianism and racism in football. The division of the two communities is more striking when considering that Catholics in Northern Ireland prefer to support the Republic of Ireland's national team, which allows them to express their Irish identity more freely. The campaign has already produced a safer environment for all to attend international matches at Windsor Park, however, "the new stadium envisaged at the Maze offers a major opportunity for a fresh start and the IFA should consider in this regard the idea of a public competition to see if a more widely acceptable anthem can be found to the playing of God Save the Queen at internationals, in line with practice in Scotland and Wales."[14]

Scotland

There is no doubt that religion played an instrumental role in the development of the game in England. It is no coincidence that nearly half of the teams that competed in the Premiership during the 2005–2006 season, namely, Aston Villa, Birmingham City, Bolton Wanderers, Everton, Fulham, Liverpool, Manchester City and Southampton, nicknamed 'The Saints,' originate from teams founded by individual churches. Besides, "the extensive use of hymn-tunes among British fans is evidence of ecclesiastical affiliations."[15] Elsewhere in Britain, religion took a different course and often manipulated football. In Scotland, the Irish are considered second-class citizens simply because of their Catholic background, since Britain's dominant religion is Protestantism. Taking into account the strong ties between religion and state, as well as the fact that the British monarchy pledges itself to defend Protestantism, the emergence of anti-Catholicism almost comes natural. These divisions are reflected in Scottish football, to an extent where the Tartan Army, pleasant supporters of the Scottish national team, do not condone the display of club colors during international matches, in an attempt to emphasize their Scottish identity instead. In contrast, Celtic and Rangers are notorious for the ethnic hatred and religious division that determine their relationship. The two clubs have managed to exploit their differences with success, particularly, from a financial viewpoint, hence the name 'Old Firm.' Murray, in his *'Old Firm in the New Age,'* encapsulated the unprecedented rivalry between Celtic and Rangers with effect when he concluded that "It is one of the ironies of Scottish identity that its two biggest football teams are its least Scottish: Rangers with their British rather than Scottish identity, their red, white and blue of the Union Jack, the Queen and the National Anthem; Celtic with their green and white of Ireland, the Pope and the Republic."[16]

Murray also argued that Irish-Catholic Celtic is the main cause that accounts for Scotland's social divisions, somehow ignoring what their city rivals stand for, and stressed that Glasgow Rangers emerged, simply, to counterbalance Celtic's obscure Scottish identity. Nevertheless, it seems that Rangers have a multidimensional personality as they represent the Scottish-British community, Protestantism, anti-Catholicism, anti-Irishness, Freemasonry and the Orange Order. Rangers' stadium, Ibrox, was actually the venue for the annual meeting of the Orange Order, indicative of the club's historic relations with Ulster, whereas their fans often sing 'The Sash,' the anthem of the Orange Order, when Rangers play host to their arch rivals. The club's commitment to Protestantism was long reflected in their unofficial policy against acquiring the services of Catholic footballers, until they signed Maurice Johnston, therefore, signaling the beginning of a new era. Indeed, the apparent no-Catholics policy was abandoned as the new trend continued with the purchase of more Catholic footballers, mainly from Europe and South America. Once in the surroundings of Ibrox, however, the new arrivals were advised against revealing their religious convictions. In other words, players were not supposed to cross themselves in the Catholic manner during football matches, so to avoid tension with their fans. Even though Jorg Albertz was reported to have had no difficulty adjusting to a new environment that dictated his personal conduct inside the football ground, it is more than obvious that Rangers' policy was a clear sign of sectarianism, if not racism. Still, at the turn of the century, Rangers were in a position to field as many Catholic players as necessary, as the board had realized that winning trophies was far more valuable than defending religion.

Celtic, on the other hand, by emphasizing their Irish-Catholic origins, facilitated the integration of people coming from a similar background into the Scottish society. In fact, Celtic take such great pride in their ethnic origins, that the Irish flag flew over their stadium, instead of the Scottish. Nevertheless, the results of Boyle's research in 1991 revealed that 43 percent of Celtic's followers favored the Republic of Ireland's national team, rather than the Scottish. His findings were probably related to the fact that the Protestant section of the Scottish supporters often abused the few Catholic players that were selected to represent Scotland. Evidently, the majority of Celtic fans (54 percent) never attended matches of the Scottish national team, with 43 percent watching Scotland's international games occasionally, whereas a poor score (3 percent) considered themselves as committed supporters of the national side. Remarkably, 52 percent of Celtic fans declared their support for the Republic of Ireland, thus highlighting their ethnic origins, at the same time as the vast majority of Rangers fans that responded to the same survey considered Northern Ireland an integral part of Britain. Bradley's research in 1990 revealed another interesting pattern, focusing on the political beliefs of Scottish football fans. As regards Scotland's duopoly, Rangers fans voted for either Labour (33 percent or the Conservative party (32 percent), whereas the majority of Celtic's fans declared support to the Labour party (85 percent). Furthermore, only a tiny 4 percent of Celtic supporters opted for the Scottish Nationalists, unlike the considerably more supportive Rangers fans (14 percent).

Regarding the absence of Asian players and fans from Scottish football, Murray argued that this phenomenon was related to the limited football ability and lack of commitment that distinguish Asian people and culture. Moreover, the relatively small Jewish community in Scotland accounts for the absence of anti-Semitism in society, while the same logic applies to the case of racism in Scotland, considering the small numbers of Afro-Caribbean and Asian people. Where racism exists, those victimized are usually of Irish-Catholic origin, whereas "the English have had little to fear so long as they kept their accents under control."[17] These arguments are firmly in line with one of Scotland's popular myths, suggesting that racism in Scottish society is nonexistent. By contrast, a strong anti-English attitude seems to characterize Scotland today, frequently observed during football matches. Most certainly, the lack of participation of the Asian community in football is manifest; however, the issue of sectarianism seems far more important.

Near the completion of the Scottish Premier League's 2005–2006 season, the Jungle Bhoys and the Blue Order, two groups of Celtic and Rangers' hardcore fans respectively, displayed banners that delivered a powerful message against racism and sectarianism during the last match between Glasgow's football giants. At the very beginning of the same season, supporters of Rangers sang sectarian anthems, the 'Billy Boys' song, during a match against Villareal of Spain, thus forcing the club's officials to respond without delay by prohibiting the infamous song. More recently, the Scottish Football Association announced the implementation of new football legislation, in time for the 2007–2008 season, which proscribes sectarianism and defines sectarian abuse. The new rules include fines for related offences, the deduction of points and even eviction from cup competitions, in line with Article 58 of FIFA's Disciplinary Code. The Scottish Football Association will also set up a supervisory body to combat sectarianism by regulating the conduct of clubs and supporters.

All in all, religion has the capacity to unify people and could become a powerful tool in combating sectarianism and discrimination. Men of faith made every endeavor to put emphasis on religion's potential for integration, just before the 2006 World Cup kicked off in Germany, when Christian ministers played against a team of Muslim imams in a friendly game refereed by Jewish officials and organized by the German protestant Church.

THE BOSMAN ERA

During the 1950s and 1960s, European football clubs were restricted to fielding native players in order to improve the prospects of their national team and so, when clubs from different countries met, those football matches were almost international in character. However, foreign players have the potential of increasing the success of a club and, therefore, its revenues, so UEFA was pressurized to liberalize the player market, but was not necessarily challenged to alter the rules concerning the number of foreigners allowed in national leagues. UEFA's first response, in 1979, was to allow clubs to field two Community players, following relevant suggestions made by the European Commission, as the European Community institution, gradually, became interested in football too. Further debates between the Commission and national football associations took place, but did not bare fruit as the Commission was reluctant to apply European legislation on football. Sport only attracted the interest of the Community after the Single European Act was initiated, when it became clear that sport provided 'a unique opportunity for promoting a sense of belonging to the single community.' The Commission aimed at banning all restrictions on players coming from a Community member by the 1986–1987 season, but UEFA, in

June 1985, proposed to ease the restrictions only on foreign footballers that had played for, at least, five consecutive seasons in a Community member and were considered 'naturalized,' that is they were treated as native players.

Continuing debates between UEFA and the Commission gave birth to the 'three-plus-two' rule in the 1992–1993 season, even though that regulation clearly violated the principles of the Treaty of Rome. As a consequence, the Commission aimed at imposing European legislation on football; however, success on that end would require the involvement of the European Court of Justice (ECJ), since a court ruling could not be objected or negotiated. The Commission, thereafter, simply awaited the right opportunity to present itself, until the case of Jean-Marc Bosman and his transfer from Standard Liege to Dunkerque was brought forward in 1990.

The fact that sports are regulated by relevant governing bodies in all member states is significant for limiting the prospects of football becoming politicized. Moreover, when the ECJ stressed that "Article 48 not only applies to the action of public authorities but extends also to rules of any other nature,"[18] it meant that sports governing bodies were considered as public authorities and, therefore, their regulations were subject to European Union (EU) treaties and legislation. Along these lines, the Bosman case was seen as contradicting Article 48 of the Treaty of Rome, which envisaged the free movement of EU workers. It is important to note that, at the same time, the ECJ supported Bosman, when he questioned the legality of UEFA's 'three-plus-two' rule on foreign players. Although the EU could not claim competence over sports, the explosion of football in the 1990s allowed the European Commission and the ECJ to recognize it as an economic activity that had to be regulated according to EU legislation and treaties. The Bosman case challenged the transfer system rules of the time, particularly, since it concerned the free movement of people within the European Union and competition law. Out-of-contract players should not be restricted from moving to other clubs and any rules regarding nationality were deemed illegal, concerning EU nationals, such as the 'three-plus-two' rule that allowed a European team to field three foreign footballers in addition to two 'naturalized' players.

There were, however, some extreme cases like the one with the German Football Association (DFB), which extended these rules to allow all foreigners based in Europe to play their football for a German club. In contrast, other European football associations interpreted UEFA's new rules strictly and intended to limit the number of foreign players in their leagues, so to protect the young talented players that had potential and could one day represent their country at national level. In fact, the apparent lack of gifted homegrown players in Germany, immediately after transfer rules changed, was often linked to the decision of the DFB. Unlike the 'liberalization' of German clubs, the 'three-plus-two' regulation had additional effects on the United Kingdom, since English clubs, for example, were restricted from selecting as many players as usual from

Ireland, Scotland or Wales, which certainly affected their subsequent performance and competitiveness. Largely, the impact of the Bosman case on national
football teams was severe, since the pool of quality youngsters was nearly
drained. In fact, the German national team included only three players from East
Germany in the 2004 European Championship in Portugal, mainly, due to the
inability of the clubs from that part of Germany to produce young talented players. Energie Cottbus was the first club to field an all-foreigners XI in a
Bundesliga match against Wolfsburg in April 2001, just as Chelsea claimed first
prize for an identical achievement in a 1999 Premiership match against Sunderland. It is no surprise, therefore, that the players' union in Spain threatened to
strike in November 1998 in protest to the large number of foreigners in the
league.

The Bosman issue became a European matter when the Liege Court of Appeal in Belgium referred the case to the ECJ. The ECJ took the matter seriously
and concluded that the treatment of the player violated Articles 48 (on the free
movement), 85 and 86 (free competition) of the Treaty of Rome. Advocate General Lenz delivered his final statement on 20 September 1995, endorsed on 15
December 1995 by the ECJ, which banned out-of-contract transfer fees and all
restrictions on players with EU citizenship. UEFA supported that the Bosman
case only concerned contractual issues and not the restrictions on foreign players, but the Commission used the case as the ideal platform for challenging all
such restrictions, particularly, since they were not compatible with EU legislation. In the pre-Bosman era, football players were virtually tied to clubs. When a
player expressed the desire to move on, his club's consent was imperative, taking into account that, in effect, the latter could retain the player's services for as
long as necessary, unless it agreed on a transfer fee with another club.

Hence, all football clubs may benefit, in theory, from the Bosman case, as
top clubs get quality players without having to pay a transfer fee, while smaller
clubs can be equally successful in attaining the services of a good player for free
or invest in younger players that have no contract. In reality, the top clubs,
which can afford to buy talent, are provided with a unique opportunity to save
money and invest elsewhere, whereas small clubs lose their important assets for
no fee—what is much needed financial resources that would be devoted to youth
academies, training facilities and the purchase of new players—and, instead, are
forced to depend on unreliable free-transferred players. Following the Bosman
ruling, the European Commission and FIFA agreed in 2001 to alter the transfer
system according to European legislation, as any reference to nationality was
deemed illegal. To this extent, UEFA introduced the homegrown player rule to
make certain that clubs register local football players, as opposed to the 'six-
plus-five' rule, which simply ensured that the majority of the players on the field
shared the same nationality. 'Homegrown' players are those trained by the club
or within the national association in which the club is based for 3 years and concerns youngsters between the age of fifteen and twenty-one. As from the 2006–

2007 season, clubs have to name, at least, four homegrown players in a 25 strong squad, increased to six and, then, eight in the 2007–2008 and 2008–2009 seasons respectively. Although both the European Commission and the European Parliament embraced UEFA's 'homegrown' plan, which seeks to address the spin-off effects of the Bosman ruling, the new regulation is much associated to the need to preserve the local identity of clubs.

Taking into account the controversy that still surrounds the Bosman case, an examination of the perceptions of certain European nations regarding the role of foreigners in football is imperative. A study conducted by Crolley and Hand (2002) revealed that football writing made references to national history on a regular basis, sometimes even making use of military terminology to comment on football matches or the attributes of a national team's players. The lack of sympathy, if not enmity, that illustrates the encounters between the national football teams of the Netherlands and Germany, for example, goes back to the occupation. Without doubt, history and, in general, nationalism, follow football closely. The print media in England employ a vast array of characteristics when describing players from different backgrounds. For example, Italian football players possess technical skills, elegance and are often hot tempered; Germans are physically strong, well organized and confident; French match the Italians' technique, but lack commitment and confidence; and the Spanish are poor performers, despite their resolve or else the occasional reference to the 'Spanish armada.' On the whole, non-British football players are, first, described in the context of their ethnic origins and, then, in terms of quality.

Likewise, the French press concentrates on the violent conduct of a section of English fans and shares the same image of German players with the print media across the channel. The Spanish press relates English fans to violence as well, which seems to be a stereotype widely used throughout Europe, but reserve special praise for players coming from Latin American nations, particularly, Brazil and Argentina. The multicultural identity of the French national team is also stressed, reflecting on the positive measures of social inclusion in the neighboring country, also mentioned in the German print media. Nevertheless, the Spanish press has sometimes produced racist remarks, concerning the black footballers of the French national team. In the same sense, Zinedine Zidane's sending off during a 1998 World Cup match transformed an exceptionally talented French player into a violent Algerian who grew up in a ghetto. With regard to the German national team, again, the same attributes are highlighted as in the English and French print media.

All in all, the print media clearly emphasize national sentiments so to boost support for the national team, often by making reference to historical and racial stereotypes, particularly, when the prestige of the nation is at stake. During international competitions, for example, age-old rivalries are revived and extreme forms of nationalism expressed through foul language and shameful banners. Football stadiums may then become political arenas ripe for extremism or else the necessary grounds for some fans to put across their racist views, obviously, at the expense of the beautiful game. In this respect, nationalism during international football matches is merely transformed into a platform ideal for launching a hateful and unethical campaign against all foreigners.

CONCLUSION

Right and Left are two incompatible political terms, yet they appeared consistent in the case of football. Both sides of the political spectrum exposed football to their decadent values and scandalous extremism by subjecting the game to an instrument of politics. Fascist and communist regimes occupied themselves with rebaptizing and merging football clubs to reflect their philosophy, moved talented players to the clubs they sponsored, transformed winning teams to propaganda machines and made good use of the more successful clubs to claim popular support as well as promote their image abroad. Despite the fact that fascism and communism served their cause well, at the expense of football, by manipulating the game in a relatively similar manner, on certain occasions their approach differed considerably. Even though the history of football reveals that clubs in Europe were largely founded by immigrants, fascism oftentimes dictated that these 'foreigners' be excluded from the game. The need to construct a national identity that would resist external influences was considered essential during the process of 'nation-building,' thus the ill-treatment of immigrant footballers and the systematic annihilation of elements deemed too foreign. Decisions concerning the banning of foreigners and, particularly, the involvement of Jewish players in football were, by definition, discriminatory enough to encourage bigotry. Likewise, communist-inspired tactics were less ruthless, but equally embarrassing for football, taking into account that some clubs were forced to relocate or simply disbanded and the fact that players were denied transfer opportunities to more competitive, West European, sides.

Ethnic divisions have obviously had an effect on the proper development of football as well. Most certainly, the founding fathers of the European Communities could not possibly have guessed that their 'Europe of regions' could one day be defined in terms of football. Had that been the Europeans' objective, the prophecy would have already been fulfilled, since the regional diversity of the continent never fails to openly express itself in stadiums, both on the terraces and the football pitch. To add to what is a distasteful state of affairs, when coupled with religion, these ethnic divisions may amount to economic, political and social ruptures that define an invisible dividing line, thus taking apart diverse societies. Policies that discriminate against non-Basques and non-Catholics, separate Catalans from Castilians or Flemings from Walloons hark back to the days of fascism when intolerance was commonplace. Alas, similar divisions were the cause of civil strife in former Yugoslavia and the intercommunal hostilities in Cyprus. Not to mention the revival of anti-Semitism, despite the bitter memories of the Holocaust. In any case, national unity is at risk, national identity crushed and national football torn apart. Moreover, considering that any given national football team represents an ethnic group more pragmatically at international level, it is no surprise that the team's composition may sometimes be questioned, therefore, clearly demonstrating the dynamics of regionalism and ethnocentrism.

There is no doubt that key to the multicultural identity of the European Union is the issue of nationality. After all, the EU's slogan is 'united in diversity.' In football, however, the distinct qualities of national identity have been oversimplified for the purpose of tackling the controversial nature of the doctrine of nationalism. The concept of dual nationality, for example, in a modern, integrated, Europe is by no means unusual, but football governing bodies often demand that some players denounce part of their background before they are considered eligible for the game. The case of Bosman further complicated the regulations concerning players' transfers in European, as it made available a plethora of 'foreigners,' including EU citizens, to clubs from around the continent, thus affecting severely the ethnic composition of teams. The football clubs that compete in the Champions League for Europe's most prestigious trophy play one another on a regular basis—with the same suspects usually making it to the last 16—and thus, attract considerable attention. As most clubs today include a number of 'foreigners,' these football matches may well be considered as international in nature, which has reduced, one way or another, the risk of fanaticism and the potential for violence. When the same clubs, nonetheless, play in domestic competitions, the ever-present football rivalries find expression in ethnic rivalries and religious divisions, which bring into existence racial stereotypes.

Notes

1. Gerry Finn and Richard Giulianotti, eds., *Football Culture: Local Conflicts, Global Visions* (London and Portland: Frank Cass Publishers, 2000), 257.

2. Simon Martin, *Football and Fascism: The National Game Under Mussolini* (Oxford and New York: Berg Publishers, 2005), 16–22.

3. Kevin Connolly and Rab MacWilliam, *Fields of Glory, Paths of Gold: The History of European Football* (Edinburgh and London: Mainstream Publishing, 2005) 50–51.

4. Connolly and MacWilliam, "Fields of Glory, Paths of Gold: The History of European Football," 56.

5. Franklin Foer, *How Soccer Explains the World: An Unlikely Theory of Globalization* (New York: Harper Perennial, 2005), 195.

6. Simon Kuper, *Soccer Against the Enemy: How the World's Most Popular Sport Starts and Stops Wars, Fuels Revolution, and Keeps Dictators in Power* (New York: Nation Books, 2003), 38.

7. Ulrich Hesse–Lichtenberger, *Tor! The Story of German Football* (London: WSC Books, 2003), 222–227.

8. Connolly and MacWilliam, "Fields of Glory, Paths of Gold: The History of European Football," 60.

9. Pete May, *Football and Its Followers* (London and Sydney: Franklin Watts, 2004), 27.

10. Simon Kuper, *Football Against the Enemy* (London: Orion, 1996), 228.

11. Geoff Hare, *Football in France: A Cultural History* (Oxford and New York: Berg Publishers, 2003), 119.

12. Stephen Wagg, ed., *Giving the Game Away: Football, Politics and Culture on Five Continents* (London and New York: Leicester University Press, 1995), 16–18.

13. Alan Bairner and Peter Shirlow, "Real and Imagined: Reflections on Football Rivalry in Northern Ireland," in *Fear and Loathing in World Football*, eds. Gary Armstrong and Richard Giulianotti (New York: Berg Publishers, 2001), 54.

14. Robin Wilson, *Football For All: A baseline study* (in association with the Irish Football Association, December 2005), 31.

15. Giovanni Carnibella, Anne Fox, Kate Fox, Joe McCann, James Marsh, Peter Marsh, *Football violence in Europe: A report to the Amsterdam Group* (The Social Issues Research Centre, July 1996), 71.

16. Bill Murray, *The Old Firm in the New Age: Celtic and Rangers Since the Sounes Revolution* (Edinburgh: Mainstream Publishing, 1998), 204.

17. Murray, "The Old Firm in the New Age: Celtic and Rangers Since the Sounes Revolution," 192.

18. Jose Luis Arnaut, *Independent European Sport Review* (2006), 23–24.

Chapter Four

European football's new 'disease'

In the summer of 1996 yet another football festival celebrated the very essence of this unique sport. English supporters sang the 'football is coming home' anthem and prepared themselves for a series of passionate encounters between their beloved national team and opposition from overseas, as foreigners invaded Britain to support their side's endeavors to claim the European championship. The competitive nature of the game, the all-attacking tactics deployed by the teams and the war-like cries of the spectators profess a spirited environment that, nevertheless, could generate hostility and aggressive behavior, even though EURO 1996 was not marred by any serious incidents. However, while football fans were returning home after Germany was crowned European champion, a team of social scientists from the Social Issues Research Centre in the Netherlands were busy publishing their report on 'Football violence in Europe.' The report stressed all possible causes of football violence and, therefore, due reference was also made to racism. As acts of discrimination were regularly witnessed in European football grounds, the researchers underlined the need for a pan-European scheme to address with effect the issue of racism in football, since far-right groups, fascist emblems and racist language threatened the integrity of the world's most popular sport.

The European Monitoring Centre on Racism and Xenophobia (EUMC) "decided in 2000 to commission research . . . to examine both the scope and the content of home pages which call for the use of football as a platform for racist and violent activities" and, eventually, published a report on *Racism, Football and the Internet*, which indicated that some 10 percent of the sites managed by football fans expressed racist, anti-Semitic and xenophobic views. The report also revealed that Italian and Spanish sites were more prone to racism, followed by German, Swiss, Austrian and UK sites, whereas France and Portugal scored considerably lower. The names of sites that contained racist, xenophobic and anti-Semitic material often pointed toward right-wing formations ('Fronte,' 'Irriducibili' and 'Camerati') and reflected the political ideology of fans ('Curva Nord Milano,' 'Ultras Verona,' 'Ultras Trieste,' 'Real Madrid Ultras Sur,' 'Salzburg Ultras,' 'Chelsea Headhunters' and 'Dortmund Rabauken') that used the internet to spread their beliefs. That was the case in Switzerland with 'Koma Kolonne 88' and 'Commando Ultra 88 Lugano,' considering that 88 is a code for the Nazi greeting 'Heil Hitler' ('8' stands for 'h,' as the eighth letter of the alphabet and first of both 'Heil' and 'Hitler'); the Austrian 'Rapid Club Wels' that targeted Africans; Spain's 'Mods e Skinheads Real Madrid,' which was full of Celtic crosses and fascist symbols; the Padova group known as 'Juventude Crociata,' whose members claimed to support the extreme right party 'Forza Nuova'; a Pro Patria supporters site from which one could download racist chants; and Lazio fans 'Irriducibili' site, the most racist of all, that not only contained a considerable amount of racist material, but also included links to other fan-managed sites inclined to the extreme right. Nearly all Italian and Spanish football sites containing racist material had a link to this site, as well as those of the English club Chelsea and the French Paris Saint-Germain.

Not surprisingly, perhaps, almost a decade had gone by, since the 'Football violence in Europe' report was published, when Kurt Wachter, FARE Project Coordinator, produced an unpublished essay on 'Racism and xenophobia in football,' which revealed that nothing much had changed in Europe. On the contrary, the incidents that Wachter described, their nature in particular, bring to light disturbing evidence to prove that racism and xenophobia are ever prevalent in the European game. During the EURO 2004, in Portugal, Croatian fans degraded Sylvain Wiltord of France and displayed banners featuring Celtic crosses; Italian fans gave the fascist salute, when the Italian national anthem was played in the game against Denmark; Holland's Edgar Davids suffered abuse from German fans; and, despite the ethnic composition of Portugal's national team, supporters from the Iberian country's various ethnic minorities were in short supply. Later on the same year, England's black players were racially abused in Madrid during a friendly game against Spain; Bayer Leverkusen's players were targeted in the very same stadium, the Santiago Bernabeu, at the Champions League match against Real Madrid; and Barcelona's star, as well as African Footballer of the Year, Samuel Eto'o still suffered abuse in away games of the Spanish league. Lazio fans maintained their racist attitude, occasionally encouraged by the team's captain, Paolo Di Canio, as he greeted them twice by giving the fascist salute, just like Paris Saint-Germain supporters continued to engage in monkey chanting. All in all, black players still have to endure racial abuse in Dutch, English, French, German, Italian, and Spanish football grounds; nevertheless, clubs too are subjected to derogatory remarks as Ajax, the 'Jewish' club from Amsterdam, is often subjected to anti-Semitic remarks, while Assyriska, an immigrant club in Norway, often became the target of racial abuse.

However, West European clubs are not alone in suffering from racist fans, since Sparta Prague from the Czech Republic and Hungarian club Ferencvaros' fans were found guilty of racist chants, Rapid Bucharest in Romania is degraded for its 'gypsy' origins, Poland suffers from groups of fans orientated to the extreme right and supporters of Slovakia's national team abused England's black players. The seemingly never ending list also included the death of an Albanian at the hands of a Greek football fan—following Greece's defeat in Albania— shortly after Greece was crowned European champion in Portugal, as well as the abuse suffered by Emmanuel Olisadebe of Panathinaikos, a Polish striker of Nigerian descent, from Olympiakos fans a few months later. Although there is certainly no room for yet another 'disease' to disgrace football, given that hooliganism has long scarred the beautiful game, regrettably, this evidence proves otherwise. Actually, "The problem of racism in European football is being described by some as 'endemic.'"[1]

RACISM IN EUROPEAN FOOTBALL

England

To a real fan, his local football stadium is a place of worship devoted to the round goddess, where offensive behavior is simply sacrilegious. It is a meeting place for like-minded people, ordinary individuals, who share a passion and wish to emphasize their sportsmanship, making good use of football's capacity to promote a sense of collective identity. Nevertheless, football grounds may also present a unique opportunity to display menacing emblems and express socially unacceptable views, thus becoming modern arenas redolent of alarming political symbols and appalling jungle-like sounds with the sole aim of intimidating players of a distinct ethnic background. In fact, these rather disturbing phenomena have succeeded in overshadowing the sport itself so often that Back, Crabbe and Solomos introduce the reader to the negative features of fandom early into their book when they stress that "Football grounds provided one of the largest public arenas in which racism could be openly expressed."[2] Britain has probably suffered most from fans that consciously violated the sanctity of football stadiums. A former Tottenham Hotspur player, Danny Blanchflower, was once quoted saying that 'The noise of the crowd, the singing and chanting, is the oxygen we players breathe';[3] however, monkey chants are anything but fresh air. This sort of abuse can only produce an atmosphere polluted enough to resist the need to breathe, which soon creates a hostile environment difficult to endure and, therefore, performing under such conditions becomes a daunting task for black players to complete. Still, racist chanting may be nothing more than a tool that serves to set apart fans supporting opposing teams, whereas the possibility that racial abuse may simply be the fans' attempt to affect the opponents' performance and the result of the match should not be ignored either.

Although visualizing Arthur Wharton, the first black player in England, play his football for Darlington as early as 1889 reflects positively on the English game, racial discrimination made a premature appearance as Dixie Dean, an

Everton player with a 'tanned' appearance, was often subjected to racist abuse in the 1930s. Coincidentally, perhaps, extreme right groups first became interested in football during the same period, when the British Union of Fascists attempted to exploit social inequalities to promote their cause by attracting the attention of fans from a working-class background, whereas some twenty years later the White Defense League publicized racist material in the *Black and White News*— a newspaper sold outside football stadiums in London. Similar fascist groups became increasingly active in the 1970s, as the National Front, along with the British Movement and, later on, groups of skinheads, turned their attention to football. In fact, some sections of football fans from clubs like Arsenal, Chelsea, Leeds United, Millwall, Newcastle United and West Ham United were closely associated with fascist elements. Evidently, far-right groups were deeply in-volved in Britain's greatest football disturbances, since leaflets of the British National Party (BNP) were found on the English section of the terraces at the Heysel stadium in 1985, while in 1995 the friendly match in Dublin between the Republic of Ireland and England was abandoned due to violent clashes between the two rival contingents of fans that, again, involved members of the British National Party and a Nazi group called Combat 18.[4] Interestingly, the number eighteen stands for Adolf Hitler's initials, following the rationale behind the website of 'Koma Kolonne 88.' The activities of these extreme right groups were facilitated to a great extent by Margaret Thatcher's policies that brought about deep social divisions and increased the gap between the lower working-class and ethnic minorities.

According to van Sterkenburg and Westland,

"The fans—almost exclusively white at this point in history—considered soc-cer to be a 'white' game. An occasional successful black player was acceptable. However, the rise of dozens of black players, including England internationals Viv Anderson, Garth Crooks and West Bromwich Albion's triumvirate, Cyrille Regis, Brandon Batson and Laurie Cunningham, posed a more sinister danger; that the game was in the early throes of an alien takeover. This has to be con-sidered against the social background of England during the late 1970s: high youth unemployment; a right-wing Conservative government; the resurgence of the far right (National Front) and especially the virulent skinhead movement, which had had a strong presence in English soccer stadiums for a decade."[5]

It seems that the waning electoral support of the National Front in the late 1970s resulted to an increase of its activities, possibly, encouraged by the election of a xenophobic Thatcher. In an attempt to produce the necessary grounds for xeno-phobia and, therefore, racism to grow, the National Front openly supported ra-cial discrimination through its magazine, *Bulldog* (first published in 1981), since one of its pages almost eulogized racist behavior by producing information on British clubs' most racist fans and rating them accordingly. However, Lowles supports that the success of these groups in recruiting new members from the world of football, either on the terraces or outside stadiums, is questionable, given that fans often presented themselves as Nazi sympathetic to terrify their opponents, with only a few being ideologically driven or, indeed, members of extreme right groups. Back, Crabbe and Solomos oppose Lowles' view and stress that "the relationship between the far-right and football culture is instrumental rather than organic."[6] Along similar lines, a team of researchers from Leuven University, in Belgium, examined the causes of the Heysel tragedy and "concluded that fascist groups across Europe were using football as a cover for networking, exchanging information and recruitment. Far-right groups seem keen to target football matches to attract recruits."[7] Apparently, the National Front had relative success in recruiting members during England's away matches on European soil, also taking into consideration that "a former leader of the National Front Flag Group, Martin Wingfield, admitted that the group had encouraged its members to be active in football stadia and had reaped benefits from this both financially and in terms of new members."[8] The account of a fan that traveled to Dublin for the game that was eventually abandoned reveals that "football was the chance to let the world know how BNP members felt about Northern Ireland."[9] Although the exact role of extreme right groups in football is widely disputed, it is certain that they have been quite influential.

The involvement of such groups in football reached unparalleled heights in the 1980s, particularly in Leeds, forcing the formation of the 'Leeds Fans United Against Racism and Fascism' group in 1987, in an attempt to contain the increasing influence of extreme right groups at Elland Road by distributing anti-racist material. Extreme right groups such as the National Front had become increasingly active and when Leeds United was relegated to Division Two, racism became even more widespread. In fact, Leeds United was so deeply affected by racism that the Football League threatened the club with expulsion, forcing the club's officials to set up a hotline for fans to report racist incidents and take a strong position against offenders by banning them from the football ground. While this part of Britain is by no means hostile to black players, particularly, when taking into account that Sheffield United fans—local rivals of Leeds United—distance themselves from their neighbors by stressing their ethical fan culture,[10] the club from Leeds suffered from yet another serious racist incident when two footballers, Jonathon Woodgate and Lee Bowyer, were implicated in an assault against Satfraz Najeib, an Asian student, on 12 January 2000. Even though the club supported the two players, the English Football Association adopted a more radical approach and did not hesitate to rule out both footballers from all future games of the national team until the court delivered judgment. Ever since, Leeds United have made great strides in combating racial discrimination and are nowadays praised by the Union of European Football Associations (UEFA) for their significant contribution in the campaign against racism in football.

Typically, racial abuse comes in the form of monkey chanting, as the more 'intelligent' members of the crowd imitate noises made by our closest relatives in the animal kingdom. This sort of immoral attitude is often complemented with the throw of bananas and peanuts, with fans, occasionally, displaying a great sense of 'creativity,' as a live monkey was set free on Liverpool's ground to humiliate John Barnes. Far worse was the case with a section of Millwall fans that made unethical remarks concerning a fire in Deptford, which caused the death of thirteen black youngsters in 1981. Certainly, such fans would not limit themselves to only denigrating black players. On the contrary, anti-Semitic chanting is also prevalent in English football stadiums, usually targeting fans of Tottenham Hotspur, due to their Jewish connections. Other incidents of paramount significance involve Chelsea's Paul Cannoville, who was abused by his own fans, and the (alleged) policy of Everton against signing black players, until Daniel Amokachi arrived at the club in 1994. Everton fans were renowned for their racist views, often calling Liverpool, their local rivals, 'Nigerpool,' which may account for the club's selective transfer policy.

Even more worrying were Ron Atkinson's comments during a 1990 World Cup match between England and Cameroon, when he insulted the intelligence of the African players presenting them as subhumans that had just climbed down the trees. Still, nothing compares to the serious race-related incidents that took place in 2001 when the football match between Oldham Athletic and Stoke City was marked by violent clashes between visiting fans of Stoke and members of the local Asian community, which caused further scuffles in the area between local ethnic minorities and members of racist groups. In a European context, Arsenal's black players were racially abused in Holland by PSV Eindhoven's fans, in September 2002, during a Champions League match. A few weeks later, it was England black players' turn to suffer similar abuse, first, in the away game against Slovakia and then in the Former Yugoslav Republic of Macedonia. On home ground, racist remarks directed at black players have subsided, however, in April 2003 the players of Turkey's national team were seriously abused and the English Football Association was fined by UEFA.

Gianluca Vialli's account, in *The Italian Job*, produced an interesting, yet precarious, approach to racial stereotypes. Prior to exploring the biological differences between West African men and others, Vialli stressed "There is clear belief that black footballers are more athletic," however,

"If blacks are naturally better athletes than whites, it's as if they have a God-given advantage, and this belittles their achievements: it implies that whites must have to work that much harder to compete with blacks. Or that blacks can afford to be lazy. This is close to ugly, long-held racial stereotypes and understandably makes people uncomfortable, particularly because of what some might see as the next logical step in this thinking: if blacks are more blessed in one department (athletic ability) surely they must be deficient in another (intelligence)."[11]

Physical attributes account for an oversimplified biological approach, with regard to the classification of footballers, which dictates that black players be placed into positions on the pitch that demand speed and strength. In this respect, blacks players are not assigned to 'intelligent' positions, which are usually occupied by 'disciplined' and 'committed' white players, and, therefore, are restricted to the wings of the team's tactical formation. Inevitably, "Black players tend to be 'stacked' into these peripheral positions due to their coaches' racial beliefs that they cannot match the decision-making skills or consistency of white players, although their speed and unpredictable style are essential on the wings."[12]

Beyond any shadow of doubt, racism is not confined to the terraces, but stretches over football's prime institutions—clubs and national/local authorities. Inapt remarks regarding black players' poor performance when playing in cold and their lack of commitment and tenacity impinge on the game itself, as well as the prospect of a career in football's upper echelons for former black players. Black players are generally commended for their physical power, athletic bodies and aggression—a classic stereotype that has its origins in the times of colonialism—and media reports often make due reference to these attributes, thus promoting discrimination in a subliminal manner. Due to these characteristics, black footballers were heavily concentrated in attacking positions and featured much less in the defense and key positions of their teams. It is essential to note, however, Stefan Szymanski's research, as it revealed that the more successful clubs contained a number of black players in their starting lineup that exceeded the average.[13] During the 1985–1986, 1989–1990 and 1995–1996 seasons, white players dominated the football grounds, but witnessed a slight reduction from 92.3 percent (1331 footballers), through 89.5 percent (1302), to 88.3 percent (1732) respectively, whereas the numbers of black players increased consistently from 111 (7.7 percent), to 152 (11.5 percent), eventually, reaching 231 players (11.7 percent). The distribution of black footballers across the four leagues was definitely uneven, nevertheless, since the Premiership absorbed the majority (9.8 percent, 15.4 percent and 17.5 percent over the three seasons), whereas the remaining three scored much less as we make our way down to the other divisions. Division One amassed more black players than the two lower leagues (8.7 percent, 10.9 percent and 11.1 percent), probably because the most successful clubs, following Szymanski's rationale, competed for promotion to the top division, draining the pool of human resources available to the lower divisions (7.3 percent, 8.1 percent and 9.4 percent in Division Two—4.8 percent, 7.2 percent and 9.5 percent in Division Three). Despite this evidence, black players in England were quite successful on an individual basis, given that their transfer cost often exceeded the amount spent for the purchase of their white colleagues.

These findings suggest that black footballers could claim parallel success in coaching positions, but only Ruud Gullit has held managerial positions at Premiership clubs, Chelsea and Newcastle United, though emphasis was probably more often put on his foreign background rather than his dark skin. Most probably, the same applies to the former manager of Fulham, Jean Tigana. Before Gullit's appointment as manager at Chelsea in 1996, Edwin Stein became the first black manager in 1993 at Barnet, which, nevertheless, was not a top-flight team, with Uriah Rennie becoming the first black referee in the top division in 1997. The relative success of black sportsmen at football's higher levels was the result of a long-lasting process that saw Viv Anderson become the first black footballer to play for England in 1978, before Paul Ince claimed his first appearance as captain of England in 1993 and Hope Powell succeeded in taking charge of England Women's team in 1998.

Nonetheless, football is generally considered 'a man's game,' yet another stereotype with racist connotations, given that the Women's national side attracts considerably less support and attention than the Men's team. Hence, Powell's personal success does not necessarily reflect the Football Association's modernized principles, but a mediocre attempt to disguise its apathy. It is noteworthy that the inclusion of black players in the squad of England's national team was facilitated to a great extent by the appointment of Bobby Robson as England manager in 1982, when he made it explicitly clear that the best footballers would be selected to represent England at international level regardless of their skin color. However, Nigerian-born John Fashanu, who earned two successive caps in England's colors during a friendly tournament but was never selected again, advised Gabriel Agbonlahor against playing for England expecting that the youngster may share his fate. Agbonlahor rejected Nigeria's call to represent the African country, opting instead to play for England after representing them at youth level.

The fact that Paul Ince at Macclesfield and Keith Alexander at Peterborough were, at the time, the only black managers in the Football League, inspired John Barnes to stress that "From an athletic point of view there will be black people because athletically we are equal, from a managerial perspective it's more to do with the intellectual aspect of it and I don't think we are regarded as intellectually equal."[14] As it happens, ten days after Barnes' remarks the number of black managers in the lower division was reduced, since Keith Alexander was sacked due to the club's poor performance. Paul Ince, too, expressed his frustration at the lack of black managers in the Premiership and recalled his experience at Wolverhampton Wanderers, when he failed to persuade the club's officials of his managerial abilities. It is important to note that Ince is convinced that "Maybe black managers will have more of a chance with foreign owners coming into the game, people who don't really see this [color] as an issue. At Macclesfield the owner's from Iraq and all he wants is this club to stay in this division. I feel wanted at this club, which is why I'm working my nuts off to make sure we stay up."[15] Despite the fact that there is no evidence to suggest that football's governing bodies in England would resent the appointment of a black manager at England Men's team, the strong opposition to Sven Goran Eriksson's appointment as England manager encourages such speculation.

In the same context, the absence of Asian football players from Football League clubs is striking. Although the Asian population is almost twice the size of the black community, a 2001 survey by the Sir Norman Chester Centre for Football Research indicated that some 0.2 percent of the youngsters that featured in football academies were of Asian origin, with only four Asians playing their football for a professional club in 2006. This disturbing evidence forced the Asians in Football Forum to request, in September 2005, that the English Football Association take action to encourage a wider participation of Asian players in football. Instead of maintaining a passive stance, by merely awaiting the Football Association's response, the Asian community put a lot of emphasis on the clubs that currently represent it. A number of teams have already witnessed considerable success, when taking into account London APSA and Sporting Bengal, the first Asian clubs to take part in the FA Cup during the 2005–2006 season, and the Bradford-based Albion Sports Club, which reached the nation-wide FA Sunday Cup Final twice.

Other notable achievements concern the contribution of two Football League referees of Asian descent, Jarnail Singh and Mo Matadar, in football's ever changing multi-ethnic composition. Despite the fact that Dimeo and Mills, in *Soccer in South Asia*, underline the Indians' desire to engage in football activities, Manchester United signed South Korean Ji Sung Park and Everton acquired the services of Chinese Li Tie, high ranking football officials—at both institutional (national and local authorities) and club level—consider Asians unsuitable for the game, due to their supposed physical inferiority and incompatible culture. Even though 'vindaloo,' an Asian dish, became the 1998 World Cup football anthem of the English, England had yet to come to terms with cultural diversity, as those media reports that concerned the performance of the national sides that took part in the competition were overflowing with racist remarks. Actually, "South American teams and players were often referred to as skilful, naturally gifted and exhibitionists, whilst simultaneously being fiery, temperamental and unpredictable," "North African teams were perceived as being somewhat light-weight and lacking in physical power" and "Other African national football teams such as Nigeria and Cameroon were naturally athletic, strong runners but with little organization and discipline, whereas the Scandinavian teams were very disciplined, possessing great power, little flair but stern commitment to shape and style (or lack of it)."[16] It comes as no surprise, probably, that during the 1998 World Cup in France, England fans racially abused nationals of the host country simply for being French and, particularly, those from the local Arab community for their skin color.

Foreign players were prevented from playing their football in England due to the Football Association's decision to put into effect a two-year residency rule in 1931, for no good reason other than reducing their numbers, until European Community laws prohibited this sort of discrimination in 1978. Obviously, Gianluca Vialli, of Italian origin, must have shocked the English Football Association some twenty years later, when he fielded on 26 December 1999 a cosmopolitan Chelsea team comprising foreign players alone. Surely, Vialli's criteria for the selection of players should not be attributed to discrimination, even though his predilection for foreigners over English talent regarding that match was more than clear. This incredible incident was not so much a celebration of globalization, as a major shortcoming for national teams. Considering that during the opening games of the 2002–2003 season only eighty-eight out of 220 players were English, with 132 foreign players coming from forty-two different countries, local talent was clearly in short supply. National teams obviously have to struggle with the new realities of the game, but so do the fans that support them with fervor, as national sentiments are often expressed through sport. More recently, Alan Pardew, manager of West Ham United, and Arsene Wenger of Arsenal made the headlines when the Arsenal manager almost called the former a racist, following Pardew's remarks about Arsenal's lack of English players after the two London clubs met in a Premiership match.

Carrington and McDonald stress that "The reason why sport has often been used politically to articulate nationalist and racist concerns is that sport is perhaps one of the clearest and most public means in demonstrating how Britain has become a multicultural nation."[17] Hence, hooliganism in England is also related to racism and xenophobia, even though the country, as a political entity, is deeply involved in the process of European integration. Based on a report produced by Sheffield Hallam University in 1996, a significant number of people (some 20 percent) from the local ethnic minority communities were made victims of racial abuse, when Sheffield United played at home. As a consequence, members of minority ethnic groups decided to spend most time indoors, merely to minimize the potential of being subject to racial harassment. Sport and football, in particular, can be extremely symbolic if not political, at international level, and thus a powerful tool at the disposal of extreme right groups that have long challenged the 'Englishness' of black players and fans. Although the concept of 'Britishness' appears to be less racist and more inclusive than 'Englishness' is, probably because the latter is also associated to England's imperial past when the English culture was a dominant force all over her colonies, the St. George cross seems to contribute a great deal toward social inclusion, as opposed to the British flag, or else the 'Union Jack,' that is much related to racism and abuse. It is widely accepted that such racial divisions within the British society and the abuse that often express them are the main causes that prevent black and Asian fans from attending football games and, therefore, limit the cultural diversity of English spectators.

Unlike France and the Netherlands, which have successfully built upon the multiracial nature of their national teams, England maintains her prejudiced stance towards non-white footballers. On one occasion, the nearly all-white English Football Association fell victim of their own lack of intelligence and brought shame on themselves when they produced a documentary-like film, the *Pride of the Nation*, which celebrated England's best players over the last forty years, failing, nevertheless, to include a single black footballer. As many complained, including Rio Ferdinand of Manchester United, the Football Association was compelled to produce a new version of England's contemporary football history that took account of a number of black players and apologized for its ineptitude. In contrast, the English Football Association has been commended by UEFA for their contribution in eliminating racism from football and, on March 2006, assisted their counterparts in Israel to combat racism at Israeli league matches by launching an anti-racist campaign, as Arab players are often subjected to racial abuse. Finally, ahead of the 2006 World Cup in Germany, the British Embassy in Berlin hosted a conference, 'Breaking Down Barriers, Celebrating Diversity, Kicking Out Racism,' in order to discuss racism in football and the underrepresentation of ethnic minorities. The conference included delegations from England and Germany, representing their national football associations, prominent campaigners from Kick It Out and Flutlicht, as well as a rare football match between Islamic imams and Christian ministers.

France

Throughout the 1970s and 1980s, French hooligans were, primarily, working-class white males, joined by upper class members that belonged to the skinhead movement and, together, formed the basis for the 'White French' racist group that was usually responsible for race-related incidents in football grounds. It was in the late 1980s when fascist symbols and racist chanting became a usual phenomenon in French football stadiums. Members of extreme right groups were often in the crowds among French hooligans, with some Paris Saint-Germain fans habitually terrorizing Arabs and blacks, even though a section of PSG supporters are made up of immigrants from Africa, Portugal and Spain, including a number of fans of Jewish descent. The Boulogne 'kop,' a group of skinheads inclined to the extreme right, is linked to the National Revolutionary Movement (MNR), as well as to the Front National, and supports that football belongs to the white community, strongly opposing multiracialism. Its members often engage in monkey chanting, publish a magazine that promotes racist and anti-Semitic sentiments and maintain good relations with foreign clubs that also have to put up with racist supporters of their own, such as Anderlecht and Bruges in Belgium, AC Fiorentina and Internazionale of Italy, and particularly, Chelsea, Leeds United and West Ham United in England.

In November 2006, the Boulogne 'kop' was indirectly involved in the death of a fan, Julien Quemener, who was accidentally shot by a black police officer that was trying to protect a Jewish supporter of Hapoel Tel Aviv chased by Paris Saint-Germain supporters outside the stadium, following the end of a UEFA cup tie between the two clubs. Evidently, during and after the game, fans of Paris Saint-Germain chanted anti-Semitic insults and made Nazi salutes. As a consequence, Mayor Bertrand Delanoë of Paris threatened to stop financing Paris Saint-

Germain, unless the club took effective steps to rid itself of hooliganism. On another occasion, the Boulogne 'kop' were involved in violent clashes with Turkish supporters when the club from Paris played hosts to Galatasaray in April 2001. In general, the Boulogne 'kop' was formed following football-related violent incidents between white French and black immigrants that fought each other to preserve their territory on the terraces of Parc des Princes. This notorious group of Paris Saint-Germain fans also objects the use of foreign players, viewed as a sign of decadence, though they support their club's black players. It is no coincidence that the Boulogne 'kop' occupy a particular part of the terrace, behind one goal, that they consider a whites-only area, thus forcing the club in April 2000 to make use of a permanently displayed banner that reads 'There is a place for everyone at Paris Saint-Germain, except racists.'

Racism in French football is often attributed to the multiracial nature of the national team. The composition of the French national football team has been a matter of dispute since 1958, when Jacques Ferran produced a piece in the 'Football France' sports magazine entitled 'Not to be confused: the French national team and French football.' Evidently, there are two "strains of French writing about immigration and football," one criticizing the heterogeneity of national team, the other stressing how it "enriches the national game."[18] Ferran's views are somehow related to the fact that during the Algerian War of Independence, the Algerian National Liberation Front asked, in 1958, French players of Algerian origins to denounce their 'Frenchness' and take part in the Algerian national football team. Among the ten players that responded with enthusiasm to the call of their motherland was Rachid Mekloufi, a talented player who played his football for Saint-Etienne, had already represented France on four occasions and, most likely, would have been called up again for the 1958 World Cup in Sweden.

The role of immigrants in French football has often been underestimated, even though L'Equipe stressed in the past that "more than 30 percent of Les Bleus down through the years came from immigrant families or had been born outside metropolitan France."[19] Regardless, the multiracial nature of the French national football team was certainly rewarded when Michel Platini led his 'foreign legion' with unparalleled success on their way to win the 1984 European Championship before a predominant French crowd. Ever since, the French national team reflects the country's multicultural nature with effect and encourages further integration. Most significantly, success in the 1998 World Cup and the 2000 European Championship certainly celebrated the multicultural values of the French Republic. Hence, it is no coincidence that "The phrase '*black-blanc-beur*' was created on the pattern of the national colours (*bleu-blanc-rouge*) to describe the special Frenchness of the team and the nation's unity in diversity."[20] However, integration is far from completed, as the November 2005 riots in Paris demonstrated. The fact that the extreme right continues to attract a significant portion of the electorate, allows the likes of Jean-Marie Le Pen to degrade ethnic minorities, question their loyalty to the Republic and even ridicule the national team for including so many colored players. France's national team at the 2006 World Cup was made up of seventeen players from minorities, in a 23 strong squad, thus prompting Le Pen to remark that "perhaps the coach went overboard on the proportion of colored players."[21] Nevertheless, the impact of anti-racist football organizations appears to be limited, due to the reluctance of the relevant football governing bodies—at national and club level—and the French government to 'politicize' football. Even though most football clubs and their fans strongly oppose racism, they consider anti-racist initiatives as political activities and, therefore, inappropriate. Unlike the somewhat awkward response of his fellow countrymen, Thierry Henry launched 'The One 4 All Foundation' to combat racism and social inequality by funding projects on sports and education in Europe and Africa.

In the past, Arsenal's prolific striker was often subjected to racial abuse, not to mention his non-white teammates in the national team. As a matter of fact, Zinedine Zidane's dismissal during the 2006 World Cup final in Germany was surrounded by premature speculations with racist connotations. Lip readers interpreted one of Marco Materrazi's words into 'terrorist,' which journalists were only too keen to put into context and relate the remarks of the Italian player to the well-known Algerian origins of the charismatic footballer.

Germany

Racism in German football became a serious issue after the country's reunification, following the fall of the Berlin Wall in 1989 and the end of the Cold War era. According to the official website of the German league, when the first ever matches of the Bundesliga kicked off in 1963, there were only three foreigners playing for German clubs, Eintracht Frankfurt's Austrian Willy Huberts, Kaiserslautern's Dutch Jacobus Prins and TSV Munich 1860's Yugoslav Petar Radenkovic. The first black player was Peruvian Julio Baylon who played for Fortuna Cologne in 1973, whereas the first Asian player would follow a few years later when Yasuhiko Okudera arrived at 1.FC Cologne in 1977. Interestingly, although Jorginho's discipline is commended, the same does not apply to fellow Brazilian football players, as 'Ailton is renowned for suddenly deciding to extend his holidays as well as for his rodeo escapades back home in Brazil, but compared to Zeze, Ailton's actions pale into insignificance. In 1964, Zeze walked out of 1.FC Cologne at the first sight of snow after just five matches and one goal.' The unprofessional attitude of Ailton and Zeze's odd response to cold may have little to do with the sort of racial discrimination that soon took over German football stadiums. By the 1992–1993 season, it was deemed necessary that all clubs in Germany's top division fielded their teams with the players wearing shirts that carried the slogan 'My friend is a foreigner' during the final matches before the winter break in an attempt to combat racism in football. As a matter of fact, the involvement of neo-Nazi groups in football and their participation in related disturbances had increased by the early 1990s, particularly, when taking into account a survey that revealed that nearly 20 percent of German football fans were sympathetic to the neo-Nazi movement, although the majority (35 percent) declared their support for either of the two main democratic parties.

Racism and fascism have long scarred the beautiful game in Germany, inspiring a section of St Pauli's supporters to form in 1986 an anti-racist group called *Millerntor Roar!*, named after the club's ground, which encouraged the club's officials to take a staunch position against racism by banning all related chants and banners inside the stadium in 1991. Their success soon attracted the attention of extreme right groups, particularly, fans of neighboring Hamburg SV, thus developing a distinctive form of local rivalry. Another group of fans orientated to the extreme right, with links to the neo-Nazi movement and even the National Democratic Party, were supporters of Borussia Dortmund, perhaps, the main reason that Julio Cesar's contract with the club had an opt out clause in case he encountered racist abuse. It seems, nevertheless, that the first 'foreigners' to suffer from racial discrimination were Turkish players, since footballers of other nationalities were rare. Nowadays, considering the size of the Turkish community in Germany, it is surprising that not many players of Turkish origin play their football for German clubs. The absence of Turkish footballers is the main cause that exclusive Turkish clubs exist in Germany, supported financially by Turkish businesses. Halm produced an account of the causes of segregation in Germany's amateur football regarding the Turkish community. It seems that the relative lack of participation of players with Turkish origins is, primarily, related to football teams made up entirely by Turkish players, which Germans regard as an obstacle to further integration, and the obvious cultural differences that separate one ethnic group from another. He also argues that "the social opportunities available to people of Turkish descent in Germany are still insufficient."[22]

When Schalke 04 kicked off the 2003–2004 season with a series of poor performances, a section of the club's fans singled out their Nigerian-born striker, Victor Agali, for failing to score goals. Although Agali enjoyed the support of the Schalker Fan-Initiative, an anti-racist group, and Rudi Assauer, the club's general manager, the player was, eventually, forced to leave the club. More recently, Asamoah, yet another Schalke 04 player, was racially abused during a German cup tie against a team from Hansa Rostock's regional league and carried on playing his game despite the fact that his coach offered to substitute him. At this point, it is important to note the player's courageous response and determination to convey a powerful message to those disgraceful supporters, which was followed by a matching performance as Asamoah scored two goals and created another three for his team. Similar incidents occurred in Germany's lower football leagues, as Energie Cottbus fans displayed an anti-Semitic banner in the away match against Dynamo Dresden in December 2005 and Lokomotive

Leipzig fans formed a human swastika during a match against Sachsen Leipzig, though little coverage was given by German media. Surprisingly, the media also ignored Asamoah's ill-treatment in the UEFA Cup away game against Levski Sofia—despite the complaints of the Schalke 04 manager during the press conference and the fact that the referee reported the incident to UEFA—and turned a blind eye to the racist behavior of German fans during international matches in France, Italy, Slovakia and Slovenia during 2005 and 2006. Eventually, the media discovered that German football was stained by racism in March 2006, after Halle fans had seriously abused Sachsen Leipzig's Adebowale Ogungbure. When the game came to an end, the player gave the fans a Nazi salute to protest his treatment and was, then, brought to justice, since fascist symbols and Nazi salutes are prohibited in Germany, but was soon after released. Even though the reasons for his unyielding behavior were never brought up, the media frenzy helped turn an otherwise 'ordinary' racist incident into a serious matter of social exclusion, thus compelling the German Football Association to launch an investigation. Racist behavior persisted albeit in different, obscured, forms, given that in a match between St Pauli and Chemnitz, during the same football season, a group of Chemnitz fans displayed "red banners with empty white circles—the allusion to far-right symbols sufficed."[23] More recently, a German referee, Michael Weiner, came close to ending the match between TSV Alemannia Aachen and VfL Borussia Mönchengladbach and warned their fans to halt derogatory chants, as a group of Aachen supporters degraded Mönchengladbach's Brazilian Kahe, with Mönchengladbach fans responding by racially abusing Aachen's Moses Sichone.

Merkel, Sombert and Tokarski described the early attempts of the German Football Association to eliminate racism, which were more or less inadequate as they usually concerned legal issues and the safety of fans in football stadiums. Among other more recent anti-racism schemes, the German Football Association supported the Dortmund fan project and launched in October 2003 the 'Kick Racism Out' campaign; screened the websites of all clubs in the top three divisions for racist and other offensive material during the 2003–2004 season; gave an official presentation on the qualities of a CD-ROM that concerned the measures available to stewards for addressing racist incidents with effect; and commissioned Nils Havemann's book *Fußball unterm Hakenkreuz*, 'Football under the swastika,' in an attempt to explore the role of the game in Nazi Germany. Moreover, statements on banners, displayed at both home and away matches of the German national team, are carefully scrutinized and any offensive behavior is recorded and put forward to the 'Central Information desk for Sport employment,' *Zentrale Informationsstelle für Sporteinsätze*, for proper analysis and, when deemed necessary, to initiate further action. Although German authorities may have had considerable experience in dealing with race-related football incidents, hosting the 2006 World Cup was probably an arduous task by any standards.

A major football tournament of the caliber of a World Cup demands attention that amounts to a great deal of organization. In the case of Germany, the local authorities had to take into serious consideration the potential impact of neo-Nazi groups, other than ordinary procedural issues. As it happens, a black German fell victim to a race-related assault almost a month before kickoff, forcing the local police to advise courts against sanctioning neo-Nazi rallies in areas close to the designated World Cup venues. Needless to say, the fact that Angola, Ghana, the Ivory Coast, Togo and Tunisia all took part in the 2006 World Cup, only added weight on the Germans' workload, as waves of colorful African supporters were expected to attend the matches of their national team.

Inevitably, the World Cup in Germany did not evade the attention of fascist elements, as one group published a different version of the 'World Cup guide' that illustrated a German player wearing the nation's colors in the number twenty-five shirt bearing the message 'White. It's not only the color of the kit. For a real NATIONAL team!' Most certainly, the fact that the player who usually pulled that jersey on was Patrick Owomoyela, whose father is Nigerian, was anything but a coincidence, thus prompting the German Football Association (Deutsche Fußball-Bund) to demand that the perpetrators withdraw all related material. However, Owomoyela was not the first black player to suffer such denigration. Gerald Asamoah, of Ghanaian descent, became in 2001 the first black player to represent Germany, encouraging a neo-Nazi group to produce a photograph of his that came with a message saying "No Gerald you are not Germany."[24]

Similar shameful activities were witnessed in a number of World Cup matches. In the match between Italy and Ghana, a number of Italian supporters made the fascist salute when their country's national anthem was played, an inflatable banana was waved whenever Ghana's players committed a foul or were in ball possession and FARE observers discovered, on their way to the Hanover stadium, an 'Ultras Italia' graffiti that featured a swastika. Germany and Poland's football encounter was preceded by violent clashes, which continued after the end of the match, including a number of far-right supporters who shouted 'Sieg Heil,' while some Polish fans wore scarves that featured Celtic crosses and the scull of the Waffen-SS. Following the match between France and Switzerland, anti-Turkish merchandise was sold outside the stadium in Stuttgart, with scarves reading: 'Bye bye Turkey—Turkish man stays at home,' probably, motivated by the violent events that took place in Switzerland's away game in Turkey during the qualifying round. Finally, Serbian fans displayed a banner with a Celtic cross in Serbia and Montenegro's game against the Netherlands. Fascist symbols and related gestures are prohibited in Germany and so, when an English football fan was detained by German police for having a swastika painted on his chest and a Nazi SS sign, he was banned from attending football matches for twenty-five months.

The World Cup's potential to attract the attention of the international community was also exploited by Iranian supporters that did not hesitate to sacrifice football's sporting ideals for the cause of political matters, as protesters gathered in Nuremberg to denounce Mahmoud Ahmadinejad. The Iranian leader was also condemned by demonstrators from the local Jewish community, because of his appalling remarks about the Holocaust, apparently, the same reason that generated support for his leadership from neo-Nazi groups. Nevertheless, it is significant that no race-related violent incidents took place during the World Cup.

Italy

Lazio's fans are, perhaps, the most racist in Italy and often sing the national anthem while making fascist salutes. They also hold anti-Semitic views, usually targeting local rivals Roma, even though there is no direct relation between the club and Rome's Jewish community, apart from having had some Jewish presidents run the club in the past. Racism in Italian football had always been a controversial phenomenon. In the city of Milan, the two local heavyweight rivals, AC Milan and Internazionale, have had different experiences with regard to racism. When AC Milan's Ruud Gullit dedicated his 1987 'European Player of the Year' award to Nelson Mandela, he automatically became a symbol of anti-racism, whereas Internazionale fans maintained their racist behavior until 1994, the year that Paul Ince signed for their club. The English black footballer soon gained the respect of the supporters and the monkey chants disappeared from the Giuseppe Meatsa. Although Ince relished a racism-free environment when playing before home supporters, he was still subjected to racial abuse when visiting other clubs. On one particular occasion, Ince collided with the goalkeeper of Cremona, at an away match in 1995, and the home fans engaged in racist chants. Astonishingly, when the player responded by applauding the supporters of Cremona, the referee simply decided to book him. In the case of Udinese, the transfer of Ronnie Rosenthal, an Israeli international, was never completed due to local anti-Semitic campaigns. In general, racism in Italian football is a mirror image of the society and the politics it is associated with, more than in other countries, as notable members of the government have supported racist views in the past, taking into account the case of Umberto Bossi, Minister for Reform, who called immigrants 'Bingo Bongo.' The Italian Football Association, in an attempt to combat racism in football, prohibited the use of banners that had racist connotations, in January 2000, after Lazio's hard-core fans displayed a banner dedicated to the 'Tiger' Arkan, a renowned Serb war criminal.

The approach of the Italian football governing body was more than necessary, considering that in 1996 Verona's fans went a step too far when they burned a black dummy to declare their opposition to the club's decision to employ the services of a black player. However, the Italian Football Association has not always responded with vigor, given that in 2005, during a match between Messina and Internazionale, Messina's Mark Zoro was abused so appallingly by away fans that, at some point and while the game was in full play, he picked up the ball and asked for the game to be halted, but no official seemed prepared to take such action. The Italian Football Association's only response was to devote the next Italian Cup and Serie A games to anti-racism. Unlike the feeble reaction of the Italian Football Association, after Treviso's fans racially abused their team's Nigerian-born Akeem Omolade in 2001, the players of Treviso took on the field in the next home game their faces painted black. Mark Zoro was also abused during Messina's away match against Internazionale, but the Italian Football Association took no action whatsoever, although FIFA's new regulations clearly mention the deduction of points and even the relegation of teams whose supporters repeatedly engage in racist activities. As if upholding a tradition, the same player was abused, yet again, when Internazionale hosted Messina at the San Siro in December 2006. Apart from the 'customary' racist chants and jeering, whenever the player from the Ivory Coast touched the ball, Internazionale fans also displayed a banner that read '*Zoro infame. Il razzismo non è un ululato ma i lamenti di un invasato,*' which translates 'Zoro is a disgrace. Racism is not wailing, but the lament of an obsessive.'

Considering that black players made their first ever appearance in Italy's football grounds during the early 1980s, the overall response of the football governing bodies to racism was some twenty years overdue and relatively weak, since FIFA's new regulations (2000) had not been applied at the time, even though both racial abuse and offensive banners stained the game. Eventually, the Italian Football Association adopted FIFA guidelines related to racism in 2006. In the meantime, Tim Parks, in his *A Season with Verona*, recorded a number of incidents during the 2000–2001 season where the fans of Verona engaged in racist chanting to an extent that the club was given a one-match ban. His book also made reference to a number of cases where the Verona fans insulted fans of clubs from the south, thus underlining Italy's regional division and the significance that was still attached to the *mezzogiorno* line. Moreover, Lazio's Paolo Di Canio twice saluted his fans in a fascist manner, first, in a match against arch rivals Roma and, then, against Livorno, a club with fans inclined to leftist politics. In the case of Livorno, Di Canio's disgraceful attitude took place only days after the 2005 Zoro incident. Nonetheless, unlike the officials of Leeds United, the Lazio board distanced themselves from the player, particularly, since Di Canio had openly expressed his inclination to fascism and admiration for Benito Mussolini. Sadly, soon after the second episode, which saw the player being handed a one match ban, "Di Canio's fascist salute features on unofficial merchandise sold outside the Stadio Olimpico."[25]

All in all, it seems that racism in Italian football is associated with radical political views. Despite the fact that the '*ultras*' merely reflected the polarization of Italian society during the 1970s, when the two extremes of the political spectrum dictated Italy's internal affairs, the influx of immigrants in the 1980s influenced to a great extent the conduct of fans and brought about a certain degree of intolerance. The emergence of xenophobic groups such as the Northern League, the National Alliance, the Lombard League and the Tricolor Flame produced the necessary grounds for racism to grow. These extreme right groups soon established relations with the '*ultras*,' as in the case of Lazio's 'Irriducibili.' Lazio were originally related to fascism and, particularly, Mussolini, however, in the 1980s the 'Irriducibili' altered mainstream trends of the extreme right, adopted a hard-core stance on the subject of immigrants and refugees, and revolutionized the perception of racism in Italy by redirecting it towards foreigners. They maintain close relations with other groups of fans of a similar ideological background and publicize their parochial views through offensive banners and chants redolent of ethnocentric symbols and old-fashioned views concerning the purity of the white race. Nevertheless, there are mixed feelings amongst the Italian academic community, with regard to the role of extreme right groups and movements in football. While some share belief that the '*ultras*' have resisted political manipulation, others are keen to emphasize the relationship between these antisocial groups of fans and extreme right elements.

Netherlands

Black players from Surinam and South Africa made their appearance in Dutch football grounds in the mid-1950s. Between the 1980s and mid-1990s, their number had increased dramatically, as they accounted for some 15 percent in the top division, the Eredivisie. Ever since the Bosman ruling, the numbers of foreign footballers amount to 30 percent of all professional players; however, the black community is still underrepresented when taking into account referees and other nonplaying positions. A plethora of quality players with origins from Surinam, like Edgar Davids, Ruud Gullit, Patrick Kluivert, Reiziger, Frank Rijkaard, Clarence Seedorf and Aaron Winter, have represented the Netherlands at the highest level, in footballing terms, with the first Surinamese player making an appearance in the national team's colors as early as 1960. In fact, their contribution to Dutch football has been so immense that when Holland beat Germany at a friendly match in 2000, six members of the team, as well as their coach, were Surinamese. Still, not all appreciate their role, as Thijs Libregts openly expressed his negative, bigot, views, which terminated his contract as Feyenoord coach in the early 1980s. Perceptions regarding the performance of Surinamese players often divide public opinion, taking into account that Seedorf was heavily criticized for missing a penalty during a World Cup qualifier against Turkey. Quite the opposite, the terrible misses of Marco van Basten in a World Cup semifinal and Ronald De Boer, again, during a semifinal match of the European Championship escaped attention. In fact, similar divisions extend over the national football team of the Netherlands, as witnessed during the 1996 European Championship in England. The mutual antipathy between black and white players materialized when members of both groups defied their common cause and refused to pass the ball to players of different color, celebrated goals with their kin and, generally, the meaning of communication had no sense. Moreover, during the same tournament, Edgar Davids revealed that black players were exempted from the team's meeting that involved tactical decisions and was, therefore, removed from the squad.

In an attempt to increase awareness, the Dutch government financed a number of anti-racist initiatives in 1991. On one occasion, it supported projects of the *Nederlandse Sporte Federatie* (Dutch Sport Federation), which organized the *Kluer Bekennen*, 'recognizing color,' conference that same year. In any case, racism in Dutch football is often disputed, since the involvement of far-right groups in racist incidents are rare, which may suggest why the Dutch Football Association (KNVB) has not done much in the front of anti-racism initiatives. In all respects, racism in the Netherlands is real enough to have the game between ADO Den Haag and PSV Eindhoven brought to an abrupt end in the 2005–2006 season by the official of the game.

Scotland

Unlike the more evident forms of racial discrimination in England, their Scottish neighbors can deceive a researcher and give the wrong impression about racism in football. Although there is evidence of intolerance, it is restricted, inaccurately, to religious divisions, thus supporting the myth that racism is absent from football in Scotland. Actually, the Scottish may well point to the fact that the first black football player to represent Scotland was Andrew Watson in 1881, almost one hundred years before the English followed their lead. Despite the involvement of black players in football so early in the development of the game in Scotland, racist incidents persist, particularly, when the rivalry between Celtic and Rangers is concerned, as Paul Elliot and Mark Walters would confirm. Had bigotry been a 'myth,' the Scottish parliament would have no reason to condemn racism in football in 2004, the work of 'Show Racism the Red Card' would have been pointless and the request that all forty-two clubs of the Football League sign up to UEFA's 'Ten Point Plan' unjustifiable. The fact that only St Johnstone FC, at the time, found it necessary to adopt the measures of the European football governing body, as opposed to England where all ninety-two professional clubs had already done so, could be interpreted as yet another sign that claims of racism in Scotland should be regarded with suspicion. In this respect, the decision of the Scottish Football Association to appoint a 'Show Racism the Red Card' Development Officer would have been superfluous.

In contrast, racism in Scotland is pretty much alive and extends over the local Asian community too. The obvious lack of both players and supporters of Asian origins in Scottish football clearly reflects the degree of racism at all levels. To this end, Celtic have actively supported the integration of Asians in football through the 'Bhoys against Bigotry' campaign, in collaboration with the 'Scotland on Sunday' paper. Celtic have also cooperated with the City of Glasgow's Ethnic Minorities Officer, appointed in the 1995–1996 season, and the Scottish Asian Sports Association. Most importantly, they strongly encouraged initiatives for setting up the Asian Soccer Academy in Glasgow, the first ever of its kind throughout the United Kingdom. The issue of the underrepresentation of Asians in nonplaying position was clearly demonstrated in the case of Partick Thistle, given that all attempts of certain local Asian businessmen to buy the club were intensely resisted. Nevertheless, Murray argued that the absence of Asian players and fans from Scottish football is much related to the limited football ability and lack of commitment that distinguish Asian people and culture.[26] It is not surprising, perhaps, that Murray's *Old Firm* (1984) was severely criticized by two scholars, namely, Bert Moorhouse, a sociologist, and, particularly, Gerry Finn, a psychologist.

Spain
Racism in Spanish football made the headlines in October 2004 when Luis Aragones, coach of Spain's national team, called Thierry Henry of Arsenal 'that black shit.' On that occasion, the Spanish coach made the racist remarks in an attempt to motivate Jose Antonio Reyes, before a game against England in Madrid, which probably encouraged Spanish supporters to racially abuse the English black football players during the match in Santiago Bernabeu. The Spanish Football Federation apologized in earnest, but did not avoid FIFA's fine, whereas the perpetrator, Aragones, was merely fined by the national association. Two years later, France coach Raymond Domenech claimed that his players were abused by Spanish supporters before their World Cup match in Germany. Furthermore, during the press conference before the game between France and Spain, Aragones refused, yet again, to apologize to the French player that he insulted. It is noteworthy that Aragones' fine was, eventually, overturned, having convinced, perhaps, the judges that he never made any racist remarks about Henry.

In the meantime, another black player, Samuel Eto'o had been racially abused during Barcelona's away game against Real Zaragoza. The player had a similar response to that of Zoro, as he threatened to leave the pitch, but was persuaded to stay on by his teammates and coach. Real Zaragoza officials asked their fans to stop the racist chanting by making an announcement from the stadium's PA system, at the behest of the referee, however, the fans ignored the pleas of their club and continued till the very end of the game. It is noteworthy that Real Zaragoza had already been fined by the Spanish Football Federation during the previous season, when their fans first abused Eto'o and, again, for their supporters' misconduct as they degraded Real Betis' Brazilian attacker Roberto a few weeks before the second Eto'o incident. Zaragoza fans have apparently developed a 'unique' kind of relationship with black players, despite their club having a few of their own, as their next victim was Levante's Ghanaian Mustapha Riga, forcing the match official to request that the home club make a relevant announcement to their fans. For the record, Samuel Eto'o was also victimized by Racing Santander and Getafe fans.

In light of this evidence, the Spanish Football Federation introduced a number of initiatives that aimed at tackling discrimination in football during international matches and also signed a response protocol with the *Consejo Superior de Deportes*, Supreme Sporting Committee, as well as with various sectors of the Spanish footballing world. This protocol was put into effect during the 2005–2006 season. However, racist chants have not subsided in Spanish football grounds. More recently, Atlético Madrid fans degraded Osasuna's Cameroonian Pierre Webo, despite their club being fined the previous season for abusing another player from Cameroon, Espanyol's Carlos Kameni, while Getafe supporters racially abused Valencia's Miguel.

Eastern Europe
Officials of Korona Kolporter Kielce, in Poland, were about to purchase a black player in 2005, Brazilian Hernani, when they met the strong opposition of their fans. On the occasion, the club prevailed, but when the newly-transferred player was introduced to the home supporters in the opening game of the football season against Cracovia Krakow, Hernani was degraded by his own fans. Contrary to the dismal response of West European clubs to similar incidents, the club provided the police with pictures of a number of fans that racially abused the player and did not even hesitate to ban six of them from entering the stadium. During a home game against Odra Wodzislaw Slaski, the players of Kolporter Kielce took to the field in T-shirts that displayed the logos of the 'Never Again Association' and its 'Let's kick racism out of the stadiums' campaign, which is coordinated by the 'Football Against Racism in Europe' network, and Hernani was distinctly applauded by the crowd each time he touched the ball. Evidently, a section of Kolporter Kielce fans qualify as neo-Nazis and have long expressed their fascist views as they often display a banner that reads 'White pride, white honor.' In another case that involved Polish fans, during the first round UEFA cup tie between FK Austria Vienna and Legia Warszawa in Vienna, the Legia fans unfurled a flag that featured a Celtic cross and displayed a banner that read 'White Legion,' including the Nazi emblem of '*Wolfsangel*,' 'Wolf's Hook,' which was the emblem of the youth organization that later became the Hitler Youth. On their turn, Austria Vienna fans abused Legia's Zimbabwean Dickson Choto and called their opponents 'car thieves' and 'Polaken.'

More recently, Wisla Krakow's Serbian Nikola Mijailovic was banned for five UEFA matches after the player abused Blackburn Rover's Benni McCarthy, following formal complaints made by Blackburn officials, the English Football Association and the referee. In Russia, the most recently recorded incidents of racial abuse concern fans of Zenit St Peterburg and Torpedo Moscow at the expense of black players from Saturn Moscow and FC Moscow respectively. In the first case, Zenit fans greeted Saturn's Brazilian captain with monkey chants when he raised the Russian flag to mark the opening game of the Russian Football Union's top division. Andre Stephane Bikey, from Cameroon, who plays his football for Lokomotiv Moscow, made particular reference to the hostile environment in Moscow and underlined his intention to leave the country while he was on trial with English club Reading.

Balkans

The fans of Bulgaria's clubs in Sofia seem to have fallen into the habit of racially abusing the black footballers of their opponents. Supporters of Slavia Sofia abused Belasitsa Petrich's black players, earning their club a fine, with the president of the Bulgarian Football Union threatening clubs with point deductions and even expulsion from the league, whereas CSKA Sofia were fined by UEFA after their fans degraded Liverpool's Djibril Cisse during their Champions League encounter in the third qualifying round. In a more interesting case, Levski Sofia were also fined by UEFA as their supporters abused Gerald Asamoah of Schalke 04 during their UEFA Cup quarter-final match. Exceeding all expectations, Levski's owner, Todor Batkov, was banned for two matches and given a fine for insulting the English referee Mike Riley.

During a friendly game between Italy and Croatia in Livorno, a number of Croatian fans formed a human swastika and made Nazi salutes. Although the conduct of the visiting supporters is, of course, alarming, it may not be a coincidence that AS Livorno fans maintain a communist culture, which has often 'invited' trouble from football-related far-right groups such as Lazio's 'Irriducibili.' Croatian media considered their fans a 'national disgrace' and made no excuse of them being, allegedly, provoked by Italian fans waving Yugoslavian flags and singing chants about the Second World War. In the domestic scene, fans of Hadjuk Split seem to uphold a tradition of racially abusing the black players of bitter rivals Dinamo Zagreb. Hadjuk has been fined by the national football association for failing to control their fans, as the latter often display racist banners.

Steaua Bucharest and Dinamo Bucharest were fined and their stadiums banned by the Romanian Football Federation due to race-related incidents. Steaua's players joined their fans and shouted racist slogans against arch rivals Rapid Bucharest, during their away game against Sportul Studentesc, while Dinamo's supporters abused Arges Pitesti's black players. Steaua's stadium was also banned for two European club competition matches by UEFA after their fans abused Shelbourne's black players during their Champions League preliminary round match.

In Serbia, during a first division football match between Borac Cacak and Vozdovac, thirty-seven Borac Cacak fans put on the notorious Ku Klux Klan hoods and displayed the United States' old-fashioned Confederate flag and banners that read 'The player should go, no one wants him here' and 'The South will rise again,' clearly declaring their opposition to one of their own players, Mike Tamvaniere from Zimbabwe. The fans also shouted 'With Hitler, Hitler and Sieg Heil' and engaged in monkey chanting, at the expense of the black player. The game was temporarily halted as the police intervened and arrested all fans involved. Sadly, a few months earlier, in April 2006, Babatune Lukmona from Nigeria, a former Borac player, was attacked and injured by skinheads in a Cacak park. Moreover, Serbian side Partizan and Italian club Livorno, during their 2006–2007 UEFA Cup match in Belgrade, presented one banner displaying the 'We don't divide, black-white, we unite' slogan, playing on Partizan's club colors, and another one that read 'Pokazi Rasizmu Crveni Karton,' Show Racism the Red Card, while the two clubs' football players and the match officials wore T-shirts that sported anti-racism messages.

THE DIFFERENT COLORS OF FOOTBALL

Poli and Ravenel, of the International Center for Sport Studies, produced in 2006 the *Annual Review of the European Football Player's Labour Market*, which clearly revealed a rather colorful picture of football, given the multinational background of players that comprised European clubs during the 2005–2006 season. In their study, the two researchers put under the microscope Europe's five most competitive football leagues, namely, the English Premier League, the French Ligue Un, the German Erste Bundesliga, the Italian Serie A and the Spanish Primera Liga. At a first glance, English clubs fielded far more full international players (62.4 percent) than France (33.8 percent), Germany (45.7 percent), Italy (37.9 percent) or Spain (33.5 percent), due to the fact that the foreign players employed by Premier League clubs ought to be footballers that have served well their national team before they secure a work permit.

Homegrown players
Before exploring the impact of foreign players in those five football leagues, it is imperative that the issue of homegrown players is briefly assessed first. All five leagues put together, the number of homegrown players occupying different positions on the pitch was more or less consistent, as 27.3 percent played in the midfield, 26.9 percent were placed in defense, 25.6 percent were goalkeepers and 23.9 percent were forwards. Overall, homegrown players accounted for 26.8 percent of all footballers; however, their contribution was disproportional, since they took part in 20.8 percent of the clubs' football matches and succeeded in scoring only 16.6 percent of all goals. It is noteworthy that the number of homegrown players in the French top division (40.2 percent) far exceeded that in Spain (31.2 percent), England (24.3 percent), Germany (22.6 percent) and Italy (14.7 percent). An additional piece of information worthy of note was that top clubs maintained a higher number of homegrown players, whereas players of similar status at middle clubs were presented with more playing opportunities and scored more often for bottom clubs. All in all, the majority of homegrown players was evenly distributed, all together, in defense and midfield positions, followed by goalkeepers and, then, forwards.

At club level, the Spanish side Athletic Bilbao, not surprisingly, trained a considerably high number of homegrown players (76.5 percent). The club's policy to employ local players of Basque origin is well known and has been discussed elsewhere. However, the fact that Athletic Bilbao was followed by four French clubs (Toulouse 64.8 percent, Nantes 61.4 percent, Nancy-Lorraine 58.6 percent and Strasbourg 57.1 percent) speaks volumes for the attentiveness that homegrown players receive in France. Three Spanish football clubs (Real Sociedad 54.4 percent, Real Madrid 48.1 percent and Osasuna 48 percent), one English side (Manchester United 49 percent) and, finally, yet another French club (Metz 53.1 percent), made up those ten European clubs that comprised the highest percentage of homegrown players. Predictably, homegrown players played in 70.3 percent of Athletic Bilbao's football matches, followed by Nantes (66 percent), Toulouse (58.9 percent), Real Sociedad (57.9 percent) and Nancy-Lorraine (52.1 percent). In the same category, Manchester United (50.7 percent) in England, Borussia Dortmund (38.5 percent) in Germany and Lecce (30.6 percent) in Italy claimed top spot in their national leagues. As for the number of goals scored by homegrown players, Athletic Bilbao led by example (64.9 percent), closely followed by Metz (61.5 percent), whereas further down the ladder were Lecce (56.7 percent), Aston Villa (56.1 percent) and Nancy-Lorraine (51.4 percent). The German Bundesliga, as the only league that was not represented in the top five, saw Borussia Dortmund scoring a poor 38.3 percent.

Despite the significance of homegrown players, at least in terms of serving the cause of national football teams, the information produced by Poli and Ravenel indicated clearly enough the limited contribution of those players. It goes without saying that the data presented does not necessarily reflect the potential of homegrown players. Instead, it seems that market forces, coupled with the phenomenon of globalization, not to mention Europeanization, have reinforced the contemporary cosmopolitan nature of European football, thus the lesser emphasis on homegrown players. Even though homegrown players made up just over a quarter of the total figure of footballers in the five leagues under examination, the near absence of those players from the clubs' starting eleven was merely highlighted by the growing numbers of foreign players. In this respect, the following section focuses on the presence and performance of foreign players in the top leagues of England, France, Germany, Italy and Spain.

Foreign players
With 55.2 percent, English clubs involved, by a long way, the highest number of foreign players, followed by clubs from Germany (41.1 percent), France (35.6 percent), Spain (31.9 percent) and Italy (30.5 percent). Furthermore, top clubs enjoyed the lion's share of foreign players (49.1 percent), while middle and bottom clubs were limited to no more than 36.1 percent and 33.4 percent respectively. In the main, during the 2005–2006 season, 998 foreign players were scattered across the five European leagues, with the majority coming from European countries (Western Europe 35.4 percent and Eastern Europe 14.8 percent). Latin American players accounted for 28.5 percent and Africans for 16.1 percent, whereas only 5 percent of foreign players came from other parts of the world.

Most foreign players of European origins came from Denmark, France, the Netherlands and Portugal. Argentina, Brazil and, further behind, Uruguay, constituted the three top Latin American footballing nations represented in the five European leagues. African players, on the other hand, usually came from Cameroon, Ivory Coast, Senegal and Nigeria. Finally, the nation most widely represented in the five European leagues, from the 'other' group, was Australia. These figures reveal the favorite 'football markets' of managers and boards of directors alike at European clubs. However, they also bring to light the ever-changing face of modern European football clubs. On the contrary, during the 1995–1996 season, just before the Bosman case reached the surface, only 463 foreigners played their football in one of the European leagues under examination. Europe, again, enjoyed the majority of foreign footballers (Western Europe 39.1 percent and Eastern Europe 29.4 percent), as players from Latin America and Africa made up 16.6 percent and 10.6 percent respectively, while 4.3 percent came from the rest of the world. European players clearly dominated football clubs prior to Bosman, but have been since much reduced taking into account that many more players arrive from Latin American and African countries at the present time.

English clubs were certainly overwhelmed by the presence of 284 foreign players, with the vast majority coming from West European countries (63.7 percent). Eastern Europe and Africa attained similar levels of representation in the Premier League (10.2 percent and 10.6 percent respectively), whereas Latin American players made up only 5.6 percent, less even than the 'other' group (9.9 percent). At the same time, it must be noted that all those foreign players came from a staggering sixty countries. Among West European players, the majority included UK nationals, Irish and Scandinavians; however, France was clearly the dominant footballing nation with forty-six players. Equally impressive was the fact that Australian and American football players overshadowed the almost predictable presence of Latin Americans, based on the findings the other four leagues produced. As regards African players, they were, primarily, from Nigeria and Senegal. Nevertheless, the numbers of West European foreign players should not confuse us. Strict policies concerning the transfer of foreign players, namely the requirements to validate a work permit, dictate that clubs focus on players that hold European Union passports, thus restricting them to markets in Western and Central Europe.

Just as in England, the 192 foreign players absorbed by German clubs were mostly Europeans. More precisely, foreign players from the west and east of Europe made up 34.9 percent and 32.8 percent respectively. Latin American players accounted for 18.8 percent and African players made up 7.8 percent, while the numbers of foreign players from the 'other' group were as low as 5.7 percent. It is noteworthy that almost half of all foreign players playing in the Erste Bundesliga came from Germany's neighboring countries. Nevertheless, the number of Brazilian players was sizeable, given that German clubs have recently turned their attention to the Latin American market too. In contrast, the low figures of African players may only suggest the lack of interest in footballers from the Dark Continent. The absence of Asian players should also be noted, as only Georgia, Iran and South Korea were represented.

The number of foreigners in Ligue Un wavered along the lines of the Erste Bundesliga with 190 players. French football clubs, however, resisted the more traditional approach, in terms of numbers, regarding the employment of European players. The odd 1.6 percent of foreign players that belonged to the 'other' group exempted, Europeans scored considerably low, as Western Europe claimed 15.8 percent and Eastern Europe 11 percent. As an alternative, African players were the dominant football force with 48.4 percent, while Latin Americans made up 23.2 percent of all foreign players in France. Despite the tremendous influence of African players in French clubs, the relatively large number of Brazilians definitely adds a distinct flavor in football in France. Still, the presence of only four Asian players was indicative of the preferences of clubs' managers in the French top division. Clearly enough, their first choice players were, indeed, of African origins, even though their quality or physical features were possibly not the only attributes to justify employment. As it happens, France maintained colonies overseas, some located in Africa, and to this day continues to enjoy a fairly healthy relationship with those countries now independent. This alone seems sufficient for French clubs to make good use of the cultural diversity that once characterized the empire and, therefore, focus almost exclusively on the African market.

Spanish clubs employed 171 foreign players from thirty-three countries, but the pattern for selection of those players, once more, was much different. Unlike France, African players were the clear minority with only 3.5 percent of the foreign players that featured in the Spanish top division, except for the 2.3 percent allocated to the 'other' category, preceded by, first, European and, then, Latin American players. While West European players amounted to 25 percent, complemented by a poor 7 percent of East Europeans, Latin American football players simply denoted to an unprecedented phenomenon with 62.2 percent of all foreign players in the league. Another odd feature of the Primera Liga, unlike the other four leagues, concerned the clear choice of Argentinean players over Brazilians. With regard to foreign players of European origins, French, Italian and Portuguese players were the dominant nationalities, followed by a relatively small Balkan contingent and even fewer players from central and northern European countries. As in the case of France, the extensive selection of Latin American players pertains to Spain's colonial, cultural and, nowadays, strong trading relations with those countries. The impact of Latin American players was probably realized soon after the impressive performances of Real Madrid's Alfredo Di Stefano, thus paving the way for many of his compatriots to disembark at Spanish shores.

Finally, Italy ranked fifth among the European nations under examination, claiming 161 foreign players. African players were the minority with 11.2 percent, although the 'other' group, once again, account for a low 3.1 percent. European players were the next most populous group of foreigners in Italian football, with 20.5 percent coming from Western Europe and 14.3 percent from Eastern Europe, but still not the leading one. As in Spain, Italian clubs were largely dominated by Latin American players, making up just over half of all foreign players (50.9 percent) in the Serie A. It is noteworthy that in the case of European players, thirteen originated from France, while other continental nations were represented by two players at most. The strong cultural relations between Italy and Latin American countries—largely influenced by the presence of Italian immigrants there—may, indeed, account for the plethora of players from this background in the Italian top division.

Naturally, of all 998 players, England accumulated 28.4 percent, Germany 19.2 percent, France 19.1 percent, Spain 17.1 percent and Italy 16 percent. Although all outfield positions were reasonably occupied by an even number of foreign players in all five European leagues, most foreign goalkeepers were concentrated in England's Premier League. Those 998 foreign players, or else 38.7 percent of all football players in the five European leagues under examination, had part in 41.4 percent of their clubs' matches and scored 50.2 percent of all goals. The percentage of matches played and goals scored by foreign players exceeded the percentage of their presence in all leagues, with the notable exception of England where the percentage of foreign players was identical to the percentage of matches they took part in and only slightly higher in terms of the percentage of goals scored. In the case of Germany the percentage of foreign players in Erste Bundesliga clubs was lower than the percentage of matches played by those footballers, while in both France and Spain the percentage of goals scored was higher.

The statistical analysis of the breakdown of foreign players into different playing positions revealed that the number of both matches played and goals scored transcended the percentage presence of the players concerned too. Despite the significance of the figures mentioned above, it is the following facts that make a strong impression. Evidently, African and West European players' percentage presence was higher than either matches played or goals scored, though in the case of African players the number of goals scored exceeded matches played. The contribution of East Europeans was quite similar, considering that the percentage presence was in line with the number of matches played, though lower than the percentage of goals scored. In stark contrast, the percentage presence of Latin American players was clearly lower than either matches played or goals scored, with the number of goals scored surpassing that of matches played. Finally, the percentage of matches played by foreign players that fit into the 'other' group was higher than their percentage presence, however, the number of goals scored failed to reach the levels of either category. On the whole, the undisputed champion was Brazil, with a stunning 139 players, followed by Argentina (eighty-eight players) and France (eighty-two). Other nations scored considerably lower, given that next in order were the Netherlands with only forty-one football players. In fact, footballers from Argentina, Brazil and France accounted for more than 30 percent of all foreign players.

At club level, Arsenal's foreign players made up 87.5 percent of the squad, while eight more Premier League clubs, together with Internazionale from Serie A and the German side Borrusia Mönchengladbach, completed the list of the ten most 'cosmopolitan' clubs, as regards the five European leagues. Given the weak presence of non-English sides in the top-ten of most 'internationalized' clubs, some additional information is necessary on the remaining four national leagues. In Italy, apart from Internazionale, foreign players made up an overwhelming majority only in the cases of AC Milan and Juventus (56.3 percent and 54 percent respectively). Apart from Borrusia Mönchengladbach, those German clubs that reflected a predilection to foreign players were Bayern München (55.1 percent), Wolfsburg (52.8 percent), Bayer 04 Leverkusen (51.1 percent) and Hamburger (51 percent). In contrast, none of the Ligue Un or Primera Liga clubs reached such levels. The squad of Sochaux included 48.2 percent of foreign players and Barcelona headed Spanish clubs with 49.1 percent. The percentage of matches played by foreign players was higher at Arsenal (93.6 percent), followed by five more English clubs, three German clubs and one side from Italy in the relevant top-ten. Foreign players also took part in more than half of their club's matches at Barcelona (64.4 percent), Villareal (55.9 percent), Real Madrid (54 percent) and Real Mallorca (51 percent) in Spain; OSC Lille (52.5 percent) in France; and Wolfsburg (60.3 percent) and Bayer 04 Leverkusen (53.7 percent) in Germany. As regards the percentage of goals scored, football giants like Arsenal, Barcelona and Internazionale were among the top five clubs that were dependent on foreign forward players, nevertheless, they were all headed by the less glamorous Fulham, which had every single goal scored by non-English players.

Quite the reverse, Athletic Bilbao ended up on the opposite side of the table on all occasions, though this fact is, of course, anything but surprising. Furthermore, the distribution of foreign players that moved between clubs affiliated to distinct national football associations was equally significant, taking into account variables such as club overall performance, playing position and zone of origin. While top clubs hired the services of 39.1 percent of the foreign players that were transferred during the 2005–2006 season, middle and bottom clubs were limited to 24.8 percent and 22.4 percent respectively. At the same time, the number of goalkeepers amounted to 15.8 percent, defenders 29.2 percent, midfielders 26.2 percent and forwards 32.6 percent. Finally, footballers from Western Europe made up 48.3 percent, Eastern Europe 53.3 percent, Africa 50 percent and Latin America 58.9 percent of all foreign players' transfers put together (52.9 percent). Hence, to suggest that foreign players simply perform well is an understatement, given that their overall contribution to the cause of the club they play for seems immense. In this respect, their services are deemed so valuable, perhaps, that neglecting the presence of homegrown players almost makes sense. Unless it is the lack of homegrown players in the first choice line up that encourages supporters to express their racist views, the performance of foreign players does not justify any form of anti-social conduct. Football fans should connect well with those foreign stars that, apparently, strive to fulfill the club's ambitions, regardless of skin color.

CONCLUSION

Karl Planck wrote in 1898 an essay on football, Fusslümmelei, which clearly reflected his perceived ugliness of the game. The physical education instructor from Germany, like other compatriots of his, despised the game and, in particular, its English origins. He even drew a parallel between the half-starved workers that played the game in England as pastime and the animal-like movement that the game required to characterize football as an 'English disease.' According to Planck, football stripped humans of their dignity and likened them to a distant relative, apes. Nowadays, his views are far from irrelevant, although it is hooliganism that was ascribed the term 'English disease' and few, if any, consider football a degrading sport. The mere reference to apes, nevertheless, and his suggestion is very much apropos, since aping has become common practice in football stadiums around Europe. Comparing dark-skinned football players to monkeys, apes and other similar quadruped animals, signifies the degree of segregation that often epitomizes Europe's otherwise sophisticated societies, thus symbolizing social exclusion and racial discrimination.

Almost every account of racism has sociopolitical connotations that denote prejudice or ignorance, exactly the 'qualities' that the extreme right never fails to exploit. Success in recruiting football fans hardly substitutes for the sensation of a decent electoral result; however, the potential of converting football stadiums into political arenas seldom is resisted. Besides, the prospect of disseminating racist material and ideas is to extreme right groups what moderate political parties intend to achieve through traditional electoral campaigns. The involvement of fascist groups in football, nevertheless, is anything but established. While certain authors underline the role of such groups in some of Europe's most violent incidents, others emphasize their lack of influence. In any case, to dismiss or underestimate the impact of extreme right groups in football could have irreparable consequences for the game, whereas to exaggerate their presence would probably tempt them to exploit the mass appeal of football even further. No matter what, it appears that racism and extreme right groups go hand in glove, which sometimes renders football vulnerable, given the game's popularity.

Even though racism in European football is an extremely significant issue, its several different guises are all the more distressing. England suffers from a lack of Asian players and black managers. The 'Frenchness' of the players that makeup the national football team of France is often questioned, as is its multicultural nature. Germany's few black players that made it to the national team have been insulted beyond comprehension, although the far stronger presence of neo-Nazi sympathizers should not be neglected. In Italy racism is intricately related to politics, since southerners and black players alike suffer similar abuse. The Dutch football players that represent country at the highest level are, reportedly, divided over racial issues—not much of a *national* team. Racism in Scotland and Spain is overshadowed by sectarianism and regionalism respectively, just as ethnic divisions in the Balkans have put racism in the shade. Likewise, racism in East European countries only reached the surface after their transition to democracy, following the collapse of certain political regimes that clearly oppressed nationalism. In this respect, the relatively low number of racist incidents in the Balkans and Eastern Europe probably pertains to a denial that racism in football exists or the delusion of the football governing bodies. The issue of racism in European football is further perplexed, when taking into account the fact that racist incidents have marred the beautiful game at national level (domestic leagues and cup), during European club competitions (the Champions League and UEFA Cup) and, of course, at international level (the 2004 European Championship in Portugal and the 2006 World Cup in Germany). Nevertheless, the performance of the players that often fall victims of racial abuse does not justify intolerance, not that it would anyhow, thus the difficulty to fully comprehend the causes of the supporters' conduct and, subsequently, combat racism in football effectively.

Notes

1. Kick It Out, "Racism in European Football," <http://www.kickitout.org> (10 Nov. 2006).

2. Les Back, Tim Crabbe and John Solomos, *The Changing Face of Football: Racism, Identity and Multiculture in the English Game* (Oxford and New York: Berg, 2001), 2.

3. Back, Crabbe and Solomos, "The Changing Face of Football: Racism, Identity and Multiculture in the English Game," 47.

4. Giovanni Carnibella, Anne Fox, Kate Fox, Joe McCann, James Marsh and Peter Marsh, *Football violence in Europe: A report to the Amsterdam Group* (The Social Issues Research Centre, July 1996), 95–97.

5. Jacco van Sterkenburg and Eelco Westland, "United Kingdom," in *Football and Racism: An inventory of the problems and solutions in eight West European countries in the framework of the Stand Up Speak Up campaign*, ed. Jacco van Sterkenburg, Jan W. Janssens and Bas Rijnen (Nieuwegein: Arko Sports Media, 2005), 34.

6. Back, Crabbe and Solomos, "The Changing Face of Football: Racism, Identity and Multiculture in the English Game," 106–107.

7. Jon Garland and Michael Rowe, 2001, *Racism and Anti–Racism in Football* (Basingstoke and New York: Palgrave, 2001), 93.

8. Anthony King, *The European Ritual: Football in the New Europe* (Aldershot: Ashgate, 2003), 231.

9. Dougie Brimson and Eddy Brimson, *Everywhere We Go: Behind the matchday madness*, Headline Review, 2006), 61–68.

10. Gary Armstrong, "False Leeds: the construction of hooligan confrontations," in *Game Without Frontiers: Football, Identity and Modernity*, ed. Richard Giulianotti and John Williams (Aldershot: Arena, 1994), 305.

11. Gianluca Vialli and Gabriele Marcotti, *The Italian Job: A Journey to the heart of two great footballing cultures* (London, Toronto, Sydney, Auckland and Johannesburg: Bantam Press, 2006), 33–34.

12. Richard Giulianotti, *Football: A Sociology of the Global Game* (Polity Press, 1999), 162.

13. Back, Crabbe and Solomos, "The Changing Face of Football: Racism, Identity and Multiculture in the English Game," 175.

14. Mike McGrath (PA Sport), "Barnes: Black bosses don't get a fair chance," <http://www.kickitout.org> (4 Jan. 2007).

15. Dominic Fifield (The Guardian), "Ince says age of most chairmen is bar to black managers," <http://www.kickitout.org> (5 Jan. 2007).

16. Sanjiev Johal, "Playing Their Own Game: A South Asian Football Experience," in *'Race,' Sport and British Society*, ed. Ben Carrington and Ian McDonald (London and New York: Routledge, 2001), 156–160.

17. Ben Carrington and Ian McDonald, eds., *'Race,' Sport and British Society* (London and New York: Routledge, 2001), 3.

18. Geoff Hare, *Football in France: A Cultural History* (Oxford and New York: Berg Publishers, 2003), 131.

19. Kevin Connolly and Rab MacWilliam, *Fields of Glory, Paths of Gold: The History of European Football* (Edinburgh and London: Mainstream Publishing, 2005) 217.

20. Hare, "Football in France: A Cultural History," 135.

21. Kick It Out, "France adjusts to racially diverse team," <http://www.kickitout.org> (9 Jul. 2006).

22. Dirk Halm, "Turkish immigrants in German football," in *German Football: history, culture, society*, ed. Alan Tomlinson and Christopher Young (Routledge: London and New York, 2006), 74.

23. Flutlicht, "Racism in a new guise," <http://www.flutlicht.org> (14 Dec. 2005).

24. Kick It Out, "Stop racist neo-Nazis at World Cup says Asamoah," <http://www.kickitout.org> (30 May 2006).

25. Football Against Racism in Europe, "Di Canio repeats fascist salute," <http://www.farenet.org> (14 Dec. 2005).

26. Gerry P. Finn, "Scottish Myopia and Global Prejudices," in *Football Culture: Local Contests, Global Visions*, ed. Gerry P. Finn and Richard Giulianotti (Frank Cass: London and Portland, 2000), 66.

Chapter Five

England tackling racism

In an attempt to address the causes of racist behavior in England, the Home Office delivered a report that produced a profile of individuals likely to initiate racist acts and examined the conditions in which such incidents took place. Given that limited research existed in this area, the report revealed disturbing facts about the nature of racial harassment and racial violence, as well as essential information regarding the social background of the perpetrators. Among the various cases discussed, one concerned racism at Findlay Park football ground in London, which stressed that "On match days, as fans passed through neighboring estates, ethnic minority residents were subjected to racist abuse and their homes were daubed with racist graffiti. So often did this appear alongside 'Findlay Park FC' graffiti, and so strong was the club's reputation for violence (including racist violence) that 'Findlay Park FC' graffiti itself took on a menacing appearance."[1] The report also revealed the links between extreme right-wing parties and football, based on the experiences of a former member of the National Front who joined the party in the 1970s through his contacts as a football fan. The same person also appears to have recruited members among train passengers on their way to football matches and met with other members of the National Front in pubs that served the purpose of meeting places for far-right groups before attending games.

Even though there is little evidence to suggest that extreme right groups have succeeded in exploiting the appeal of football to promote racist material and recruit members, racism became extremely vocal through its association with right-wing movements that took up hooliganism. In fact, a couple of incidents demonstrate the relationship between football's two plagues. In February 1984 England played France in a multicultural Paris, where English hooligans, including members of the National Front, physically abused local fans and engaged in racist chanting. On another occasion, members of the National Front were on board the same plane with the England squad and abused the team's black players, as they returned from a football match in Chile. Both incidents, nevertheless, pale in comparison to what happened before the 1985 European Cup Final kicked off at the Heysel Stadium in Brussels, where the National Front, allegedly, had part in the tragic events that caused the death of thirty-nine football supporters.[2] The presence of extreme right elements and neo-Nazis, in particular, encouraged a number of fans from several clubs to establish close relations with the Anti-Nazi league. However, those groups of fans often stood alone as football clubs were reluctant to support their cause and condemned them to inaction. Tottenham Hotspur, in 1979, threatened the '*Spurs against the Nazis*' campaign with legal action, whereas Leyton Orient decided to ban '*Orient against the Nazis*' members, following violent clashes with the '*British Movement*' of West Ham United supporters.

Despite the debate surrounding the involvement of extreme right formations in football, allegedly, for the purpose of recruiting new members, the English Football Association, for one, supports the theory that such groups were in the past. In fact, the national football association of England stressed in the *Football For All* report that "The practice of political parties of the far-right using football as a propaganda tool has been broken."[3] Even though the influence of extreme right groups in football, generally, seems to have been diminished, it is certain that discrimination has yet to be defeated, given that the very same report argued that "There is also widespread xenophobia and racism expressed by some England fans when travelling abroad, attitudes that need to be addressed as part of longer-term campaigning work."[4] Still, racism in football in England remains a thorn in the flesh that football governing bodies ought to address to all intents and purposes and at all levels of the game. Football's less violent, than hooliganism that is, but equally distressing 'disease,' has been rekindled and necessitates a novel line of attack.

ETHNIC MINORITIES AND FOOTBALL

Football Task Force

Beyond any shadow of doubt, racism and xenophobia only emphasize divisions in society and discourage members of ethnic minorities from taking part in social events like football. The UK government supports the idea that football, among other sports, has the capacity to enhance integration by promoting a sense of local identity, given that football clubs often represent either regions of a country or part of a city. According to the *Investing in the Community* report, produced by the Football Task Force and submitted to the Minister of Sport, "Football clubs in England have deep roots in their communities. The club–community relationship has traditionally been based on mutual support. Clubs draw strength from the goodwill of local people, who have nurtured and supported them over the generations. Clubs repay this by providing a community focus and source of civic pride. Many of the country's oldest football clubs have their origins in community institutions such as churches, social clubs or works teams. Clubs that sprang from such humble beginnings are today global brands and bring enormous economic and social benefits to their towns, regions and the country. They fulfill a number of roles: generators of wealth; providers of employment; ambassadors for regions and the country. The FA Premier League and its clubs are one of this country's most successful and prominent exports."[5]

Considering the impact of racism in football grounds across the country, the British government asked the Football Task Force 'to make recommendations on appropriate measures to eliminate racism from football and encourage wider participation by ethnic minorities, both in playing and spectating.' The *Eliminating Racism from Football* report was primarily concerned with the low number of professional football players of Asian origin; the more than obvious poor attendance records of spectators from ethnic minorities; the disproportionate number of black players to black spectators; the underrepresentation of blacks and Asians in administrative positions at football clubs and local football organizations, including their absence from the English Football Association; and the existence of few black and Asian referees and coaches. During the 1970s and 1980s, black English football players were severely abused as their own fans engaged in racist chanting and threw bananas at them. Football clubs and the national team, in particular, often attracted the attention of extreme right groups that were interested in publicizing racist material; however, English football was primarily concerned with hooliganism and, therefore, racism was simply overshadowed. In the 1990s, hooliganism was largely defeated, thus pushing the issue of racism high up on the agenda of the football authorities.

The state responded with effect when the Commission for Racial Equality launched the *Let's Kick Racism Out Of Football* campaign in 1993, thus producing the necessary grounds for setting up 'Kick It Out,' Britain's prime anti-racism organization devoted to football. Action taken by both clubs and players contributed to a considerable decline of racist incidents in football grounds, but the report stressed that racism had yet to be eliminated, as it existed at boot rooms and boardrooms of football clubs. There was evidence to suggest that racism was still around, taking into account that there were no Asian footballers playing for clubs in the top division, even though the Asian community comprised some 3.5 percent of the total population; few blacks had management, coaching or senior administrative positions; the Football Association council contained no members from ethnic minorities; black and Asian people made up barely one percent of attendance at Premier League games, but comprised some 7.5 percent of the English population; and few black and Asian people held non-playing positions at football clubs.

The report revealed that a number of professional football clubs' officials regarded Asian people as physically inferior, thus unsuitable for the game, with Asians often being forced to join local Asian leagues to avoid racist abuse. Hence, to encourage wider participation from ethnic minorities, the Football Task Force recommended that football be promoted at schools; highlighted the significance of making good use of positive role models; emphasized the nature and scope of relevant community schemes; underlined the responsibilities of local authorities, as most football grounds are owned by the local councils; and supported the introduction of match officials from ethnic minorities. In light of the distressing evidence that the Task Force brought together, the team of experts made further recommendations to stamp discrimination out of football, which concerned clubs most. As a first step, stewards should be asked to undertake proper training in order to address problems related to racist behavior with effect, as envisaged in the *Stewarding and Safety Management at Football Grounds* (1995) document that was jointly published by the Football Association, the FA Premier League and the Football League.

Moreover, confidential 'hotlines' should be made available to fans that wished to come forward and complain about offenders, while clubs should be prepared to take action when dealing with racist supporters and even consider banning them from attending future matches. As for the low attendance of spectators from a distinct ethnic background, anti-racist organizations should be established to work closely with ethnic minority communities and local clubs, so to encourage wider participation. In Sheffield, for example, the Football Unites Racism Divides anti-racism organization enjoys the support of Sheffield United, local youth clubs and the local council aiming 'to increase the participation of local black people in the life of Sheffield United FC, as either spectators, players or employees, and to decrease the level of racial harassment and abuse in and around the football club.' The report also stressed that the prospect of clubs establishing better relations with local communities is the essence of cultural assimilation and the ideal means to promote diversity and people of all ethnic backgrounds to participate.

By the turn of the century, much remained the same, as the issue of racism continued to command the attention of England's football governing bodies and all pertinent actors. In this respect, Sport England produced in 2000 the *Sports Participation and Ethnicity in England* report, which revealed that participation in amateur football amongst males from ethnic minority groups was relatively high. Actually, black males, in particular, enjoyed participation rates as high as 31 percent, three times the national average, while Asians were close to the national average and Pakistani men exceeded it (16 percent). Even when taking into account those that never took part in the game of football, but expressed an interest in doing so, black African men scored 19 percent, followed by Bangladeshi (18 percent) and 'Black Other' men (13 percent), while Pakistani men, Indians and men in the 'Other' ethnic group scored 8 percent each. Evidently, racial abuse had a key role in impeding the endeavors of men from ethnic minority background to participate more widely in football. The report indicated that 'Black Other' men were more likely to suffer from racial discrimination in football, whereas Chinese men were the least likely of all ethnic groups to experience discrimination because of their ethnic background.

Likewise, Bradbury's *The New Football Communities* study, concerning the relationship between football clubs and local ethnic minority communities, revealed more disturbing facts. From a total of ninety-two football clubs, all playing in the FA Premier League or the Football League, eighty-eight clubs responded to the questionnaire, including forty-five clubs located in areas where ethnic minorities accounted for at least 5 percent of the local population. In fact, all of the football clubs based in London and nearly three-quarters of the football clubs in the Midlands were to be found in areas with significant, in terms of numbers, ethnic minority communities, but only some 60 percent of all the clubs that responded admitted they encountered difficulties in recruiting spectators from minority groups. Several clubs (24 percent) attributed the low participation of minority ethnic groups in football to a perceived interest in other sports, while a number of clubs (11 percent) linked the same issue, inaccurately as it was, to religious and cultural factors. Surprisingly, perhaps, 76 percent of the clubs argued that no particular measures needed be taken into consideration to increase participation among members of ethnic minority backgrounds, 52 percent stated that they had in place those policies deemed necessary to become more accessible to all sectors of society and 57 percent claimed that no racist incidents had ever taken place when the club played before its home crowd. Despite the deceptive absence of racial discrimination, 77 percent of the clubs provided their supporters with vital information concerning possible avenues for dealing with racial abuse, eight clubs made 'hotlines' available to fans, while forty-one clubs had already received complaints related to discrimination during games at home.

Commission of Racial Equality
The Commission of Racial Equality concerned with the apparent underrepresentation of ethnic minorities in the sport of football, regarding both playing and nonplaying positions, produced the *Racial Equality in Football* report in an attempt to address the issue of racism in football more effectively. The rate of response to the posted questionnaires was as follows: Premier League clubs 95 percent (nineteen out of twenty clubs), Division One clubs 79 percent (nineteen out of twenty-four), Division Two clubs 67 percent (sixteen out of twenty-four) and Division Three clubs a low score of 46 percent (eleven out of twenty-four). Apart from Division Three, today known as League Two, the majority of the clubs that responded stated that a written Equal Opportunities policy was in place (seventeen clubs in the Premier League, fifteen in Division One, twelve in Division Two and only five in Division Three). In the Premier League, or else Premiership by today's standards, and Division One, renamed Championship, those policies seemed to concern channels available for dealing with complaints regarding racial discrimination and harassment, though it was clear from the clubs' responses that their officials made reference to mere actions taken by spectators, rather than their own staff. It is noteworthy that two football clubs, one in Division Two, nowadays League One, and another club in Division Three, stated that they had no intention of drawing up an Equal Opportunities policy.

On the basis of the data provided, it became clear that ethnic minority communities were underrepresented in the case of management staff (2 percent in the Premier League, 4 percent in Division One, 2 percent in Division Two and 0.02 percent in Division Three); administrative staff (4 percent, 2 percent, 1 percent over the top three divisions and none in Division Three); coaching staff (6 percent, 5 percent, 11 percent and 15 percent respectively); and other staff (20 percent, 10 percent, 5 percent and 3 percent across the four divisions). Sadly, only one Premier League club specifically encouraged applicants from underrepresented groups to apply for a job with the club, whereas another club stated that one non-white director sat among a board of seven. In Division One, the size of boards varied from three to seven, with only two directors coming from the black and Asian communities in two different clubs. Similarly, in Division Two only one director was said to be from an ethnic minority group, whereas in Division Three four directors, spread equally over the boards of two clubs, were identified as members from ethnic minorities. Regarding the ethnic breakdown of the playing staff in all four divisions the combined figures of fourteen Premier League clubs revealed the presence of only two Asian players (0.4 percent), four from the 'Chinese' or 'Other' group (0.7 percent) and twenty-three from the 'Mixed Race' group (4.1 percent), compared to 113 players from the 'Black' group (20.3 percent) and 415 white players (74.5 percent). In Division One the proportion of black players amounted to 17 percent of the total number, 8 percent were of mixed race and, naturally, 75 percent of the football players were white, whereas only one member of playing staff was Chinese and none were Asians. Likewise, in Division Two 17.6 percent of playing staff were from ethnic minorities, whereas in Division Three, from the eight clubs that provided such data, the number of ethnic minority players came up to 19.5 percent. Twelve Premier League clubs (63 percent) also provided an ethnic breakdown of the under-16 academy players, which followed a similar pattern to their senior team, including nine Chinese/Other players (0.7 percent), ten Asian/Asian British players (0.8 percent), fifty-nine Mixed Race players (4.6 percent), 156 Black/Black British players (12.2 percent) and 1,049 white players (81.7 percent).

Obviously, black/black British players were significantly overrepresented (12.2 percent compared with 2.19 percent of the population in England and Wales), whereas Asian and Chinese players, taken together, were significantly underrepresented (5.23 percent of the total population). It is important to note that Division One clubs employed several different approaches in answering the 'ethnic background' question, when, for example, they made reference either to actual numbers and percentages or vague estimates, such as 'mixed,' 'small number of Black and Asian,' which clearly made any detailed statistical analysis impossible. It became obvious, nonetheless, that there were virtually no Asian players in the academies. Similar problems, regarding the accuracy, or lack of it, of the information provided, characterized the response of the two lower divisions as well. Apparently, the average ethnic minority representation in Division Two and Three was a considerably poor 11 and 7.6 percent respectively.

Further, a considerable number of the clubs that responded to the questionnaire made genuine attempts to increase ethnic minority attendance (thirteen Premier League clubs, fifteen clubs from Division One, nine in Division Two and seven Division Three clubs). Considering the overall result of their campaign, ten Premier League clubs and five clubs from Division One found their strategies effective; however, one club from Division One, five from Division Two and three clubs from Division Three expressed no interest in encouraging more support from ethnic minority communities, whereas the remaining clubs either did not produce enough details or failed to answer the question. In the top division, seventeen clubs (89 percent) also mentioned certain policies for tackling racism and an equal number of clubs said that stewards received anti-racist training. All Division One clubs that responded stated that strict measures for dealing with racist behavior at matches had been adopted and sixteen clubs claimed that arrests and/or life bans were imposed whenever race-related incidents occurred. Moreover, stewards in seventeen clubs had received anti-racist training, although they did not produce any further details. In Division Two and Three, those clubs that made reference to anti-racism initiatives, all mentioned the involvement of Kick It Out, local anti-racism campaigns, *Football in the Community* projects and links with local ethnic minority groups. Division Two clubs also stated that an ethnic minority liaison officer had been appointed to represent the club in local communities, while clubs in Division Three often distributed free tickets to members of ethnic minority communities in order to boost attendance rates. In Division Two, four of the clubs that aimed at raising the numbers of spectators from ethnic minority background found their policies successful and five clubs provided details on a small number of racism-related arrests, thus indicating how well they monitored their policies on one hand and that stewards were equipped with the necessary training to deal effectively with racist incidents. On the whole, twelve Division Two clubs said their stewards received anti-racism training, though they submitted no further information. Finally, in Division Three only two clubs that sought to increase ethnic minority attendance considered their efforts effective and eight clubs stated that their stewards had undergone anti-racism training.

Most certainly, the survey that the Commission for Racial Equality conducted was not limited to football clubs; it was also extended to the relevant football authorities, in an attempt to assess the degree of institutional racism in football. The Football Association had a very detailed equal opportunities policy that was widely disseminated, included definitions of discrimination, made reference to a 'complaints and disciplinary' procedure and listed all groups that could possibly be discriminated against. Regarding the ethnic breakdown of the Football Association personnel, 8 percent and 9.5 percent of managerial and administrative staff members, respectively, were from ethnic minorities. However, all fourteen members of the Football Association board and the ninety-two members of the council described themselves as white. The Football Association formally monitored the ethnic breakdown of referees and revealed, in a 2003 survey, that 2.2 percent of referees were from an ethnic minority group, with 0.3 percent choosing not to answer the relevant question. The FA Premier League had a written equal opportunities policy too, which included definitions of different types of discrimination and harassment, as well as a 'complaints and disciplinary' procedure, much like the Football Association. The FA Premier League had seven managerial staff members at its disposal, one of whom was from an ethnic minority group, and forty-one administrative staff, six from an ethnic minority background.

Likewise, the Football League had a written equal opportunities policy, though it was merely a basic statement of intent. Unlike both the Football Association and the more glamorous FA Premier League, the equal opportunities policy of the Football League offered no definitions on discrimination and harassment, but contained the usual 'complaints and disciplinary' procedure and included all the groups that could suffer abuse. The only ethnic minority staff members (6.9 percent) held administrative positions and all directors were white, however, one 'White British' was a Greek-Cypriot. Finally, the Professional Footballers' Association had a written equal opportunities policy that applied to all staff. The policy contained definitions of various forms of discrimination and harassment, discussed the 'complaints and disciplinary' procedure and listed all the groups that could be discriminated against unlawfully. The policy also included a firm commitment to take positive action to address the issue of underrepresentation with effect. The data provided revealed the strong presence (29 percent) of managerial staff from ethnic minority groups (all were Black British), but none in administrative or coaching posts. The Professional Footballers' Association said it had 'several black committee members,' but failed to produce any figures. However, the Professional Footballers' Association monitored the ethnic background of delegates to its AGM. In this respect, the last audit revealed that 7 percent of its members were 'Black British' or 'Mixed,' while 1 percent belonged to the 'White Other' group and the rest were 'White British.'

Taking into account the location of most clubs' football grounds and the proportion of ethnic minority communities, the results of the survey were certainly embarrassing. Whereas black players were overrepresented and well established in the professional game of football, Asians were largely ignored, despite the several Asian leagues that run throughout the country. Various interrelated factors may account for this phenomenon, such as education, social status and culture, nevertheless, the fact that black players were clearly exempted from these parameters underlines the paradox of the Asian football players' absence. Still, the relative success of black players, in terms of participation at the top level of the game, vanished into thin air when their playing career was over and access to the higher echelons of football became constrained. The Independent Football Commission, too, recognized the underrepresentation of ethnic minorities in football. As a consequence, it made a number of recommendations to the Football Association, the Premier League and the Football League to address the issue of racism more effectively. The recommendations of the

Independent Football Commission concerned integration projections, the enforcement of related sanctions, special training of clubs' officials, equal opportunities in employment and plans to increase ethnic minority attendance. Not surprisingly, all suggestions were welcomed by the relevant authorities, apart from the recommendation to restructure the Football Association, which was obviously rejected by the very same body.

According to the *Increasing BME Participation in Sport & Physical Activity by Black and Minority Ethnic Communities* report, the Football Association has been collecting evidence regarding the background of fans and the ethnic origins of officials and staff in county football associations since June 2002 and in 2003 it commissioned a survey on participation and racism from the British Market Research Bureau. The results of that research were more than just revealing. Some 57 percent of non-whites seemed to be somehow involved in amateur football, which certainly exceeded the national average (53 percent). Participation in football amongst black and minority ethnic groups was also higher (52 percent), when compared to the white population (41 percent). Contrary to previous studies, Asian people were more likely to experience racism than other ethnic groups. About 25 percent of adults reported that they had witnessed discriminatory behavior in football, even though 52 percent argued for the opposite and 23 percent had not come across any racist incidents. Interestingly, as children grew older, they registered more racism.

As a matter of fact, 11 percent of youngsters in the 7–9 age group reported racism, increased to 19 percent in the 10–12 age group, reaching 20 percent in the 13–15 age group. Finally, some 68 percent of adults involved in football stressed that more action was necessary to eliminate racism, a view that was strongly supported by young people in the 16–24 age group. Regarding support for the national team, 62 percent of England fans were aged between 31 and 50, of which some 99 percent were white. Another survey of the same year revealed that 97.4 percent of referees were white, whereas only 1.1 percent were 'Black' or 'Black British,' 0.6 percent belonged to the 'Asian' or 'Asian British' group, 0.4 percent were of 'Mixed' race and the same percentage applied to 'Chinese' or 'other.' Equally disturbing was the evidence produced by a 2002 survey, which revealed that 97 percent of the Football Association staff and volunteers were white; the FA Council was all white; 99.6 percent of County FA council members were white; 98 percent of referees, coaches and medical staff were white; and none of the international players described themselves as 'Asian,' 'Asian British,' 'Chinese' or 'other.' Obviously, the report also indicated the low numbers of managers and coaches at the top divisions from black and minority ethnic groups, despite the increasing number of players from the same background. Alas, one commonplace, prejudiced, 'explanation' was their lack of organizational skills. Finally, one in five of black and minority ethnic groups' players, coaches, administrators and spectators have experienced racism, perhaps, due to football's "popularity and the confrontational culture of the game."[6]

Asians Can Play Football

The *Asians Can't Play Football* (1996) report should have had a tremendous impact upon the issue of racial discrimination in football, at the expense of the Asian community, and contributed, at least, to raising awareness about an important issue that concerned an equally significant part of the British society. Since the report made a number of recommendations to address the problem with effect, the Football Association responded by hosting the same year a national conference to assess the prospects of increasing the participation of Asians in football and set up the 'Asians in Football' working group. Nevertheless, some ten years later, the *Asians Can Play Football, Another Wasted Decade* report indicated that the number of Asian football players did not increase over the years, nor did their involvement in administrative, managerial and coaching positions. The same applied for Asian spectators, even though several football clubs were located in areas with large Asian communities. Moreover, the fact that all-Asian football leagues continued to exist merely because of the apparent lack of opportunities for Asians to play their football with a professional club confirmed that racism was still an issue. Evidently, at the time when the report was published, only four Asians played professional football, Adnan Ahmed (Huddersfield Town), Michael Chopra (Newcastle United), Zesh Rehman (Fulham) and Harpal Singh (Stockport County).

The report also stressed the significant contribution of a number of all–Asian football clubs. Albion Sports, for example, is a team made up of British Asians in Bradford that witnessed considerable success in nationwide football competitions, which provides opportunities to all children—regardless of their background—and cooperates with local schools and with Leeds United to promote young players from ethnic minority communities and pave their way to professional football. Luton United, founded in June 2000 as Luton Asians FC but was renamed two years later, was awarded the National Development Award for their work with ethnic minorities in 2003 and, particularly, for having addressed the issue of the underrepresentation of Asians in football at local level. Just as Albion Sports, Luton United also witnessed success in national, amateur, football competitions. In London, the West Ham United Asians in Football Project was set up in 1998, aiming to encourage Asian participation in football, in cooperation with the Football Association, the Football Foundation, Sport England and the London Boroughs of Newham, Tower Hamlets and Enfield. Leicester Nirvana, founded in 1994, is yet another football club that caters to the needs of young Asians. The club has long suffered from inadequate facilities, apparently, a common problem for Asian clubs across the country, and depends largely on support from the local authorities. It is noteworthy that the club was created after Nirvana FC decided to take a new course in the early 1990s, when racism on the pitch reached alarming levels. Today, Leicester Nirvana maintains close links with Leicester City FC, a local professional club that strive to combat racism in football.

The contribution of the anti-racism organization Football Unites Racism Divides was commended, since their people have been instrumental in supporting teams with a distinct ethnic background, such as Sharrow United, Sharrow Athletic, Porter United and the African Dream Team. The Scottish Ethnic Minority Sports Association, originally known as the Scottish Asian Sports Association (SASA) when they were founded in 1990, to encourage the wider participation of local Asian communities in football. The growing enthusiasm behind Asian teams, eventually, led to the formation of SASA FC. The club begun in the lower levels of the Glasgow Sunday league, moved up to the Saturday Glasgow Central League in 1998 and, ultimately, to the Scottish Unity League. Successful as it was, SASA FC proved that Asians had good technical ability and the necessary physical capacity to play football. Inspired, perhaps, by their memorable achievements, the UK Asian Football Championship was established in 1999 to address the issue of Asian underrepresentation in the popular game.

FAN PROFILE, RACISM AND LEGISLATION

Fan surveys
In the mid-1990s, black footballers accounted for almost a quarter of all professional players; however, the numbers of non-white fans in the Premier League were as low as 1 percent. More recently, national fan surveys carried out during the 2000–2006 seasons, six football seasons all together, revealed interesting facts. Without a shred of doubt, white supporters dominated the terraces, as their numbers never failed reaching at least 96 percent of the crowd, whereas black and Asians made up some 1 percent. The rest of the seats were occupied by a constantly increasing number of foreign nationals. Evidently, from all Premier League clubs, Arsenal and Tottenham Hotspur consistently attracted many more non-white supporters than other clubs, while Leicester City (and Bradford City in the 2000–2001 season) 'specialized' in attracting more Asians during the 2000–2002 seasons, when the club played top-flight football. The ever-present issue of racism, most probably, accounts for the perceptible underrepresentation of ethnic minorities on the terraces. It is important to note, nonetheless that younger fans were more likely to be frustrated by racism, an omen, perhaps, that future generations will not subscribe to discrimination.

For the moment, a survey conducted by the Sir Norman Chester Centre for Football Research indicated that spectators were more sensitive to foul language, when attending a football match together with their partners or children, than to racist language, even though the presence of black players in football was anything but unusual, given that they made up some 13–15 percent of professional footballers in the Premier League. To add to the negative image of some supporters, 60 percent of football fans felt there were too many foreign footballers playing for English clubs. Along similar lines, the Working Group on Football Disorder stressed that a certain degree of racism and xenophobia also characterized England supporters, usually expressing their national sentiments through foul language, since they were more likely to oppose anything that is not English. In this respect, an on-site recording of the initial reaction of the Chelsea fans to the manager's overwhelming decision to field a team that failed to include a single English player on December 1999 would speak volumes for their views on the role of foreigners in football. Four years earlier, a fan survey indicated that the majority of football supporters (79 percent) were in favor of foreign players, whereas only a 10 percent argued for the opposite.

However, fans also stressed the need to promote young English players and some even suggested that foreign players should be restricted to quality internationals from the most competitive football nations. The 1997 survey showed, for a second time, that fans were supportive of quality foreign players (59 percent), though their numbers dropped significantly, while a third of supporters (33 percent) felt that their numbers and sheer presence in the starting lineups constituted a credible threat to the future development of young English footballers. Nevertheless, that 33 percent mostly reflected fans that followed small clubs with relatively few foreign players in their squads and, therefore, their views may lack substance. Following the Chelsea 'incident,' the 2001 fan survey indicated that supporters were more in favor of an effective combination of illustrious foreign players and local talent, while those concerned with the lack of local talent grew to 60 percent of the respondents. It is noteworthy, nonetheless, that the inflated prices of English players was just another reason for clubs to target foreign players as, for example, after the 2002 World Cup Manchester United paid some thirty million pounds for the transfer of Rio Ferdinand from Leeds United, whereas Arsenal spent only four million on Gilberto Silva, a member of the winning Brazilian national squad. As the football market expanded, some key signings for the Premier League clubs in 2002 concerned players from China, Japan, Nigeria, Senegal and Turkey. However, the subsequent multinational nature of football clubs may suggest that fans will not only support their national team, but also follow those nations that feature their club's foreign stars and thus, lessen the impact of nationalism.

Today, English fans may be accustomed to foreign players, particularly those of a high caliber, however, professional football clubs fail to increase participation from ethnic minority groups. Instead, members of the black and Asian communities are more likely to take part, in all forms, in ethnically exclusive football teams, thus providing evidence of both their eagerness to participate in the beautiful game and that racial discrimination persists. The fact, however, that football has the capacity to promote integration should not leave the football governing bodies unimpressed. Given that the majority of fans (51 percent) choose to support a football team by virtue of locality, national football associations may well pin their hopes on the rare qualities of the game so to consolidate relations among distinct ethnic groups and promote cultural diversity.

Arrests in football grounds

Indeed, supporters of England belied the expectations of their critics, since the 2004 European Championship in Portugal and the 2006 World Cup in Germany did not witness the extremely embarrassing effects of hooliganism, unlike the 2000 European Championship that was cohosted by Belgium and the Netherlands. On the other hand, racism was still troubling the football authorities in England. According to reports produced by the Home Office (Statistics on Football-related Arrests and Banning Orders), over a period of six football seasons, from 2000 to 2006, 428 arrests related to racist chanting were recorded in both domestic and international competitions. It is noteworthy that the Home Office reports reveal that racist conduct, in the case of certain clubs, seems to be a recurring phenomenon.

The majority of these episodes took place in the Premier League (124), which revealed a relative symmetry (twenty-two incidents in the 2000–2001 season, nineteen in 2001–2002, twenty-four in 2002–2003, twenty in 2003–2004, twenty in 2004–2005 and nineteen in 2005–2006), and in Division One (120), where there was no such pattern of consistency (ten, seventeen, twenty-eight, twenty, nineteen and twenty-six offences over the same seasons). In contrast, the second and third divisions scored considerably lower (sixty-three and thirty-one arrests respectively). In Division Two, racist incidents were almost constantly increasing (eleven in each of the 2000–2001 and 2001–2002 seasons, fourteen in 2002–2003 and sixteen in 2003–2004), until they were considerably reduced during the last two seasons (six recorded incidents in the 2004–2005 season and five in 2005–2006). On the other hand, Division Three demonstrated exceptionally low levels of racist offences, apart from the 2000–2001 season when fifteen arrests were recorded, given the numbers of incidents that took place during the five subsequent football seasons (one offence in 2001–2002, four in 2002–2003, five in 2003–2004 and three in each of the 2004–2005 and 2005–2006 seasons). Likewise, the two domestic cup competitions had their own share of racist incidents; however, the League Cup witnessed far less racism (nineteen recorded offences). In the FA Cup, twenty-nine racist incidents alone were recorded during the 2002–2003 season (from a total of forty-two). As a matter of fact, the number of racist incidents recorded during the 2002–2003 season (103 offences) far exceeded any one of the other five football seasons under examination (eighty-two in 2000–2001, forty-eight in 2001–2002, seventy-one in 2003–2004, fifty-seven in 2004–2005 and, finally, sixty-seven in 2005–2006).

At a glance, there seems to be no obvious numerical correlation between the figures mentioned above, except for the fact that the top two divisions, the Premier League and Division One, and the FA Cup, the more prestigious cup competition of the two, reached their peak—in terms of arrests made related to racist conduct—during the 2002–2003 season. Yet those numbers alone bring out the inner meaning of racism in English football, given that the majority of clubs that competed in the Premier League or Division One were, and usually are, located in large urban areas. According to the *Racism in Rural Areas* report, produced by the European Monitoring Centre on Racism and Xenophobia, the degree of discrimination that occasionally illustrates the relations between the local population and immigrants in rural areas is more clearly recognized, due to the socio-economic forces that dominate such 'closed' societies. In contrast, the inherent dynamics of a multicultural environment, as in the case of urban areas, do not pertain to the distinctly higher number of arrests made during matches that involved clubs from the top two divisions (244 in total), compared to the ninety-four offences committed in the bottom two divisions. Certainly, clubs in the Premier League and in Division One attract considerably larger crowds, because of the seating capacity of their stadiums and the football stars that feature in the starting eleven, which may account for the disproportionate distribution of racist offences across the four divisions—even though this oversimplification fails to satisfy our academic curiosity. Unless, of course, socioeconomic forces—similar to those encountered in rural areas—and political issues, emphasize those social divisions so often expressed through racist language at football matches.

The same Home Office reports not only provide a breakdown of the number of arrests related to racist chanting by competition and year, they also mention the clubs that suffer from racist supporters, though they only cover the past five football seasons (from the 2001–2002 season to 2005–2006). Evidently, a number of clubs figured without fail on the lists of shame. In the Premier League, Aston Villa and Chelsea claimed five appearances, followed by Everton and Middlesbrough (four each during the 2001–2005 seasons). Leeds United, too, featured in the relevant lists on four accounts (during the 2001–2004 seasons and in the 2005–2006 season), though on the last occasion the club was relegated to Division One. In the 'most offences per year' category, the title went twice to Leeds United (six and five offences respectively) and Chelsea (five offences in each season), though in one case Leeds United shared top spot with Everton (five offences during the 2003–2004 season). Divisions One and Two demand a parallel examination, since the degree of success or failure was for some clubs associated with promotion or relegation. Burnley and Millwall are the only two clubs that featured in the same lists in one single division (Division One), the former on four accounts (2001–2005 seasons) and the latter on three occasions (2003–2005 seasons) respectively. In contrast, Grimsby Town appeared twice in Division One (2001–2003 seasons) and once in Division Two (2003–2004 season); Barnsley featured once in Division One (2001–2002 season) and twice in Division Two (2003–2005 seasons); and Brighton & Hove Albion, Plymouth Argyle and Stoke City were included once in Division One and twice in Division Two. Nevertheless, the ultimate champion was Sheffield Wednesday, which stayed in the 'charts' over the entire five-year period, having spent three seasons in Division One (during the 2001–2003 seasons and in 2005–2006) and two in Division Two (during the 2003–2005 seasons). From those clubs, in Division One, that really stood out due to their fans' racist conduct, Millwall occupied first position twice (eight and five offences during the

2004–2006 seasons), while Sunderland, too, made one appearance that leaves no one cold (seven offences in the 2003–2004 season). In Division Two, Grimsby Town had a similar fate in the 2003–2004 season and Port Vale the season before with 5 and 6 offences respectively. Stoke City claimed top spot twice, once in Division Two (seven offences during the 2001–2002 season) and the next season in Division One (nine offences). In Division Three, race-related incidents were kept at moderate levels, however, Lincoln City made three successive appearances in the relevant lists during the 2003–2006 seasons. Taking into serious consideration the information mentioned above and, particularly, the propensity of some Stoke City fans to racist conduct, the 2001 riots that took place in the north of England, ultimately, may be anything but a coincidence. Naturally, football clubs ought to take action and eliminate racism from their grounds, even though there is this argument that football clubs fail, intentionally, to take action regarding racist incidents, given the compulsion to avoid drawing the attention of the public to this sort of matters.

Football legislation

To this end, legislation has enabled the football governing bodies in England to combat racism with effect. Section 3 of the Football Offences Act (1991) was the first attempt to eradicate racial discrimination from football, however, one could be charged for racist chanting only when the individual in question engaged in such conduct together with other supporters and, therefore, was clearly ineffective. Instead, an individual could only be legally prosecuted under the Public Order Act (1986) for making use of 'obscene and foul language at football grounds.' Still, the Public Order Act failed to describe the contents of such language more accurately. Taylor, whose brainchild was the well publicized Taylor Report that modernized football stadiums in England, stressed the limited efficiency of the Public Order Act as well, but his views were most probably "centred upon the potential risk to public order rather than the social unacceptability of racism."[7] Eventually, Section 9 of the Football (Offences and Disorder) Act of 1999 amended Section 3 to extend the offence over individuals too. The Football (Offences and Disorder) Act of 1999 also amended the definition of racist chanting. Whereas the 1991 Act defined racist chanting as "consisting or including matter which is threatening, abusive or insulting to a person by reason of his color, race, nationality (including citizenship) or ethnic or national origins," the 1999 Act included "the repeated uttering of any words or sounds whether alone or in concert with one or more others."[8]

Nevertheless, equally problematic was the definition of racial aggravation in the Crime and Disorder Act of 1998, which stated in Section 28(1) that "An offence is racially aggravated . . . if: (a) at the time of committing the offence, or immediately before or after doing so, the offender demonstrates towards the victim of the offence hostility based on the victim's membership (or presumed membership) of a racial group; or (b) the offence is motivated (wholly or partly) by hostility towards members of a racial group based on their membership of that group."[9] These loopholes clearly demonstrated that offenders could evade justice and maintain their unethical conduct. Furthermore, the Football Spectators (Prescription) Order 2004 and the Football (Offences) (Designation of Football Matches) Order 2004 came into force on 11 October 2004 and amended the definition of a 'regulated' football match (Football Spectators Act 1989) and the definition of a 'designated' match (Football (Offences) Act 1991), since it obstructed the application of football disorder and football banning order legislation. Only matches that involved Premier League and Football League clubs were considered 'regulated' and 'designated,' which means that individuals banned from football matches could attend matches in the Football Conference and in minor cup competitions. Moreover, racist incidents at Football Conference matches were not considered an offence, with the courts being unable to impose banning orders.

With focus on racism among football players, Gardiner and Welch supported that racial discrimination on the pitch should warrant a red card. They also emphasized that the Race Relations Act of 1976 made clear that clubs were responsible for protecting their players against discrimination and even suggested that the inclusion of a relevant clause in a player's contract would probably have the desired effect, since it would then prevent them from abusing their colleagues. The main problem that the Race Relations Act failed to address with effect, nevertheless, was the fact that it did not allow room for clubs to take such action in case a player abused an opponent. Still, making it an offence for a player to abuse another footballer would enable club to take disciplinary action against them.

Recently, thirty-nine football supporters were arrested as regards racist chanting and violent conduct by Staffordshire Police, following the end of the FA Cup match between Stoke City and Birmingham City. The arrests took place after police authorities made relevant photographs public that were, first, processed by the Football Intelligence Unit. A fan of Lincoln City, Benjamin Davis-Todd, was found guilty of racist chanting and was banned from attending football matches until 2008. A Burnley fan, George Jackson, "was given a 12-month conditional discharge and a three-year order banning him from any town or city in the UK where Burnley or England are playing for three hours before and after any game," for having racially abused Paul Ince of Wolverhampton Wanderers. Jackson was found guilty of misdemeanors, after the nearby steward, Mark Jackson, "saw [George] Jackson doing monkey impressions and moving his arms up and down in a monkey impersonation."[10] Another football fan that shared Davis-Todd's fate is Robert Bell for racially abusing a player of Turkish side Galatasaray during their Champions League match against Liverpool at Anfield. It is noteworthy that the incident came to a steward's notice following complaints from fans seated close to the perpetrator. Two more fans were banned from football matches for three years—as they engaged in racist chanting, though in separate incidents—by the Chester Magistrates' Court. Concerning a different, but equally important offence, a Wolverhampton Wanderers fan was banned for two years from attending football matches, after he was caught by closed circuit system giving the Nazi salute during his club's penultimate game of the season against Tottenham Hotspur at home.

THE ENGLISH FA AND PREMIER LEAGUE CLUBS

The Football Association

'Football For All' is the English Football Association's *Ethics and Sports Equity Strategy* of 2002, which focused, intrinsically, on "fairness and respect for all people; equality of access and opportunity; recognizing that inequalities exist and taking practical steps to address them; and that football needs to ensure it is equally accessible to all members of society."[11] The English Football Association takes pride in not having received any complaints related to discrimination against any of its bodies since 1997, "possibly even before this but records are not held any further back."[12] As one might expect, the national football association has an equal opportunities policy in place and advertises "in the National Press and sector specific to encourage a wide selection of candidates to apply."[13] Moreover, the Football Association also advocates that courts adopt an uncompromising policy towards dealing with all racist offenders, thus highlighting its commitment to combating racism in football. The *Ethics and Sports Equity Strategy* clearly indicated the determination of the English football governing body to tackle discrimination in football by taking into serious consideration the sheer absence of Asian football players from the top division, the apparent underrepresentation of ethnic minorities in the various bodies of the English Football Association and the limited involvement of blacks in managerial and coaching positions.

On the whole, 'Football For All' was concerned, particularly, with the more than obvious lack of black coaches, even though the number of black football players was constantly increasing. Most certainly, the fact that Hope Powell became the first black coach to take charge of England women's team in 1998 simply underlines the belated recognition of black people in the game. However, the English Football Association is not alone in combating racism, as quite a few County FAs (regional football bodies) aim at bringing ethnic minorities closer to football through relevant community schemes. For example, the County FA in Cambridgeshire supported the local Chinese community in their attempt to found a football team that was promoted to the local Cambridge University League. Along the same lines, the Manchester County FA maintains that the successful integration of the local ethnic minority groups in Oldham is imperative, particularly, since the well publicized violent, interracial, clashes of 2001 in the north of England. At European level, the English Football Association hosted in March 2003 the UEFA-sponsored Unite Against Racism conference, which was held at Chelsea's football ground, Stamford Bridge, with the participation of delegations from more than fifty countries, as well as European-based football oriented anti-racism organizations. Most importantly, the report stated:

"The FA has a direct role to play in tackling racism through the application of rules and regulations. We have introduced a number of amendments to our rules and regulations to ensure that effective measures can be taken against racist behaviour in the game, both on and off the pitch. FA Rules specifically cover discrimination in all its forms as a key element concerning conduct, as follows:

Laws of the game
Guidance has been issued to referees that racist remarks constitute a dismissal offence in accord with Law 12 the use of offensive, insulting or abusive language and/or gestures and must be punished accordingly.

Rules of The Association
Rule E.2: A Participant shall not use any one or combination of the following: violent, threatening, abusive, indecent or insulting words or behaviour.

Rule E.3: A Participant shall not carry out any act which is discriminatory by reason of ethnic origin, colour, race, nationality, religion, sex, sexual orientation or disability.

Guidance for Punishments for Disciplinary Commissions
Guidance for offences under Rule E2 are listed in The FA's Handbook and circulated directly to every player in the FA Premier League and the Football League. Where a racist factor has been accepted or proved then for the first offence the suspension and fine to be doubled, and for a second offence, be trebled. Any subsequent offence proved should result in a substantial period of suspension from all football related activities together with a fine.

The Guidance for Punishments for Disciplinary Commissions outlines measures for dealing with cases where discrimination is proved: 'the discrimination offence should be seen as serious, with double the penalty being the minimum for the discrimination charge being proved.'"[14]

To increase participation of ethnic minority communities in football, several football clubs distribute free tickets for members of a distinct ethnic background to attend matches of the reserve team, while others seem to have adopted similar measures to encourage ethnic minority groups to attend first team matches. The Football Volunteer program, supported by the Prince's Trust and funded by the Premier League, managed to successfully recruit members (26 percent) from ethnic minorities, whereas the Premier League developed a novel scouting scheme at Leicester City, which aims at increasing the numbers of professional football players from ethnic minority groups. As a result, the local club appointed a member of their scouting staff to maintain links with amateur clubs that feature youngsters from ethnic minorities with the purpose of encouraging them to join football club academies. Moreover, the Premier League, in cooperation with the Professional Footballer's Association, expressed concern about the absence of blacks from managerial and coaching positions and produced the Racial Equality Standard with the support of Britain's leading anti-racism organization Kick It Out. The Standard "contains three stages of achievement; preliminary, intermediate and advanced. Each stage is then divided into three areas of work; stadiums and outreach work, policy and planning, and administration and management,"[15] thus holding football clubs responsible for encouraging wider participation from ethnic minorities, adopting the necessary measures to tackle racism with effect and increase the participation of people from ethnic minorities in administrative and management positions. Stewards, too, must undertake the Football Stewarding Qualification to ensure a standard approach towards racism. At this point, it is important to note that Kick It Out emerged through the Advisory Group Against Racism and Intimidation, which was founded in 1995 to serve and promote the cause of anti-racism initiatives assumed by the football governing bodies. As it happens, the Advisory Group Against Racism and Intimidation materialized after the Commission for Racial Equality launched the 'Let's Kick Racism Out of Football' campaign and, soon after, endorsed the 'Let's Kick Racism' and 'Respect All Fans' as its guiding principles.

Kick It Out also organized a conference on citizenship, in June 2005, at Old Trafford, to make good use of football and promote diversity, racial equality and social inclusion, particularly, since these issues are all part of the Citizenship curriculum. The English Football Association also aimed at adopting novel measures to increase ethnic minority participation in football, given that the population of such groups increased by 44 percent, with black Africans, Bangladeshis and Chinese growing fast in numbers. At the same time, it became evident that the British society is aging, which means that for stadiums to maintain attendance, football would have to adapt to the new realities. These facts become all the more important when taking into account that a BBC program revealed that football, more than any other sports, was widely viewed among ethnic minority communities, unlike white audiences, even though spectators from a similar background ranged between 2 and 8 percent at Premier League matches. All in all, increasing participation among ethnic minority communities remains high on the agenda of the English Football Association. In this respect, the main objective of the English Football Association is to increase the average attendance of ethnic minority members from 1 percent, the typical figure for the 2003–2004 season, to 5 percent by 2008. To this extent, the English Football Association supported the Asian 5-a-side Football Challenge Cup, on 14 July 2002, which was a huge success considering that forty-five junior teams and forty-five adult teams took part in this unique competition. Most certainly, the commitment of the English Football Association to combat racism did not escape notice, as UEFA has fully acknowledged the contribution of the English football governing bodies to the popular game. In Chief Executive Lars-Christer Olsson's words, "England is a good example in the way they have campaigned and addressed the behavior of fans and players towards each other in the fight against racism."[16] To suggest that Britain was the first to devise anti-racism initiatives may not be far from reality.

Premier League clubs
It is encouraging, of course, that Premier League clubs participate through a variety of channels in the struggle against racial discrimination, as the 2001– 2002 and 2003–2004 Annual Charter Reports of the English Football Association (FA Premier League) indicate. With no doubt, their contribution to anti-racism campaigns across the country and the genuine support to the cause of the English Football Association are of immense significance.

Arsenal
Arsenal, for one, has been committed to increasing participation from ethnic minority communities—successfully so, as mentioned above—by making good use of various channels, such as offering free tickets, as competition prizes, through local press, like *The Voice, New Nation, The Asian Times, The Jewish Chronicle* and *Parikiaki*. Arsenal has actively demonstrated its commitment to the elimination of racism from football by employing Kick It Out initiatives and has also had some of its football stars feature on the organization's anti-racism material. The club's more illustrious French players also made an appearance in an anti-racism video intended for schools in France.

Taking into account that Arsenal's black players have had the unfortunate experience of being racially abused on more than one occasion, including appearances with their national teams, the club's active role in, and overall dedication to, anti-racism campaigns is certainly not surprising. Moreover, the club was instrumental in smoothing the progress of integration through the *Arsenal and Maimonides* project, which aimed at strengthening relations between Jews and Muslims through football and held Sunday morning football training sessions for children and volunteer coaches from the two communities.

Birmingham City
Birmingham City, in partnership with the West Midlands Police and sponsored by the Neighborhood Renewal Fund, appointed a Development Officer for Asian Football in June 2003. The Development Officer's main task is to encourage the local Asian community in Birmingham's Small Heath, an area largely populated by ethnic minority groups, to take part in the club's coaching program. The club supports the cause of Kick It Out and even encouraged pupils from local schools to become involved in anti-racism campaigns, in an attempt to represent with effect the several ethnic minority communities located in the area. Birmingham City has certainly not ignored the local ethnic communities. The club's commitment to increase participation from ethnic minority groups is when taking into consideration the fact that Birmingham City recently appointed two Asian officers to support the club's Community Department. Obviously, the need to establish closer links with local communities and schools in the area are among the key responsibilities of the two officers. Given that some members of these ethnic minority groups cannot always afford to attend Birmingham City's football matches, to increase their participation in the game, the club provides them with tickets at lower prices.

Blackburn Rovers

In an attempt to promote integration, Blackburn Rovers, in 2002, set up a football tournament open to teams from ethnic minorities and local schools, and established the Minority Communities Working Group to encourage wider participation from ethnic minority groups. The club also supported the 'Religious Studies/Citizenship' program, which fosters respect for cultural diversity, as pupils from different religious convictions are encouraged to visit local Mosques and Cathedrals in order to develop a better understanding of the concept of religion and its various practices. Blackburn Rovers, too, are committed to eradicateing racism from football and have held local anti-racism campaigns, such as 'Racism: Not Under Our Roof' to raise awareness.

At the same time, the club's officials sought to develop certain strategies, compatible with their Racial Equality Standard, in an attempt to quantify those supporters from ethnic minority background. To this end, it was decided to include a relevant question on ethnicity in the season ticket application form from the 2004–2005 season onwards. Moreover, the Asian Policy Group was established in 2003, with the sole purpose of bringing the club closer to local ethnic minority communities. On a few occasions, club officials have also cooperated with local football clubs, such as Darwen BC and Blackburn United, to organize and promote the 'East Meets West' football competition devoted to teams from distinct ethnic backgrounds. Blackburn Rovers' intention to establish closer relations with local ethnic communities is also reflected in the club's support of local Asian entrepreneurs, football-related events and an ethnic minority newspaper, *Asian Image*. The club also maintains links with the Ethnic Minorities Development Association.

Bolton Wanderers

During the 2003–2004 season, a unique football event took place at the Reebok Stadium, home of Bolton Wanderers. The club held the 'Bolton Inter-Mosque Football Tournament,' together with the Bolton Council and the valuable cooperation of local mosques that made up the participating football teams. All matches of the tournament were referred by Football In The Community officials, who may also claim credit for both their novel idea and the organization of the event. Bolton Wanderers support the cause of Kick It Out too and are also interested in increasing participation from local ethnic minority communities. In this respect, Bolton Wanderers appointed an Ethnic Minorities Community Development Officer to fulfill the purpose of the club's Football In The Community scheme. It is noteworthy that the club mentioned in both Annual Charter Reports that no complaints about racist behavior were received.

Charlton Athletic

Charlton Athletic has also been quite active, devoting time and resources to eliminate racism from football. As a matter of fact, the Charlton Athletic Race Equality Partnership is a project supported by the club, in an attempt to address issues related to racial discrimination with effect. It is important to note that the Charlton Athletic Race Equality Partnership was set up in 1993 by the club, the supporters' club and the Greenwich Council, as a response to the racially motivated murder of a young black boy named Stephen Lawrence. Charlton Athletic, together with the supporters' club, holds the annual 'red, white and black' anti-racism campaign. The relevant event of the 2003–2004 season took place during the home match against Fulham under the motto 'South Africa Day,' accompanied by all necessary African-style festivities, since the club decided to become involved in the construction of a football centre near Johannesburg.

Chelsea
The violent and racially discriminatory conduct of a section of hard-core Chelsea fans is well publicized and has been discussed earlier. In this respect, it comes as no surprise that the club has often collaborated with local police authorities in the past, by taking part in covert operations during league matches, which resulted to the suspension of many football supporters (season ticket holders and club members). As unorthodox as it may seem, Chelsea encouraged their supporters to come forward and report racist incidents by offering them, in exchange, vouchers for the purchase of the club's merchandise from the Chelsea Megastore. Nevertheless, committed to the cause of anti-racism campaigns in football, Chelsea has been working closely with the London Tigers, a club that plays its football in the Asian Football League, to encourage the wider participation of Asians in football.

Derby County
Another club that actively supports the cause of Kick It Out is Derby County. The club has demonstrated its interest in increasing support from ethnic minority communities by providing the Derby Racial Equality Council with complimentary tickets, which are then distributed among members of minority groups in the area. Derby County deserves credit for having arranged a charity football game between the Normanton Allstars, a team made up of players from ethnic minority background, and Derbyshire Constabulary, a team representing the local police force. The main purpose of the match was to improve communication and establish closer links between the police authorities and a community that has suffered from race-related crimes in the past. The income received from the football game was offered to the Afghanistan Children Appeal.

Everton
The only football club, in both FA Premier League Annual Charter Reports, mentioned for having adopted the Ten-Point-Plan of Kick It Out, concerning the elimination of racism from football, is Everton. The fact that the club developed the Everton Against Racism project, further illustrates Everton's determination to tackle racism in football. The main task of the Everton Against Racism project is to monitor all complaints related to racist incidents, considering that the project was actually set up to facilitate the effective implementation of the Ten-

Point-Plan. Furthermore, Everton also developed a protocol together with Merseyside Police, which is reviewed on an annual basis, regarding the proper handling of racist behavior and/or incidents in and around the club's football ground.

What really stood out, however, in Everton's endeavors to reach out to people from an ethnic minority background, primarily, concerned people of Chinese origins. The Chinese community in the greater area of Liverpool constitutes, apparently, one of the largest in Europe. Hence, the club aimed at establishing closer relations with that minority group and was quite successful in doing so; partly because of the decision to employ—literally and metaphorically speaking—Chinese star Li Tie. Moreover, Everton was also successful in encouraging support from overseas, by putting great emphasis on the city of Liverpool's 'City of Culture' award.

Fulham

Fulham supported the nationwide Kick It Out campaign under the 'Black and White Help Fulham Unite' slogan, by distributing free tickets to members from ethnic minority communities, devoting part of the matchday program to antiracism and making a variety of ethnic food available to their fans during the event. The club launched in October 2003 the 'Different Cultures—Same Game' project, which is funded by the Western Union and Sportsmatch. The two-year project supported the anti-racism initiatives of both Kick It Out and Show Racism The Red Card and intended to promote cultural diversity, integration and the participation of ethnic minority groups in football. The club strives to raise awareness and seeks the support of their fans in the campaign against racism in football so to create a safer environment. In partnership with the Metropolitan Police, Fulham proved quite resourceful in promoting their anti-racism campaign. The club adopted "a scheme where stickers can be stuck to seats around areas where racist supporters have been identified; the stickers detail how to deal with racist crime and how to report it."[17] Fulham also held 'Search for a Star' events, in cooperation with the Western Union, to provide children from ethnic minorities with the opportunity to display their football skills and, if successful, come into contact with Premier League clubs.

Leeds United

Leeds United commitment to the struggle against racism is known and, perhaps, expected, given the club's troubled history of extreme right groups and racist conduct. In this respect, the club actively urges young people to both support its anti-racism campaigns and openly express their opposition to racial discrimination. The club maintains close relations with Kick It Out, the Leeds City Council Equal Opportunities, the Race Equality Advisory Forum, the Leeds United Fans Forum, the Hindu Charitable Trust and the Sheikh Temple, in its attempt to combat racial discrimination. Leeds United is also involved in local ethnic minority projects and works closely with schools in the area.

The Leeds United Against Racism Schools Project was launched in partnership with the Yorkshire Evening Post to address the issue of racism and includes
visits from Glasgow's football giants, Celtic and Rangers, and the Glasgow City
Council, while Leeds United and the local authorities offer similar services to
the city of Glasgow. With no doubt, the anti-racism education pack—compatible
with the National Literacy Strategy and the New Citizenship curriculum—that
the club produces in association with its Fans Forum, certainly epitomizes the
contribution of Leeds United to the nationwide campaign against racism. This
initiative, clearly the brainchild of the club's Learning Centre, is definitely a
very considerate effort to provide teaching personnel and relevant staff at
schools with the necessary anti-racism material to educate people on issues pertaining to cultural diversity, with the purpose of combating racial discrimination
in society. As a matter of fact, the education pack has proved such a major success that Leeds United officials were, every so often, struggling with the growing demand from schools. Apparently, the club's officials do not consider their
input significant enough to draw a line and simply relish the praise they so often
receive, including the European football governing body, considering that Leeds
United, as is the case with most clubs, also distributes free tickets to increase
participation from ethnic minority communities.

Leicester City
Leicester City is yet another highly active football club that takes pride in its
contribution to combating racism in football. Making good use of the Football In
The Community scheme, Leicester City has been successful in bringing the local
Asian community closer to the club, thus increasing attendance at football
matches, as well as encouraging Asian youngsters to join its football academies.
The club is a member of the Foxes Against Racism project, which is also supported by the Leicester City Council and local community leaders. The activities
of Foxes Against Racism include:

> "Conducting an extensive survey of clubs about racism in local football
> in Leicestershire. The survey findings received plenty of local media
> coverage and are being used by the local County FA to look at their
> policies in relation to dealing with racist incidents locally.
>
> Continuing to work with the Club through articles and features in the
> match programme and other outlets to reinforce its message about deal-
> ing with racism among fans—and inside the club.
>
> Helping to initiate a new community coaching initiative involving
> Leicester City working with young Asians and based at Rushey Mead
> School. This is part of our determination that the club should improve
> its recruitment of local ethnic minority players for its excellence pro-
> grammes."[18]

Given Leicester City's attempts to increase participation from Asian communities, one of the club's coaching staff, Rashid Mama, was specifically working to meet that end and even visited schools to encourage more Asian youngsters, among other pupils from an ethnic minority background, to play the game of football.

Liverpool

The contribution of Liverpool to the Kick It—Kick Off project, a course supported by the Knowsley Local Education Authority that ran over a period of six weeks during the school curriculum, was fundamental, since the project aimed at raising awareness about racism among children. The club also held a poster competition, open to pupils from local schools, in order to commemorate the tragic events that marked the Holocaust and to educate young people about issues concerning racism and anti-Semitism. Moreover, the Community Department of the club organized a football tournament for ethnic minority teams, including players of Arabic, Somali and Swahili origins.

Manchester United

Just as local rivals Leeds United, Manchester United have deeply been involved in the production of an education pack specially designed for schools, colleges and youth groups. To this end, the dominant club of Manchester works with the Youth Charter for Sports group, based in Salford, to develop a community scheme, a citizenship project rather, intended for children from deprived areas. The project, supported financially through the Barclaycard 'Free Kicks' program, makes good use of football's capacity to further promote integration. In addition to taking part in the annual anti-racism campaigns held by Kick It Out, Manchester United appointed an Education Officer, who is also a member of Trafford's Racial Harassment Forum, which is known as 'Diverse,' so to address the issue of racial discrimination with effect.

Southampton

Southampton, together with the Southampton City Council and Friends Provident, launched the 'Racism Just Ain't Saintly' project, playing on the club's nickname, the 'Saints.' The main objective of the project was to increase participation from ethnic minority communities and, therefore, promote integration. Added emphasis should be put on the fact that Southampton built its new stadium in an area largely populated by ethnic minority groups, which reveals that the club is genuinely interested in establishing close relations with local people. Needless to say, Southampton has participated in the nationwide anti-racism campaigns of Kick It Out and encouraged people from a distinct ethnic background to take part in the game, by making available football-related programs.

West Ham United

West Ham United launched the Our Asians in Football project, in association with Sport England, to increase the Asian community's involvement in football. In the past, 1,276 football training sessions were provided to 25,520 participants, in an attempt to provide players from this ethnic background with the opportunity to play a part in football and even join professional clubs. Other than promoting the interests of Asian youngsters that wish to pursue a career in football, the project provides Coach Education opportunities for football players from Asian communities to gain the FA teaching qualification. As one might expect, West Ham United received due praise by the Home Office, for strengthening the process of integration and increasing participation from ethnic minority communities. Apart from supporting the cause of Kick It Out, in yet another attempt to attract the attention of the Asian community, the club's under-19 side played hosts to Abhani Football Club from Bangladesh, before a predominantly Bangladeshi crowd.

On the whole, all Premier League clubs, including those that were not mentioned here, have actively supported the activities of Kick It Out, have had their stewards receive proper training on how to treat racist incidents and cooperate with local police authorities to lessen the potential for discriminatory conduct around the football ground. It is noteworthy that for a number of clubs, namely Aston Villa, Leicester City and Middlesbrough, it is a condition for season ticket and matchday ticket holders that they do not engage in racist conduct. Likewise, in the case of Everton, Leicester City and Middlesbrough, ground regulations make it clear that any form of racist behavior constitutes an offence. Under these circumstances, a number of fans were banned by Chelsea, Everton, Fulham, Leeds United, Leicester City, Manchester City, Newcastle United and Sunderland. Evidently, 'hotlines' installed in the football grounds of Everton, Leeds United and Sunderland proved a valuable source of information, with regard to racist incidents. Similar Kick It Out 'hotline' services are available at the stadiums of Aston Villa, Birmingham City, Fulham, Leicester City, Manchester United, Tottenham Hotspur and West Ham United.

Although it seems that anti-racism campaigns and all relevant measures have somewhat contributed to the elimination of racism in football, it is certain that all pertinent actors ought to intensify their efforts. In particular, it is evident that football clubs alone cannot claim much success in dealing with racist offenders, unless the police authorities adopt firm policies that harmonize well with the persistence of clubs to rid football of racial discrimination. In the 2003–2004 season, during Manchester City's home matches, even though four fans were ejected, on different occasions, by the club's officials from the football ground due to racist conduct, "the police were not on hand to make an arrest."[19] Paradoxically, similar incidents took place, during the same season, when Chelsea played at home, as "4 supporters were arrested, 3 ejected and 23 were banned for racist behaviour."[20] Evidently, the number of arrests does not add up to the number of fans that were banned by the club or the records of the Home Office, which reported only one arrest made on grounds of racist chanting.

CONCLUSION

As difficult as it is to establish whether racism plagued football in England first, it is almost certain that the English football governing bodies are pioneers in addressing the issue effectively. Multiculturalism is definitely an inherent feature of English society that can be traced back to the times of colonialism, therefore, the determination of the British government to tackle racial discrimination and xenophobia is not surprising. In the case of football, however, racism has only recently been addressed in effect. The main reason that accounts for the authorities' apparent lack of sympathy, as regards the predicament of the popular game, answers to the name of hooliganism. What is also known as the 'English disease' continues to be football's omnipresent concern, thus dominating the agenda of the football governing bodies throughout the continent. Evidently, football disorder in the stadiums of England was, eventually, treated by an English therapy inspired by the Taylor Report; nevertheless, violence in football still haunts authorities elsewhere in Europe. Racism, on the other hand, emerged gradually from the shadows of hooliganism, almost taking European football by surprise. Given that the European Union is confronted by the arduous task of constantly promoting further integration, at the same time emphasizing the continent's vibrant culture and overwhelming diversity, the need to tackle racism is fundamental. In contrast to hooliganism, however, racial discrimination requires a more innovative approach.

By the turn of the century, English authorities realized the dimension of the problem, as a number of studies devoted to sport and ethnicity revealed that minority groups were alienated from the popular game. In this respect, the contribution of the Football Task Force, the Commission of Racial Equality and the valuable research conducted by the Sir Norman Chester Centre for Football Research was immense. Although racist chanting is by no means as frequent a phenomenon as in the 1970s and 1980s, bar the odd incident, it appears that an equally distressing issue torments the game of football. Nowadays, racist offenders are, indeed, a rare commodity, but football and ethnic minorities in England constitutes an unusual combination. The absence of supporters, directors, administrators and coaches from black and Asian background confirms that the biggest stumbling block in increasing participation from ethnic minority communities is not confined to a small segment of fans that ridicule themselves by imitating monkeys. Instead, exclusive black and Asian football leagues, as well as the lack of Asian players in professional football, indicate the strong presence of a far more shocking issue. It is common knowledge, by now, that institutional racism has the capacity to overshadow the beautiful game and harness its wide appeal to sustain White domination. In the case of England, at least, institutional racism may simply serve the purpose of keeping football as white as the skin color of an 'authentic' Englishman. Moreover, the poor representation of ethnic minority groups among football supporters may suggest that football terraces are an inhospitable environment to non-whites, thus defining the color of the game.

Hence, it was imperative that the English Football Association, in close collaboration with professional football clubs, adopt those measures necessary to eliminate racism from the game. The national football association, in particular, strives to alter old-fashioned perceptions and obliterate racial stereotypes, so to facilitate the proper development of the game. Although the implementation of racial equality standards is likely to bring about the desired result, novel measures are required to encourage more members from ethnic minority background to participate. The fact that the English Football Association aims at increasing the attendance of this part of society proves that the authorities are on the right course of action, even though their estimates seem rather ambitious. Still, the football governing bodies in England have been successful in raising racial awareness, by publicizing the nondiscriminatory nature of the game, through a series of anti-racism activities. Besides, the football-related legislation that is in place should establish, ideally, a most appropriate regulation of the game. Professional football clubs, on the other hand, ought to contribute to the public good as well. Even if the significance of maximizing profits dictates their core policies, the prospect of attracting a wider audience from all quarters will surely serve their cause well. At the same time, clubs would reach out to ethnic minority communities and, therefore, represent better their locality. No matter the diversity of their fans, it is in the clubs' best interest to increase support, considering that well supported clubs tend to perform well too. And it seems they have realized it, given their commitment to anti-racism campaigns and relevant community projects. In simple terms, clubs must be open to all, just as football is for all. Ultimately, it is national football associations and their affiliated members that are greatly indebted to the popular game; not the exact opposite, which comes close to blasphemy.

Notes

1. Rae Sibbitt, *The perpetrators of racial harassment and racial violence*, Home Office Research Study 176 (London: Home Office, Research and Statistics Directorate, 1997), 24.

2. Sir Norman Chester Centre for Football Research, University of Leicester (UK), Fact Sheet 6: Racism and Football, 4–5.

3. The English Football Association, *Football For All*, 2004, 18.

4. The English Football Association, "Football For All," 18.

5. Football Task Force, *Investing in the Community* (Submitted to the Minister for Sport, 11 January 1999), 9.

6. *Increasing BME Participation in Sport & Physical Activity by Black and Minority Ethnic Communities* (A Report by Ploszajski Lynch Consulting Ltd, To The BME Sports Network East, January 2005), 43–44.

7. Steven Greenfield and Guy Osborn, "When the writ hits the fan; panic Law and football fandom," in *Fanatics! Power, identity and fandom in football*, ed. Adam Brown (London and New York: Routledge, 1998) 205.

8. HOC 34/2000, *Home Office guidance on football–related legislation* (Home Office circular 34/2000, 2000), 26.

9. Home Office Research Study 244, *Racist offences—how is the law working?, The implementation of the legislation on racially aggravated offences in the Crime and Disorder Act 1998*, Elizabeth Burney and Gerry Rose, with the assistance of Sandradee Joseph and Rebecca Newby, Institute of Criminology, University of Cambridge, (Home Office Research, Development and Statistics Directorate, July 2002), 13.

10. Kick It Out, "Football fan banned for racial abuse," <http://www .kickitout.org> (13 Sept. 2006).

11. The English Football Association, "Football For All," 3.

12. The English Football Association, "Football For All," 4.

13. The English Football Association, "Football For All," 4.

14. The English Football Association, "Football For All," 25.

15. The F.A. Premier League, *The F.A. Premier League Charter Report 2003/04* (2004), 12–14.

16. The F.A., "England the example", http://www.thefa.com (14 Dec. 2005)

17. The F.A. Premier League, "The F.A. Premier League Annual Charter Reports Season 2003/04," 189.

18. The F.A. Premier League, *The F.A. Premier League Annual Charter Reports, Season 2001/2002* (2002), 196.

19. The F.A. Premier League, "The F.A. Premier League Annual Charter Reports Season 2003/04," 287.

20. The F.A. Premier League, "The F.A. Premier League, Annual Charter Reports Season 2003/04," 155.

Chapter Six

Anti-racism in European football

Racism in football was a thing of the past until the 1990s, when the game's modern disease returned with a vengeance. People involved in the sport of football, directly or indirectly, have on many occasions embarrassed the popular game irreparably. The unpredictable mass that are football fans, for example, have been held accountable for disturbing racist incidents that attacked the dignity of players and supporters alike, inside and outside football grounds. Some fifteen years ago, Lazio fans expressed their antithesis to the club's decision to hire the services of Aaron Mohammed Winter, a player of Surinamese-Indian origins, when they stained the club's walls with a rather hateful message that read 'we don't want neither nigger nor Jewish' (July 1992). Far worse, German racist fans made their views heard during a European Championship qualifying game against Turkey, when they chanted 'Kreuzberg must burn'; Kreuzberg is a district of Berlin populated by a large Turkish community (October 1993). More recently, fans of Dinamo Bucharest displayed a banner during a match against fierce rivals Rapid Bucharest that read 'More Tigane,' death to the gypsies, (August 2001). Sadly, it is not always football supporters that are responsible for racially abusing rival fans and players. On one occasion, the president of Turkish side Trabzonspor spoke of Kevin Campbell in a depreciatory manner, when he was quoted saying that 'We bought a cannibal who believes he is a forward' (February 1999). Nothing compares, nevertheless, to the notorious-for-his-personal-racist-views Jean-Marie Le Pen, who once suggested that French players coming from ethnic minority background should refrain from singing the national anthem, thus questioning their Frenchness and loyalty to the nation (June 1996). Regrettably, this pattern of racist behavior is not exclusive to non-playing staff either. The infamous Eric Cantona kicked a football fan who, allegedly, hurled abuse at him during Manchester United's away game against Crystal Palace, though it should be noted that it was the player's nationality and not his skin color that caught the attention of the supporter's vicious remarks (November 1995). Ten years later, Nenad Jestrovic of Anderlecht was sent off by the match official during a Champions League game at Anfield, after racially abusing Liverpool's Momo Sissoko (November 2005). Another referee that disturbed the waters was Gurnam Singh, who took the English Football Association to court on grounds of racial discrimination (December 2001). Speaking of institutional racism, though from a wholly different standpoint, ITV sportscaster Ron Atkinson made a last-minute effort to redeem what was left of his honor and gave up his job, for having called Chelsea's Marcel Desailly 'a fucking lazy, thick nigger' (April 2004).

INTERNATIONAL FOOTBALL GOVERNING BODIES

Fédération Internationale de Football Association
The ultimate governing body in the world of football is, of course, the *Fédération Internationale de Football Association* (FIFA). Among a plethora of international organizations, highly praised for their diverse membership, the prominence of FIFA stems from its 207 affiliated national football associations, which compares well with the widely acclaimed United Nations of 192 members. To discuss FIFA's contribution to the development of the popular game would have been a pleasant voyage no doubt, however, it is imperative to focus on the task at hand and assess the response of football's supreme governing body to racism. FIFA's prime concern is to improve communication among all pertinent actors and convey a strong anti-racism message. In this respect, the president of FIFA, Joseph Blatter, set up the FIFA Ambassadors Against Racism. This unique 'embassy' is headed by Thierry Henry and includes prominent figures from the world of football such as Bobby Charlton, Sven Göran Eriksson, Jürgen Klinsmann, Michel Platini and Pelé, to name a few. No matter the world-wide reputation that followed the team of ambassadors, nevertheless, FIFA felt compelled to address the issue of racism to all intents and purposes, taking into account the dimensions of the problem and its impact on football.

The Extraordinary Congress of FIFA met in Buenos Aires on 7 July 2001 and adopted a resolution that urged all relevant parties to combat racism and purge those extreme elements that endorse discrimination. Key to the successful implementation of the resolution was the concept of cooperation, as the need to have football's governing bodies establish closer links with governments was soon realized. Given that racism in football reflects political, economic and social trends of society, it is fundamental that football and state authorities support the campaign against racism actively. The capacity of football to promote integration and cultural diversity became the driving force of FIFA's resolution, which stressed the potential of education in eliminating racism from the game and the need to assess the causes of racial discrimination. For the most part, however, the resolution addressed football clubs. It underlined that clubs should make an example of racist offenders by banning them from the football ground; monitor the behavior of fans during matches that are more likely to instigate racist incidents; and advertise anti-racism material in the stadium. The resolution also promoted cooperation between police authorities and stewards, so to deal with racism without delay, and highlighted the significance of encouraging fans to come forward with information regarding racist offenders. Clubs should strive to produce a racism-free environment in concert with their players, whose contribution is more than just instrumental. Central to the success of clubs in their endeavors is the education of players, as regards the principles of social inclusion, so to help shape their behavior toward teammates, coaching staff, spectators, referees and opponents. Moreover, the resolution urges clubs to take action against players that endorse racial discrimination whether on the pitch, in public or in private. Not surprisingly, the resolution dictates that football governing bodies adopt racial equality standards, to increase participation from ethnic minority groups in football and at all levels. Along these lines, match officials are required to follow games with a vigilant eye and reprimand racist offenders. The resolution also recommends that football clubs and national football associations make good use of their official websites to promote and support anti-racism campaigns, and urges the Confederations to observe anti-racism initiatives and inform FIFA's Executive Committee accordingly. Finally, the media should resist the need to publicize race-related incidents that may cause further disturbances.

Furthermore, certain statutes of FIFA make particular reference to non-discrimination. FIFA's Article 3 on 'Non-discrimination and stance against racism' stipulates that "Discrimination of any kind against a country, private person or groups of people on account of ethnic origin, gender, language, religion, politics or any other reason is strictly prohibited and punishable by suspension or expulsion."[1] In the same line of reason, Article 1 on 'Ethical obligations and non-discrimination' of the FIFA Code of Ethics specifies that "All persons bound by this Code (Note: Official is every board member, committee member, referee and assistant referee, coach, trainer, and other persons responsible for technical, medical and administrative matters in FIFA, a Confederation, Association, League or club) shall adhere to the principles and objectives of FIFA in all actions within or outside of FIFA, the Confederations, Associations and clubs, and refrain from any undertaking injurious to FIFA or its principles and objectives. These persons shall respect these ethical obligations in the performance of their duties as an Official of FIFA, the Confederations, the Associations, or clubs. While discharging their duties, Officials shall under no circumstances act in a discriminatory manner, especially in terms of ethnic background, race, cultural values, politics, religion, gender or language. They shall also pledge to behave in a dignified manner."[2] Evidently, both articles put great emphasis on human values and stress the essence of equality. Despite the fact that fundamental principles of sport, probably, render these regulations excessive, at least in the case of such a popular game, professional football commands that directives be in place to make certain its proper functioning.

Hence, to facilitate the campaign against racism in football and create the necessary environment for all to participate, FIFA revised the now famous Article 55 of the disciplinary code on nondiscrimination to state:

"Par. 1: Anyone who publicly disparages, discriminates against or denigrates someone in a defamatory manner on account of race, color, language, religion or ethnic origin, or perpetrates any other discriminatory and/or contemptuous act, will be subject to match suspension for at least five matches at every level. Furthermore, a stadium ban and a fine of at least CHF 20,000 will be imposed on the perpetrator. If the perpetrator is an official, the fine will be at least CHF 30,000.

Par. 2: If spectators display banners bearing discriminatory slogans, or are guilty of any other discriminatory and/or contemptuous behavior at a match, the appropriate body will impose a sanction of at least CHF 30,000 on the association or club that the spectators concerned support and force it to play its next official match without spectators. If the spectators cannot be identified as supporters of one or the other association or club, the host association or club will be sanctioned accordingly.

Par. 3: Any spectator who is guilty of any of the offences specified under par. 1 and/or 2 of this article will be banned from entering any stadium for at least two years.

Par. 4: If any player, association or club official or spectator perpetrates any kind of discriminatory or contemptuous act as described by par. 1 and/or 2 of this article, three points will automatically be deducted from the team concerned, if identifiable, after the first offence. In the case of a second offence, six points will automatically be deducted, and for a further offence, the team will be relegated. In the case of matches without points, the team concerned, if identifiable, will be disqualified.

Par. 5: The confederations and associations are required to incorporate the provisions of this article in their statutes and to enforce the sanctions stipulated. If any association infringes this article, it will be excluded from international football for two years."[3]

Given the ever-increasing trend of racial discrimination in German, Italian, Spanish and Eastern European football stadiums, FIFA announced on March 2006 that racist incidents during the World Cup in Germany would be dealt with severely, in line with Article 55. The seemingly newfound strength of FIFA, however, which stemmed from Article 55 and its novel, hard-core, measures on combating racism in football, proved ill decided and premature, while FIFA's enthusiasm was cut short in an abrupt manner. Hardly a month had gone by and Joseph Blatter was already forced to adopt a much more moderate approach. In light of new evidence, the president of football's world governing body stated that the national teams that took part in the 2006 World Cup need not fear the deduction of points, where their fans are found guilty of racist conduct, though the rules stipulated in Article 55 would still have an effect on players, coaching staff and team officials. Following an investigation by FIFA and UEFA's legal representatives, it became clear that not even football clubs could be subjected to Article 55, not to mention national teams. As a matter of fact, William Gaillard, UEFA communications director, stated that "It has had to be watered down because it was on shaky legal ground. The legal committees of UEFA and FIFA felt an automatic points' deduction would not have stood up in a civil court."[4] Subsequently,

> "FIFA sent out a circular to national associations in July amending the original rules and giving disciplinary bodies the option to reduce sanctions. The amendment said: 'Sanctions imposed on the basis of this article may be reduced or even disregarded if the player, team, club or association concerned can prove that it was not or was only minimally responsible for the offences in question or if other significant mitigating circumstances exist, particularly if the offences were provoked intentionally to cause a player, team, club or association to be sanctioned in accordance with this article.'"[5]

Despite FIFA's international status, it is certain that the organization lacks the legal posture to dictate the behavior of its affiliated members effectively, whereas Article 55 too, in its own merit, has only witnessed partial success. Except for Paragraph 3, on the whole, the application of Article 55 has certainly been limited; therefore, the response of the European governing body to the issue of racism in football becomes all the more intriguing, taking into account the Confederations' responsibility to promote and support anti-racism initiatives.

Union of European Football Associations
The Union of European Football Associations (UEFA) guide to good practice, *Unite against racism in European football*, stressed the significance of encouraging the involvement of ethnic minorities in anti-racism campaigns, given the absence of black supporters on the terraces.[6] In this respect, UEFA produced the *Ten Point Plan of Action for Professional Football Clubs* to promote the participation of ethnic minority communities in football, suggesting that clubs:

1. Issue a statement saying the club will not tolerate racism, spelling out the action it will take against those engaged in racist chanting. The statement should be printed in all match programmes and displayed permanently and prominently around the ground.
2. Make public address announcements condemning racist chanting at matches.
3. Make it a condition for season ticket holders that they do not take part in racist abuse.
4. Take action to prevent the sale of racist literature inside and around the ground.
5. Take disciplinary action against players who engage in racial abuse.

6. Contact other clubs to make sure they understand the club's policy on racism.
7. Encourage a common strategy between stewards and police for dealing with racist abuse.
8. Remove all racist graffiti from the ground as a matter of urgency.
9. Adopt an equal opportunities policy in relation to employment and service provision.
10. Work with all other groups and agencies, such as the players union, supporters, schools, voluntary organisations, youth clubs, sponsors, local authorities, local businesses and police, to develop proactive programmes and make progress to raise awareness of campaigning to eliminate racial abuse and discrimination.[7]

Much unlike Article 55, the *Ten Point Plan of Action for Professional Football Clubs* seems more plausible, even though it lacks the austerity of FIFA's scheme. It is precisely the nature of the approach of the two organizations that may determine their success or not in eliminating racism from football. While FIFA's attitude is far more radical, given that Article 55 focuses exclusively on sentencing racist offenders, the rationale behind UEFA's concept depends entirely upon football clubs reaching out to ethnic minority groups and promoting anti-racism campaigns. The resolution that FIFA adopted in Buenos Aires exempted, football's world governing body may seem more determined in eradicating racism, however, the more gentle approach of UEFA has the potential to claim more success.

UEFA's response to racism prompted the Norwegian Football Association to adopt a similar stance and suggest to its affiliated members a number of measures to combat racism in football with effect. The Norwegian Football Association's code of ethics concerns:

1. Recognition of human worth by all who participate in sport.
2. All discrimination must be fought.
3. Nonacceptance of prejudice.
4. Be alert to, and prepare to fight against, racism.
5. No to violence.
6. The participation of all in football.
7. Football exists because of voluntarism, encouraging people to work together as a team.
8. Parental participation is essential if children are to be encouraged into sport.[8]

The German Football Association assumed a similar role in national football and urged its members to eradicate racism from German stadiums, by suggesting the:

1. Adoption of an anti-racism clause in stadium rules and regulations stating that racism and xenophobia and the displaying and calling of extreme-

right signs and symbols will not be tolerated and will lead to the persons concerned being banned from the stadium.

2. Instruction of stewards with regard to forbidden symbols attributable to the extreme right.

3. Publication of statements in match programmes informing fans that the club does not tolerate racism, condemns racist chanting and the displaying of extreme right symbols and salutes, and will take appropriate action.

4. Insisting that owners of season tickets commit not to take part in racist abuse, racist chanting or any other form of aggressive behaviour such as the use of pyrotechnic devices and that they report persons who behave otherwise to the stewards or the police.

5. Introduction of appropriate steps against the sale or distribution of racist and xenophobic literature on stadium property on matchdays.

6. Influencing of players, coaches and officials not to make racist comments.

7. Removal of all racist graffiti on stadium property.

8. Development of action plans or projects in association with the authorities, the police, the fan projects, supporters clubs, sponsors, the social services, and players and coaches to raise awareness against racism and xenophobia.

9. Use of regular announcements against racism and xenophobia by the PA announcer.

10. Use of messages on the scoreboard stating that the club and the fans are against discrimination and racism.[9]

Although both national football associations deserve credit for their contribution to the campaign against racism in football, there are striking differences that distinguish the two schemes. The Norwegian version looks relatively vague, as it fails to make the necessary recommendations that could produce tangible results, regarding the measures that ought to be adopted for the purpose of eliminating racism from football. Nevertheless, it certainly is as epigrammatic as any proper code of ethics, therefore, rendering any further details excessive. In contrast, the German account is far more descriptive and purposeful, though it should be noted that race-related incidents in Norwegian football pale in comparison to Germany's predicament. The German plan clearly summarizes an assortment of guidelines that clubs need implement to rid their football grounds of racial discrimination and produce a healthy environment. All in all, the Mission Statement of UEFA, outlined in *Vision Europe*, stressed the need to "Increase access and participation, without discrimination on grounds of gender, religion or race" and "Promote positive sporting values, including fair play and anti-racism."[10] The vision of UEFA is to promote football among people of distinct backgrounds, so to facilitate their integration and peaceful coexistence, taking into account the game's democratic nature and scope, as well as its capacity to bring people closer together and enhance social cohesion, particularly, since UEFA is a nonpolitical and nonreligious organization.

In this respect, following the second Unite Against Racism conference, UEFA published the *Tackling racism in club football* report that, in effect, was a guide for clubs that touched upon the following principles:

"UNDERSTAND THE PROBLEM — It is easy to argue that issues such as racism are not within the domain of your club, that they are broader societal issues which should be left to other authorities. Most clubs will find it helpful for key staff to undergo an awareness training programme.

BE CLEAR ABOUT YOUR OBJECTIVES — Are you running a campaign to tackle racist chanting, or to reach out to local ethnic minority communities, or both? Develop principles for action that can be widely publicised, that all internal and external stakeholders within the club can support. Encourage publicity and ownership of these ideas.

WRITE A PLAN OF ACTION — Include practical outcomes for implementing your objectives. Use the UEFA ten-point plan as a basis for the measures your club can take. Set targets for progress and monitor regularly.

DEVELOP A CLEAR IDENTITY for your campaign, to help recognition and spread ownership among supporters. You may wish to develop a specific brand name.

MONITOR AND REPORT PROBLEMS — Develop systems for monitoring and reporting racial abuse and discrimination in all areas of your club.

PARTNERSHIPS — Work with fans, players, stewards, NGOs and community organisations with expertise in the field to implement your action plan. Make sure you involve ethnic minority and migrant communities.

FAN CULTURE — Use the culture and traditions of fans to help get your message across. Use message boards and other media associated with fans.

USE YOUR ICONS — Draw on the support and appeal of players to endorse anti-racist and anti-discriminatory messages.

MEDIA ACTIVITIES — Work with the media to publicise your activities.

ENCOURAGE NEW AUDIENCES — Work towards making your club as open as possible. Take specific measures that encourage ethnic minorities, migrants and women to get involved as fans, players and employees."[11]

The guide made explicit reference to the significance of involving players and managers who have been discriminated against in anti-racism campaigns, so to dissuade both fans and players from engaging in racist conduct. Football clubs should encourage players that have been racially abused to come forward and publicize their unpleasant experiences to attract public attention and discourage future perpetrators. It also stressed the potential contribution of the game to the successful integration of ethnic minority communities into society and underlined that "The sheer physical presence of a stadium with thousands of visitors every two weeks gives it a presence within local communities that is unmatched by most other institutions. It is often argued that clubs should be using the appeal of football to get involved in their local communities, working with young people, the disaffected and other marginalized groups. The 'community capital' that clubs can bring to effect social change in their environments is significant."[12] Apart from the obvious economic benefits that stem from the participation of ethnic minority supporters, these new fans would also contribute to the elimination of racism from football grounds. At last, but certainly not least, more opportunities should be made available to managers from ethnic minorities to lessen the degree of underrepresentation and dismiss all relevant racist connotations.

The European football governing body has, no doubt, been instrumental in addressing the issue of racism in football with effect. It has certainly achieved in inspiring its affiliated members and their clubs to take genuine action and combat racism. FIFA has also been alarmed by the rapid increase of racist incidents in European football and has contributed to the elimination of racial discrimination, at all levels, from the beautiful game. On many occasions, the two governing bodies have supported the initiatives of national football associations and football clubs, and have never failed to condemn racist offenders, whether players, fans or nonplaying staff. However, the sheer multitude of football clubs throughout the continent weighs heavily on both FIFA and UEFA, as regards their endeavors to monitor the conduct of all pertinent actors involved in the game. For all the commitment of football's supranational authorities to the eradication of racism, the regulation of such a popular game would probably be unsuccessful, but for the several anti-racism organizations devoted to football alone and their decisive contribution.

ANTI-RACISM ORGANIZATIONS IN FOOTBALL

Football Against Racism in Europe

In February 1999, the European Commission sponsored a unique seminar in Vienna dedicated to the issue of racism in football. The seminar, Networking Against Racism in European Football, brought together football officials representing more than forty organizations from thirteen European countries. Among those attending the event were anti-racism groups, national football associations, professional players' associations and fan clubs, all gathered to discuss issues pertaining to racism and xenophobia. When the seminar was concluded, all parties pledged their unabated commitment to the eradication of both phenomena from the sport of football. Most significantly, the participants declared their support to a pan-European organization devoted to their cause, as Football Against Racism in Europe (FARE) was founded.

The mission of FARE, a network of anti-racism organizations in Europe, is to combat racism at local, national and European level. Hence, its Plan of Action states that:

> "FARE calls upon football governing bodies and clubs to:
> recognise the problem of racism in football;
> adopt, publish and enact anti-racist policy;
> make full use of football to bring people together from different communities and cultures;
> establish a partnership with all organisations committed to kicking racism out of football in particular with supporters groups, migrants and ethnic minorities.
> FARE commits itself to:
> challenging all forms of racist behaviour in stadia and within clubs by making our voice(s) heard;
> include ethnic minorities and migrants within our organisation and partner organisations;
> work together with all organisations willing to tackle the problem of racism in football."[13]

Apart from the European Commission's valuable contribution, considering that the European Union institution has also financed projects and campaigns carried out by the premier anti-racism organization in the continent, FARE gained the support of the European Parliament too, when the latter adopted a resolution on racism in football in March 2006. The resolution received tremendous support from the Members of the European Parliament, more than any other resolution before in the history of the institution, which urged all actors anyhow related to football, primarily, the European football governing body, national governments and national football associations, to maintain their relentless campaign against racism and implement the necessary measures to rid the game of discrimination. As it happens, the resolution was initiated by Emine Bozkurt, a Dutch Member of the European Parliament, who stressed that "A united parliament scored a brilliant goal against racism but the game continues. I will tell Employment Commissioner Spidla to urge football clubs that they have to create a racism free working environment as outlined in Article 13a of the Amsterdam treaty."[14] Undoubtedly, the wholehearted support of the two European Union bodies underlined the prominence of FARE, thus producing the necessary grounds to combat racism more effectively.

Needless to say, UEFA's contribution to the cause of FARE deserves attention too. FARE's partnership with UEFA kicked off during the 2001–2002 season, when UEFA CEO Gerhard Aigner presented a check of one million Swiss Francs to FARE, intended to launch the organization's anti-racism campaign. In October 2002, with only a year's experience, FARE was hugely successful in launching the second European-wide Action Week Against Racism. Among other anti-racism activities, fans of PSV Eindhoven organized the 'PSV fans against Racism' action, after Thierry Henry was racially abused in a UEFA Champions League match against Arsenal; ethnic minority groups set up a football tournament in Vienna to assist flood victims in Austria, with the participation of amateur teams from Bosnia-Herzegovnian, Romanian, Turkish and Yugoslavian backgrounds; Standard de Liège staged an anti-racist choreography prior to a home match; Girondins de Bordeaux players sported the 'South Stand Against Racism' slogan just before the game against AS Monaco; English clubs devoted two weekends to anti-racism campaigns; Schalke 04 led by example the anti-racism campaign in Germany; the *Progetto Ultrà* group in Italy published a magazine, in both Italian and English, called 'Ultras unisce-Razzismo divide'; Swiss football fans formed an anti-racism coalition named 'Fans United'; and leaflets that condemned racial discrimination and violence were handed to fans before kickoff at various football venues in Serbia.

FARE's presence was even more impressive during the 2004 European Championship in Portugal. With the support of the Football Supporters International network (FSI) and UEFA, FARE publicized its cause widely, by distributing among fans a football magazine translated in several languages and publishing an anti-racism supplement in the Portuguese sports newspaper *O Jogo*, which featured statements from all sixteen team captains. FARE also set up a hotline for fans to report racist incidents and hosted a media event in Oporto, on the opening day of the competition, with the participation of UEFA and all competing teams. In the event, Pat Cox, president of the European Parliament, stressed the need to combat racism. The rising tide of public discontent towards racism in football and the apparent contribution of FARE in Europe's premier competition at national level soon became evident.

The 2004 Action Week was FARE's most successful anti-racism campaign, involving a whole host of events in thirty-three European countries. Sporting du Pays de Charleroi, RSC Anderlecht and KSK Beveren, all in Belgium, made reference to FARE's Action Week in match-day leaflets distributed to fans and displayed banners, in cooperation with their football supporters, which read 'All Different—All Equal.' The *Bröndby Fans Mod Racisme* group, set up in response to racist incidents at home matches, organized a free concert and circulated anti-racism leaflets before Bröndby's match against OB. Flutlicht, an anti-racism organization in Germany devoted to football, distributed stickers displaying anti-racism messages, whereas supporters of St Pauli staged a fine choreography in their away game against Werder Bremen. In Scotland, all thirty clubs of the Football League took part in anti-racism initiatives, had messages against discrimination included in matchday leaflets intended for fans and made relevant announcements inside their football stadiums. Austria devoted a weekend's league fixtures to anti-racism and, in particular, players of Austria Vienna and Rapid Vienna displayed anti-racism banners, as the stadium's PA system repeated related messages. England's main anti-racism organization, Kick It Out, organized a nationwide campaign that included all ninety-two professional football clubs, while the players of the national team completed a training session wearing Kick It Out T-shirts, before the World Cup qualifying game against Wales. Young Boys Bern fans, in Switzerland, produced unique postcards that featured prominent football players and displayed the 'Together against violence and racism' slogan in the match against Thun. Romania's National Council for Combating Discrimination displayed in all top division football grounds huge posters that read 'We are all DIFFERENT, we are all EQUAL and we are all a TEAM! We fight against discrimination! Join us!,' while anti-racism messages were delivered through the stadiums' PA systems. UEFA held similar events during the fourth leg matches of the Champions League group stage, as children accompanied all clubs' football players to the field wearing Unite Against Racism T-shirts. Children wearing FARE T-shirts also had a key role before the match between PSV Eindhoven and Ajax, holding up red cards against racism, while anti-racism messages were displayed on the stadium's screen and FARE's Action Week featured in the match-day program. In France, Metz's *Horda Frenetik '97* fan club distributed anti-racism leaflets and displayed relevant banners; Girondins Bordeaux fans also took part in the Action Week; and LICRA, an anti-racism organization dedicated to all sports, hosted a number of youth football tournaments under the motto 'Let's put racism off-side!' Another similar organization in Ireland, Sport Against Racism, set up a nationwide campaign against racism. Spanish clubs Cadiz and Celta Vigo displayed an anti-racism banner in their Primera Liga match and distributed red cards to all fans before kickoff. Italian '*ultras*' held anti-racism activities in schools, produced relevant banners and organized a number of football-related events. What made the 2004 FARE Action Week a major success, however, was the participation of Central and Eastern European countries that suffered from racism in football, like Armenia, Azerbaijan, Belarus, Bulgaria, Croatia, Czech Republic, FYR Macedonia, Hungary, Latvia, Poland, Romania, Russia, Serbia and Montenegro, Slovakia, Slovenia and Ukraine. Ethnic minority communities in that part of Europe, nevertheless, lack the necessary support of football governing bodies, as regards the organization of anti-racism campaigns.

No matter the success of FARE at European level, the 2006 World Cup in Germany, the first international competition in Europe since the organization's inception, was an exceptional opportunity for FARE's publicity, given the media hype and the participation of national teams the world over. During the World Cup, FARE, FIFA and the World Cup Local Organizing Committee aimed at raising awareness about racism. On the World Cup opening day, FARE launched the '*Football Unites!*' program during a press conference with the participation of FIFA and the Local Organizing Committee. FARE's activities included "an eleven city tour by the 'StreetKick' mobile football game, bringing together fans to celebrate shared cultures; a multilingual hotline for fans to report racism at the World Cup; the distribution of fifty thousand anti-racism fanzines during the tournament, and a touring exhibition detailing the history of anti-racism activities in football across Europe; activities with young Germans from an ethnic minority background; and monitors to identify racially discriminatory banners, chants and other forms of racism inside and around stadiums."[15] FIFA, too, made good use of football matches to convey a strong message against racial discrimination in sport and dedicated the quarter-final matches to anti-racism, as all team captains of the remaining eight teams (Argentina, Brazil, England, France, Germany, Italy, Portugal and Ukraine) read a statement against racism, while the teams stood together behind a banner that read 'Say No to Racism.' On the whole, the 2006 World Cup took place under the motto 'A time to make friends.' During every single match of the competition, a total of sixty-four games, a huge banner covered the centre circle of the field that read 'Say No to Racism' and anti-racism video spots were displayed in every single venue. Furthermore, all 736 football players and all delegation members of the thirty-two contestants signed a declaration concerning fair play, as well as racism and discrimination. It is noteworthy that the Polish national team wore T-shirts that featured the 'Let's kick racism out of stadiums' motto, to declare their support to the Never Again Association, before kickoff in the group stage match against bitter rivals Germany.

Soon after the World Cup came to an end, the never-ending activities of FARE had to expand over the Balkans, or else Europe's 'powder keg,' to promote peace, order and stability in war-torn former Yugoslavia. In partnership with Serbian club Smederevo and the Balkan Alpe Adria Project, FARE organized in Serbia an unusual youth football tournament against racism and nationalism, from 4 to 6 August, sponsored by the King Boudewijn Foundation and UEFA. The teams that took part in the tournament were Sarajevo from Bosnia-Herzegovina, CSKA Sofia from Bulgaria, Orient Rijeka from Croatia and Vardas Skopje from FYR Macedonia, together with Partizan Belgrade, OFK Belgrade, Mladost Apatin and Smederevo, all from Serbia. To add color to the tournament, pupils from Smederevo schools displayed banners and sang in support of the guest teams.

The recent, and even more successful, Action Week Against Racism was launched by FARE in October 2006, with the cooperation of UEFA, at the highest level of club competition. During the Champions League group stage matches, the captains of all clubs wore Unite Against Racism armbands, players were accompanied by children in Unite Against Racism T-shirts, announcements against racism were made by the PA systems and Unite Against Racism adverts were placed in match-day programs, as well as in the official UEFA Champions League magazine *Champions*. Although a record number of more than 600 groups from thirty-seven countries were anticipated to make a stand against racial discrimination, part of FARE's European-wide campaign against racial discrimination, one of UEFA's affiliated members failed to become involved. On behalf of the European University-Cyprus (formerly known as Cyprus College)—a leading private academic institution—and the Cyprus Footballers Association, the author intended to organize anti-racism events in all top division football matches. The activities, sponsored by FARE, would include a short announcement against racism, banners that read *Μόνο τα χρώματα των ομάδων διαφέρουν, πείτε ΟΧΙ στο ρατσισμό*, 'Only the clubs' colors differ, say NO to racism,' and a press conference to raise awareness about racial discrimination. Unfortunately, the banners that the two groups produced were never displayed. Instead, they wait patiently in a corner of my office, until the opinionated members that comprise the executive committee of the Cyprus Football Association alter their dogmatic attitude and embrace our endeavors. Beyond all expectations, the Cyprus Football Association decided against our activities, even though the official websites of both FARE and UEFA made due reference to the fact that the Cypriot authorities had yet to organize such a campaign. While the problem of institutional racism is self-explanatory, one feels compelled to ask whether the incomprehensible response of the Cyprus Football Association adds a new dimension to the issue. The Cyprus Football Association claims that racism in Cypriot football is not an issue, thus their decision to reject in 2005 UEFA's offer of 50,000 Swiss francs—the governing body of European football made the same amount available to each and every one of its affiliated members—for the purpose of organizing nationwide campaigns with the intention to eradicate racism from the popular game. Under these extraordinary conditions, Apollon Limassol constitutes the only oasis available to all football supporters who wish to combat racial discrimination in Cyprus. The club launched its highly praised anti-racism campaign in November 2005, including anti-racism material such as posters, banners, leaflets and T-shirts, as well as school visits and the organization of related seminars.

Contrary to the disgrace that is the Cyprus Football Association, the remaining participants succeeded in carrying out their anti-racism activities effectively. Among others, the Centre for Equal Opportunities, in Belgium, organized the 'Don't act like a monkey' campaign, with the participation of all professional football clubs, the Belgian Football Association, fan groups and the football players' association, in an attempt to combat racism in stadiums. Likewise, the players' associations in Hungary and Portugal also organized nationwide campaigns against racial discrimination. In Germany, in response to the racist incidents that took place during the 2006 World Cup, all professional clubs took part in FARE's Action Week, with a staggering 750,000 red cards distributed to fans. Austria's professional clubs also staged anti-racism events and team captains read an anti-racism statement before kickoff. Finally, in the aftermath of the horrendous racist incident that involved Borac Cacak fans (see chapter 3), anti-racism campaigns took place at all football grounds of Serbia and relevant FARE leaflets were distributed to fans.

Kick It Out

Kick It Out emerged in 1993 through the Commission for Racial Equality's *Let's Kick Racism Out of Football* campaign, which aimed at eliminating racism from football by making good use of education and community projects. The anti-racism campaign was sponsored by the English Football Association, the Professional Footballers Association, the FA Premier League and the Football

Foundation. At international level, Kick It Out is a partner of the FARE network and has been praised by UEFA, FIFA, the Council of Europe, the European Commission, the European Parliament and the British Council for its overall contribution in the fight against racism in football. The main priorities of Kick It Out concern discrimination in professional and amateur football, the underrepresentation of black and Asian communities in the game, the participation of young people in race-related educational projects and the development of partnerships throughout Europe. All in all, the *Let's Kick Racism Out of Football* campaign was much related to the 'Football in the Community' scheme of the Professional Footballers' Association, which aimed at increasing the participation of ethnic minorities in football. The *Racial Equality Standard for Professional Football Clubs* concerns a number of measures to combat discrimination in football. The *Racial Equality Standard* was developed by Kick It Out, based on material from Sporting Equal's *Achieving Racial Equality: A Standard for Sport*, with the support of football's governing bodies. The *Racial Equality Standard* seeks to commit football clubs to create a racism-free environment for all spectators, players, managers and administrators, as well as to bring the popular game closer to ethnic minority communities.

Hence, the successful implementation of the *Racial Equality Standard* by clubs necessitates the completion of three interrelated levels, with all relevant evidence validated by an independent accreditation panel. All levels consist of three related stages, namely, 'stadiums and outreach,' 'policy and planning' and, finally, 'administration and management.' At the 'Preliminary Level,' "The club will have demonstrated a commitment to racial equality by producing a written equal opportunities policy and a race equality action plan for all areas of activity. The plan will be monitored. The plan will include an assessment of the club's current supporter base, community development targets and clear guidelines for dealing with abuse." Then, at the 'Intermediate Level,' "The club will have demonstrated clear improvements in services as a result of monitoring, consulted local ethnic minority communities and implemented its action plan. The club will be able to show clear evidence of the implementation of an equal opportunities policy." Ultimately, at the 'Advanced Level,' "The club will be an exemplar in the way it encourages the participation of ethnic minorities at all levels, and areas of activity, as employees, supporters and of community outreach."[16]

As a first step towards eradicating discrimination, within the nature and scope of the 'Preliminary Level,' clubs are asked, at the 'stadium and outreach' stage, to raise awareness and publicize their cause in their football stadiums by displaying anti-racism messages and making relevant announcements; commit season ticket holders to refrain from discriminatory conduct; adopt a policy regarding racist incidents; investigate race-related complaints; promote Kick It Out's hotline to report racist abuse; gather the necessary data to project the participation of spectators from ethnic minority backgrounds and those in their academies; and organize anti-racism events. Regarding the 'policy and planning' level, clubs are required to commit themselves to embracing racial equality; develop a racial equality plan and an Equal Opportunities Policy; make their commitment known to ethnic minorities; and appoint a racial equality officer. Finally, the 'administration and management' level dictates that the racial equality plan and the Equal Opportunities Policy require approval and provide information of the ethnic background, among others, of all nonplaying staff employed by the club.

The 'Intermediate Level,' at the first stage, stresses the need for clubs to produce anti-racist material; make certain that tickets and club merchandise are available to members of distinct ethnic background; build bridges with ethnic minority communities; and provide all stewards with the necessary training to deal with racist incidents. At the 'policy and planning' stage, clubs need to set up a network that will defend and promote their racial equality plan, including members of ethnic minority communities and fans. As for the third stage, clubs are required to produce background information of all those employed on match-days only, like stewards and catering staff; apply the racial equality plan on recruitment techniques and job advertisements; and to effectively address the problem of underrepresentation in playing and coaching positions.

Finally, at the 'stadiums and outreach' stage of the 'Advanced Level,' clubs must hold anti-racism campaigns and take part in community events, offer the facilities of their football ground to ethnic communities and increase participation of supporters from ethnic minority groups. The 'policy and planning' stage concerns a review process to verify the effective application of the racial equality plan and that all staff are properly trained, whereas the final stage of the third level urges clubs to increase the number of employees that come from minority backgrounds.

Evidence that clubs have completed with success all levels is then submitted to the accreditation team before any club claims the relevant award. Clubs have to prove their determination to combat racism in football and serve the cause effectively, as "The award is valid for three years in the expectation that clubs will be aspiring to the next level of achievement. If after three years the next level has not been achieved, the club will be asked to resubmit evidence to maintain the existing level. Clubs that are successful will be awarded a kite mark for each level for use on official documents."[17] At the time of writing, Manchester City became the first football club to achieve the Intermediate Level in September 2006, followed by Blackburn Rovers and Everton, both in December 2006.

Kick It Out is also involved in education, at school level, and every year holds a competition where pupils are asked to produce work on topics related to race, cultural diversity and citizenship. In 2004, for example, pupils wrote essays on famous Muslims, as the Week of Action coincided with Ramadan. The work of Kick It Out in education also involves the allocation of funds to school projects. In the past, Villers High School, at Middlesex, organized a conference devoted to racism in sport; pupils from Matthew Murray High School, at Leeds, worked on a project concerning the life of Albert Johannson, the first black footballer to feature in an FA Cup final and former Leeds United player from South Africa; and Temple Primary School, from Manchester's Cheetham Hill, initiated a project, with the participation of several local primary schools of ethnically diverse pupil population, that involved work in class and a interracial football games. As far as the nationwide anti-racism campaign of Kick It Out is concerned, it is no coincidence that the Week of Action takes place every year on October. Ever since 1987, October in Britain is the Black History Month, which celebrates the contribution of all black players to the game of football. The key objectives of Black History Month concern the promotion of knowledge of black history, information on black football players and to raise racial awareness.

Football Unites Racism Divides

Football Unites Racism Divides (FURD) was founded in November 1995 and seeks to create a racism-free environment for all to play and watch the game of football, improve the supporters' conduct and increase the participation of ethnic minority groups. It is important to note that members of FURD often have the opportunity to sit in disciplinary hearings, when racist incidents are assessed by the English Football Association, which is crucial to identifying and comprehending the factors that cause racist behavior. The main objective of FURD, therefore, is to produce the necessary grounds for players, coaches, referees and administrators from ethnic minority backgrounds to enter the world of football, considering, at least, how costly and, therefore, prohibitive the game may prove. In this respect, FURD has helped a number of teams gain access to the necessary financial resources, such as the Awards For All grants—Sharow United and Surud United are two of these teams. Moreover, FURD, in cooperation with the County FA Development Officer, Sheffield First For Safety and the Refugee Housing Association, organized the Sheffield All Nations League in 2003. The competition was held at the University of Sheffield and involved seventeen football teams, with players from Afghani, Albanian, Eritrean, Kosovar, Kurdish, Liberian, Somali and Yemeni origins. The first ever winners of the All Nations League was the African Dream Team, which joined a local Sunday league in 2004 and help organize the event ever since. Another refugee team, Red United, won the Unity Shield, a Barclaycard kit and several other prizes. In the All Nations Summer League, later on the same year, eight teams took part with players from Afghanistan, Albania, Chile, Iran, Iraq, Jamaica, Nigeria, Sierra Leone, Somalia and Yemen.

Nevertheless, the attention of FURD is not solely focused on amateur football. To enhance the prospect of eliminating racism from the popular game, FURD maintains good relations with the two Sheffield clubs, Wednesday and United, as well as with Barnsley and Rotherham United. Most significantly, however, FURD worked with the Institute of Citizenship in developing a new curriculum related to the subject of citizenship. FURD underlined the fact that an improved Citizenship Resource Pack would help raise awareness and advance the understanding of young people. As a matter of fact, anti-racist education has already contributed to minimizing the damage Islamophobia has caused in Britain, since the tragic events of 11 September 2001. Subsequently, in May 2002, a conference devoted to education, football and anti-racism took place at the football ground of Manchester United, with the cooperation of the Department for Education and Skills and the Association for Citizenship Teaching. The conference aimed at making good use of football to educate children on anti-racism, since the introduction of Citizenship into the national curriculum provides a unique opportunity to teach children from a young age about the meanings of diversity and the several national, regional, religious and ethnic identities that coexist in the United Kingdom. FURD also appointed an education worker in July 2001, funded by the Football Foundation, to promote the values of social inclusion in schools, youth centers and even prisons to raise racial awareness. Moreover, FURD was instrumental in developing the Young Footballers Against Racism education pack, intended for secondary schools, which includes sessions in classrooms and on the football field. Usually, the pupils selected for these classes share racist views that engage in antisocial conduct or feel alienated from their peers. FURD also maintains a Resources and Information Centre, dedicated to collecting documentation related to racism in sport and, particularly, football.

Yet the most popular anti-racism activity of FURD answers to the name of Streetkick, first launched in 1998. The game of Streetkick facilitates the integration of young people and enlightens all participants of the crucial contribution of black football players to the game, by utilizing anti-racism and educational material displayed and distributed during relevant events, and staff and volunteers from distinct ethnic backgrounds to advance the values of cultural diversity. The three central objectives of Streetkick focus on combating disadvantage, by targeting areas where youngsters from ethnic minority background are offered limited opportunities to play organized football; anti-racist work and education, primarily, applied in areas disturbed by racial issues; and community cohesion, concerned with the integration of young people from various different racial, cultural and religious backgrounds together in positive ways. Another FURD initiative relates to a football tournament that first took place in Manchester, *The Unity Cup Festival*, in 2003. The teams that participated in the Unity Cup are unique in that they consist of refugees and asylum seekers from all over the United Kingdom, while the 2005 competition, held in Leeds, included a team from Slovakia that comprised players of Roma background. Among other activities, all participants were offered advice on asylum rights and how to establish relations with professional clubs and local football governing bodies.

Show Racism The Red Card
Show Racism The Red Card (SRTRC) is an anti-racist charity, founded in January 1996. Just as with all other partners of the FARE network, the main objective of SRTRC is to combat racism by promoting the image of high-profile football players and managers as role models, as well as publicizing anti-racism

material. Moreover, in an attempt to both raise awareness and educate children, SRTRC holds an annual competition at school level, for pupils to produce art, poetry, essays and videos related to core principles of anti-racism. The SRTRC campaign, other than having players from the black and Asian communities, like Andy Cole, Rio Ferdinand, Dwight Yorke and Shaka Hislop, take part in its projects, also joined the Norwegian Players Union and the Norwegian People's Aid organization in setting up a competition that brought pupils closer to anti-racism activities. The winning parties were awarded their prizes during the interval of the match between Norway's two football heavyweights, Lyn and Rosenborg.

With regard to the organization's contribution to anti-racism, officials from SRTRC stressed that UEFA's 'Ten Point Plan' should be complemented by action from the national football associations, clubs, players, fans and, in general, all pertinent actors that have some role in football. More accurately, a spokesperson for the SRTRC stressed in 2004 that they:

"welcome the wholehearted support Scottish clubs and footballing authorities have given our campaign this year. However we must ensure the scenes of racist abuse we have witnessed at Scottish grounds, both large and small, are not repeated again next year. The UEFA ten point plan is a good starting point particularly point seven of the plan. A clear agreement must be established between the police, stewards and the club as to the course of action that will be taken against those engaged in racist abuse at games. This agreement must be seen to be implemented and should be widely publicised so all supporters know the consequences they will face if they break the law in this way. Many clubs have made good progress on this issue in the last few years and all SPL clubs SRTRC have met have shown a willingness to implement the plan. Supporters also have a role to play in this. Fans, the vast majority of whom are not racist, have a responsibility to be self-policing to some extent. They have a duty to create an environment that makes it clear that racism is not welcome at their club."[18]

Furthermore, the SRTRC campaign appointed a Development Officer in Scotland to liaise with clubs, the football governing bodies and local authorities to combat racism in football and to deliver a strong message against discrimination. The Development Officer conducts serious work in schools, based on disseminating anti-racism material and a relevant video that features high-profile footballers playing in the Scottish league. The post of the SRTRC Development Officer is sponsored by the Scottish Executive, UEFA, the Scottish Football Association, Show Racism The Red Card and the Educational Institute of Scotland. Referring to the overall contribution of the SRTRC and the role of the Development Officer, the Deputy Communities Minister, Mary Mulligan, stressed that "Nobody should suffer because of their race, nationality or beliefs. Racism must not be tolerated. We support this high profile campaign because it will educate and influence attitudes in young people. It complements our own 'One

Scotland. Many Cultures' campaign which highlighted the problem of racism in Scotland, particularly since one of the key targets for the next phase is raising awareness in young people." Nevertheless, not all shared Mulligan's views, since Bill Aitken, Member of the Scottish Parliament, said "The fact of the matter is, this is just another time when public money is being used for one of those politically correct notions that the executive follows from time to time. Of course we all condemn racism in sport and we recognise it's a problem down south but I don't think it's the most pressing issue in Scottish football."[19] Nevertheless, the impact of SRTRC on Scottish football cannot be underestimated. Officials from SRTRC work closely with primary and secondary schools in Scotland, which utilize an anti-racism education pack and a relevant video that features players from the Scottish Premier League. SRTRC also holds a school competition, related to anti-racism themes, and workshops intended to advance the merits of its nationwide campaign.

Progetto Ultrà
With funding from Emilia Romagna Region and the European Commission, *Progetto Ultrà* was founded in 1995, as part of *Unione Italiana Sport Per Tutti* (UISP), Italian Sports for All, and aims at defending football's edifying values and creating an environment free of racism. In this respect, the organization facilitates communication amongst supporters and other relevant organizations, mediates between rival fans and promotes anti-racism campaigns in Italy. Most significantly, *Progetto Ultrà* maintains an impressive archive on football fan culture that includes some 18,000 titles, as regards books, fanzines, newspaper articles and press cuts, dissertations, magazines, photos of football supporters and '*Ultras*,' as well as documentation dedicated to violence, racism and youth culture. Officials of *Progetto Ultrà*, together with football fans from several rival clubs, assess the impact of laws related to football violence, since it is their intention to alter the stereotype of supporters and separate ordinary fans from extreme elements that occasionally resort to violence, as in the case of the '*ultras.*' Unlike most other similar organizations, *Progetto Ultrà* members mediate between rival groups of fans to avoid violence or between fans and police authorities in order to serve the very same cause. As a matter of fact, some excessive stadium bans were reduced, as a result of the efforts of *Progetto Ultrà*. As one might expect, *Progetto Ultrà* is a founding member of FARE and during the Action Week Against Racism organizes anti-racism campaigns throughout Italy, with the support of football clubs and fans.

However, the most valued contribution of *Progetto Ultrà* concerns the organization of *Mondiali Antirazzisti*, Anti-Racism World Cup, every year, which includes a five-a-side football tournament where people from different nationalities play to deliver a powerful message against racial discrimination. The tournament first kicked off in 1997 at Montecchio, in the region of Emilia Romagna in northern Italy. Teams are made up by migrants, people from ethnic minority communities all over Europe and anti-racism organizations. During the same summer that Germany hosted FIFA's World Cup, *Progetto Ultrà* celebrated the tenth, successive, *Mondiali Antirazzisti*, organized together with *Istoreco*, an antifascist historical association. On the occasion, 204 teams took part in football and other sports' tournaments, like basketball, volleyball, cricket and martial arts, organized by fans and NGOs from Italy and local Asian communities. Overall, the contribution of *Progetto Ultrá* in Italian football is more than crucial. The '*ultras*' are renowned for resisting the authority of the state and the game's governing bodies; therefore, any sort of interference, in political and football terms, is treated with suspicion. For that reason, *Progetto Ultrá's* endeavors to establish closer links with these fan groups are essential in prevailing over racial discrimination and, of course, violence.

Bündnis Aktiver Fussballfans

The *Bündnis Aktiver Fussballfans* (BAFF), Federation of Active Football Fans, was founded in 1993 and, today, comprises some forty groups that represent fans from several clubs and is the only nationwide football supporters' organization in Germany that aims at combating racism, among other issues. BAFF hosts an annual meeting with the participation of fans from clubs all over Europe, an event that never fails to draw the attention of local media, ever since the second congress of 1997 witnessed the participation of the German Football Association, the Professional Footballers Association and police officials, also broadcasted by the TV station SAT.1. The organization cooperates with the German football governing bodies, clubs and fans to eliminate racism and has even developed a nine-point plan that inspired, in 1998, the German Football Association to introduce in the Specimen Stadium Regulations (Musterstadionordnung) sections that pertain to anti-racism. It also maintains links with FARE, takes part in the annual Anti-Racism World Cup in Bologna and supports the campaign of Show Racism The Red Card. BAFF also held the *Target Stadium: Racism and Discrimination in Football* exhibition sponsored by the European Union, which produced an insight to racism in football since the 1980s and the relationship between hooliganism and extreme right politics like the neo-Nazi movement. In addition, it stressed the potential of football to eliminate racism in society and thus, aimed to raise awareness about racial discrimination. The exhibition, which targets supporters, pupils, football governing bodies, political institutions and the media, was first held in Berlin in November 2001.

Schalker Fan-Initiative

The *Schalker Fan-Initiative*, 'Independent Schalke Supporters Association,' was founded after some Schalke 04 fans took part in a peaceful demonstration, on 9 November 1992, in Gelsenkirchen, to commemorate the 1938 persecution of Jews. As those supporters felt dejected concerning racism in their stadium, they marched with a 'Schalke fans against racism' banner and circulated a leaflet with anti-racism material. The leaflet was such a success that it was re-produced in a local sports paper (Revier-Sport) and drew much attention from people who simply wished to get involved. The degree of interest and involvement of those fans in meetings, campaigns and media, brought about the *Schalker Fan-Initiative* in February 1993. Next, the *Schalker Fan-Initiative* produced, in April 1994, a fanzine called *Schalke Unser*, 'Our Schalke,' which also addressed issues related to racial discrimination. The publication was so successful that *Schalke Unser* soon became the biggest-selling fanzine in Germany, as it initially sold two thousand copies, today reaching an astonishing eight thousand copies. Moreover, the Schalker Fan-Initiative played an instrumental role in setting up the *Bündnis Antifaschistischer Fussballfans*, 'Federation of Antifascist Football Fans.' By 1996, the *Schalker Fan-Initiative* had grown significantly, enough to move into an office and Schalke 04 provided them with club merchandise that is sold to cover the organization's expenses. More recently, the *Schalker Fan-Initiative* launched, in 2001, a project named '*Dem Ball is' egal, wer ihn tritt*,' 'The ball doesn't care who kicks it,' which is a nationwide scheme that produces anti-racism material intended for education purposes at school level.

Nigdy Wiecej
Nigdy Wiecej, Never Again, was founded in 1992 to combat racism and anti-Semitism, as well as to defend human values and multiculturalism. Poland's leading anti-racism organization produces the '*Nigdy Wiecej*' magazine, a publication that contains information on extremist and racist groups in Poland and Europe in general. It cooperates with the London-based, international, anti-fascist magazine named 'Searchlight,' the European anti-racist network UNITED for Intercultural Action, FARE and other relevant organizations in Eastern Europe. As with *Progetto Ultrà*, *Nigdy Wiecej* also maintains a valuable archive on racist, anti-Semitic, and neo-fascist publications produced in Poland since 1989 and often acts as a consulting agency to the Parliamentary Committee on Ethnic Minorities. The key objective of the organization is to raise awareness about racial discrimination and defend cultural diversity. To this end, *Nigdy Wiecej* coordinates anti-racism activities in Poland and works with anti-racist and antifascist groups, including minority organizations. From 1995 to 1997, together with the Polish Union of Jewish Students, *Nigdy Wiecej* held a campaign demanding to ban neo-Nazi, fascist and racist organizations, and to introduce similar measures in the Constitution of the Polish Republic. More recently, the 'Let's Kick Racism Out Of Football' campaign was launched by the organization in April 2002, complemented with the simultaneous release of a CD entitled 'Let's Kick Racism out of the Stadiums.' The 'Let's Kick Racism Out Of The Stadiums' campaign concerns the monitoring and reporting of racist incidences, the production of two anti-racist magazines, 'Stadion' and 'Never Again,' and the organization of an annual anti-racist football tournament. The activities of *Nigdy Wiecej* were successful enough to draw the attention of the Polish Football Association and football clubs alike to the alarming issue of racist symbols displayed in stadiums. As a result, the Polish Football Association, in cooperation with *Nigdy Wiecej*, developed an anti-racism manual that served as a guide for clubs. Furthermore, officials from *Nigdy Wiecej* also made

good use of Emanuel Olisadebe, the first ever black football player to represent Poland at national level, as a role model.

There is no doubt that anti-racism activities are much needed in Eastern Europe, taking into account its fairly recent transition to democracy, as well as the fact that the lack of financial resources, too, often constitute obstacles difficult to overcome. Hence, in October 2003, FARE made a significant contribution to the cause of organizations similar to *Nigdy Wiecej* by offering them all funds, after it received the MTV Free Your Mind Award. Ever since, *Nigdy Wiecej* is no longer a mere partner of FARE, but also the main representative of the esteemed pan-European anti-racism network in Eastern Europe, by allocating those funds to relevant schemes devoted to raising awareness about racism through football. The essence of this partnership becomes evident when considering that *Nigdy Wiecej* officials often encountered the inexcusable denial of the local authorities and media that racial discrimination existed in Polish society. Therefore, to further publicize its cause, as well as the issue of racism in Poland, the organization hosted a conference of the UNITED network in November 2003, with the participation of nearly seventy anti-racist groups from all over Europe. Determined to eradicate racial discrimination, officials from *Nigdy Wiecej* and FARE will be promoting anti-racism initiatives in Eastern Europe, particularly, in Belarus, Estonia, Latvia, Lithuania, Moldova, Russia and Ukraine. The two anti-racism organizations will provide local authorities with essential information on how to eliminate racism by making good use of the game of football and promoting the necessary anti-racism campaigns.

INTEGRATION THROUGH SPORT

State sponsored activities

The European Commission's DG Education & Culture commissioned a study on Sport and Multiculturalism, which was published in August 2004 as part of the series on education and sport. Given the interest of European Union bodies in continental football, coupled with the fact that national governments and football authorities have realized the impact of sport on society, it is not surprising that the popular game has come to be recognized as a valuable ingredient of assimilating diverse populations. The integration of ethnic minorities has long been an issue in the United Kingdom and sports have often served as the means to an end, including initiatives such as *Sporting Equals*, produced by both the Commission for Racial Equality and Sport England (2001), and the *Equality and Diversity Strategy* of UK Sport (2004). Germany's diverse population, on the other hand, remains deceivingly unreported, as no official documents provide any definitions of the term 'ethnic minority.' Instead, reference is made to the apparent distinction between 'German' and 'foreigner,' also reflected in sport, considering that the participation of ethnic minority communities is limited, due to xenophobia. One initiative that focused on tackling these issues was the *Street*

Soccer for Tolerance project of the German Football Association. The Netherlands is yet another multicultural country that promotes the integration of ethnic minority groups through sport, as in the case of the *Als racisme wint, verliest de sport* (If racism wins, sport loses) campaign, however, funding devoted to such activities has recently been decreased. The Institute for Sport Management, in Belgium, organizes the annual Neighborhood Ball campaigns in areas populated by ethnic minority groups. In addition, the Belgian Football Federation (KBVB-Koninklijke Belgische Voetbalbond), together with clubs and FIFA, launched the 'Fighting Racism in Football' campaign in the 1990s, which includes projects such as 'The United Colours of Football' and 'Show Racism the Red Card.' The FairPlay-vidc campaign, in Austria, aims at integrating ethnic minorities through sport and makes good use of football, in particular, to combat racial discrimination, while the Swedish Sports Federation (SISU) has adopted a similar approach. The Portuguese Council for Refugees, State Secretariat for Sport, Ministry of Defense, Higher Sports Council, High-Commission for Immigrants and Ethnic minorities, Cape Verdian United Association, Guinea Association, Casa do Brasil, SOS Racism and Olho Vivo, are all concerned with the integration of ethnic minorities in Portugal through sport. Even though Poland is a relatively homogeneous country, her authorities have adopted a similar multiagency approach to promote sports among ethnic minority communities, often through organizations related to religious affiliation, such as the Lutheran Sports Organizations, Greek Orthodox Sports Organization, Jozef Kalasancjusz Associations 'Parafiada,' the 'MACABI' Sports Club, the Katolickie Stowarzyszenie Sportowe RP and Salezian Sports Organization. The Parafiada, in particular, has been praised for bringing closer together Catholic young people from Poland and other European countries like Belarus, Estonia, Latvia, Lithuania, Moldova, Russia and Ukraine, through an annual festival that first took place in 1988. Hungary is another example of a homogeneous country that promotes sport to integrate ethnic minorities. The National Anti-Racism Day, for instance, organized in 2004 by the Ministry of Sport, the Hungarian Football Association and the Ministry of Interior, included football games that involved local Roma and Slovene communities. Nevertheless, the European Union's study on Sport and Multiculturalism also revealed a number of countries that failed to benefit from the unifying force that is sport. For example, measures relating sport to integration in Denmark are clearly pointless, due to the tight immigration policies in place. Italy, too, has few sporting activities that aim at integrating ethnic minorities. It seems that Unione Italiana Sport Per Tutti is the only organization that strives to create a better environment for Italians and immigrants. In this respect, the organization devoted to combating discrimination in Italy through sport:

> "has five sets of aims:
> • to promote recreational, cultural and sport activities that aim at maintaining specific cultures and identities of immigrant communities in Italy

- promoting intercultural dialogue, in particular the project of Centro Olympic Maghreb in Genoa aiming at immigrants from North Africa, South America, Eastern Europe
- promotion of events such as the Anti-racist World Cup which involves mixed teams (men and women) from different ethnic minorities
- initiatives to combat ethnic and social prejudices such as the 'Ultra Project' targeting football fans at national and international level
- projects at the international level, for example:
  – the Peace Games which aims to promote peace through sport and other recreational activities in areas of crisis in Africa, Middle East and the Balkans
  – the campaign 'Una speranza per il futuro' (A hope for the future) which provides funds for the reconstruction of a sport camp in Mostar."[20]

Apart from the *Sport Against Racism in Ireland* campaign, Irish authorities employ few sporting activities that aim at integrating ethnic minorities, though it is important to note that Ireland is a fairly homogeneous country that recently became a destination for immigrants. The Czech Republic has quite a homogeneous population too, with the notable exception of the Slovak minority and other much smaller German, Polish and Romany minorities. Consequently, few organizations use sport for integration, such as the Centre for Refugees and the Society of Citizens Assisting Emigrants. Similarly, Slovakia has few minorities, namely, Czechs, Germans, Hungarians, Roma, Russians and Ukrainians, however, the authorities have not adopted any sporting activities to integrate these ethnic groups, even though the Hungarian population feels its rights are not adequately served, often advancing related claims by involving the neighboring Hungarian government. Notwithstanding the perspective of these five countries, the impact of sport on integration should not be underestimated. As a matter of fact, the European Monitoring Centre on Racism and Xenophobia (EUMC), with the cooperation of Europe's football governing body, launched the 'Fighting Racism and Xenophobia through Sport' campaign, to defend the European Union's core principles of diversity and equality. Likewise, the Committee of the Regions, UEFA and EUMC, held an international conference in Braga, Portugal, on 19 May 2004, to discuss the potential of sport in combating racism in football. On the whole, the main purpose of the conference was to equip the Portuguese authorities with the necessary means to address effectively the issue of racial discrimination on and off the pitch, given that the Iberian country was about to host the 2004 European Championship finals.

Sports projects in Europe
The Sport and Multiculturalism report also mentioned a number of projects related to football, among other sports, all emphasizing the uplifting principles of the world's most popular game. The Open Fun Football Schools Project, launched in 1998, makes good use of the beautiful game to promote peace and

stability in the Balkans. Schools from Bosnia and Herzegovina, FYR Macedonia and Serbia and Montenegro take part in the project. In a more straightforward mission, the French club Toulouse has been instrumental in the *Let's Play Together* project, launched in 2002, which is devoted to the integration of local young people from distinct ethnic backgrounds. In Germany, Türkiyemspor—Türkiyem means 'my Turkey'—was established in 1978 to attract young Turks from Berlin and, then, integrate them in the local society. Today, Türkiyemspor is open to all young people, regardless of their origins, and is regarded as a highly successful program, in terms of promoting integration. The Leicester Racial Equality Sport Project, in England, was launched in 2001 with the intention to increase participation from ethnic minority communities, after research conducted by Sport England revealed the limited access to sport of members from distinct ethnic groups. The Voluntary Action Leicester, Asylum Seekers and Refugee Sports Development Project is yet another local scheme, launched in 2002, which aims at the integration of asylum seekers and refugees in Britain by organizing football games. During the same year, the Algerian Association in Nottingham was set up to bring closer together immigrants, refugees and asylum seekers of Algerian descent through weekly indoor and outdoor football sessions, considering the game's capacity to ease the sense of isolation and depression that usually dominate the emotions of a migrant when settling in a foreign country.

Another project in Britain concerns the activities of the Bosnia-Herzegovina Community Centre, founded in 1996, which is devoted to the integration of Bosnian people through 5-a-side football sessions and relevant tournaments, with the participation of other refugee groups and members of the local ethnic community. In divided Cyprus, the Trust Games were meant to produce the necessary grounds for the two communities, Greek-Cypriots and Turkish-Cypriots, to restore confidence in one another, ever since the tragic events of July 1974. Not surprisingly, the project only included volleyball during its early stages, given that physical contact between opponents is a rarity. Later on, the success of the project resulted to the introduction of football and basketball games, thus encouraging wider participation from the two communities. The project was supported by the United Nations and a number of citizens from the two communities, since issues of political recognition did not leave room for official channels to be utilized. Sadly, politics was the main cause that the project came to an abrupt end in 2004, when the referendum on the Anan Plan was held. From the Eastern Mediterranean to Central Europe and Austria, more precisely, the Vienna Institute for Development and Cooperation (vidc) launched in 1997 the 'FairPlay. Viele Farben. Ein Spiel' (FairPlay. Different Colours. One Game), aiming at the elimination of racial discrimination from football. FairPlay-vidc has stressed the very essence of education in raising racial awareness and organized in the past anti-racism activities involving Austria's top two football divisions. In support of the organization's endeavors to combat racism in Austrian football, the Ugandan national team toured Austria in October 1998 and played a match against Vorwärts Steyr, which attracted considerable media attention.

Furthermore, the two Vienna clubs, SK Rapid and Austria, together with thirty-nine amateur teams and Maccabi, Vienna's Jewish representative in football, took part in FARE's second anti-racism campaign. The Coloured Sport Clubs project, in Belgium, was launched in 1996 by the King Boudewijn Foundation to develop the necessary policies to eliminate discrimination and advance the relationship between Belgians and ethnic minority communities. In this respect, the key objectives of the project centered on the need:

> "to raise the number of migrant participants,
> to stimulate the active involvement of foreigners in the club,
> to provide qualitative tutors and coaches and to stimulate youngsters to follow coaching programmes,
> to develop connections to local actors
> to react on long term social challenges and developments."[21]

Finally, in the Netherlands, the VV Roodenburg almaar beter (FC Roodenburg is getting better all the time) project, launched in 2000, aimed at encouraging a football club from Leiden to allow young people of Moroccan origins to participate more in the popular game. Despite the obvious intrinsic worth of the project, the study also brought to light a more interesting, but also disturbing, aspect of Dutch football. Although the majority of players seemed to have Surinamese origins, when the report was prepared, only Ruud Gullit was managing a football club, which highlights the lack of black managers in Dutch football. At the same time, Frank Rijkaard and Henk ten Cate were part of the coaching team at Barcelona, whereas Stanley Menzo had only just been employed by the national football association to coach the goalkeepers of the Dutch national team. Beyond any shadow of doubt, the underrepresentation of blacks in managerial positions is not exclusive to England.

CONCLUSION

There is no doubt that the educational value of sport and the good use of sports, particularly football, are central to tackling racial discrimination effectively. As a matter of fact, Article III (282) of the draft Constitutional Treaty makes explicit reference to sport, for the first time ever at Community level, as an integral part of the campaign against racism. Hence, the decision of the European Commission's DG Education & Culture to commission a study on Sport and Multiculturalism is hardly surprising. The number of football-related projects devoted to assimilation across Europe, clearly underline the game's potential. Evidently, the European Union, FIFA and UEFA seek to employ football with the intention of advancing integration, though from distinct perspectives. While the European Union puts emphasis on the values of sport to illustrate the sheer magnificence of the continent's cultural richness, football's leading governing bodies have employed diversity to preserve the interests of the popular game. In this respect, FIFA and UEFA's response to racism lack the sort of prudence that exemplifies the approach of the European Union. Indeed, it seems that both FIFA and UEFA are, for the most part, concerned with disciplinary measures, rather than producing the necessary grounds for football to rid itself of racial discrimination and xenophobia. Moreover, except for several documents and public announcements condemning racist incidents in football, the supranational authorities of the game have only recently become seriously involved in anti-racism activities. UEFA has supported relevant campaigns and organizations over the past few years, whereas FIFA's endeavors to combat racism materialized during the 2006 World Cup in Germany and will be extended over the next tournament in South Africa (2010).

Anti-racism organizations devoted to football, highly praised for their contribution to the popular game, have been remarkably active. As with all sports projects mentioned above, these organizations came to being in the mid-1990s. Therefore, their response to racial discrimination and xenophobia in football was timely enough to adopt novel measures intended to eradicate these issues and reach out to ethnic minority groups. Given that racism in European football is a deep-rooted menace, a mirror image of those ingrained prejudices characteristic of several societies across the continent, the majority of anti-racism organizations also have part in educational activities. Every single one of these groups has been heavily involved in nationwide campaigns against racism and, all together, in pan-European initiatives promoted by FARE. It is no coincidence that all anti-racism organizations have been commended for various successful, innovative, schemes such as the Streetkick game designed by FURD and the phenomenal *Mondiali Antirazzisti* organized by *Progetto Ultrá* in Italy. Likewise, Kick It Out and FARE are also unique in that both collect information related to racist incidents in European football. However, to maintain such high levels of efficiency, it is imperative that the attempts of these anti-racism organizations attract the necessary support of national governments and football associations alike. In any other case, the endeavors of these groups will be irreparably harmed.

Anti-racism activities have definitely succeeded in raising awareness about racism. These organizations deserve credit for bringing the game's governing bodies, clubs and groups of fans closer together in a joint effort to combat racial discrimination in football. In essence, the indisputable success of all relevant initiatives stems from the fact that anti-racism organizations, particularly the FARE network, have convinced European and national authorities that the game of football offers fertile soil for the eradication of racism. The case of England is evidence of the likely results, when all pertinent actors decide to collaborate. Nevertheless, anti-racism in England also has a considerable advantage over many other European countries, taking into consideration the presence of football-related legislation. Cyprus exempted, anti-racism campaigns in football command much attention throughout Europe and, therefore, related organizations have mustered the necessary encouragement to persist with their activities and prevail over football's modern plague. Their inspiring commitment to the elimination of all forms of discrimination from football as well as their endeavors to increase participation from ethnic minority groups will continue to be applauded.

Notes

1. Fédération Internationale de Football Association, "FIFA Endeavours" <http://www .fifa.com/en/fairplay/fairplay/0,1256,5,00.html> (13 Sept. 2006).

2. Fédération Internationale de Football Association, "FIFA Endeavours."

3. FIFA, Amendment to article 55 of the FIFA Disciplinary Code.

4. Kick It Out "Racism sanctions reduced," <http://www.kickitout.org> (6 Sept. 2006).

5. Kick It Out, "Racism sanctions reduced."

6. UEFA and FARE, *Unite against racism in European football, UEFA guide to good practice* (UEFA Communications and Public Affairs Division, June 2003), 26.

7. UEFA and FARE, "Unite against racism in European football, UEFA guide to good practice," 37.

8. UEFA and FARE, "Unite against racism in European football, UEFA guide to good practice," 30.

9. UEFA and FARE, "Unite against racism in European football, UEFA guide to good practice," 31.

10. UEFA, *Vision Europe* (Nyon, April 2005), 7.

11. Second Unite Against Racism Conference, *Tackling racism in club football, A guide for clubs* (Produced by FARE for UEFA, 2006), 14.

12. Second Unite Against Racism Conference, "Tackling racism in club football, A guide for clubs," 29.

13. Football Against Racism in Europe website <http://www .farenet.org> (22 Dec. 2005).

14. Football Against Racism in Europe, "European Parliament team up against racism," <http://www.farenet.org> (15 Mar. 2006).

15. Football Against Racism in Europe "World Cup summary" Number 1 – June 12th 2006 <http://www.farenet.org> (12 June 2006).

16. Kick It Out, *Racial Equality Standard for Professional Clubs*, 10.

17. Kick It Out, *Racial Equality Standard for Professional Clubs*, 20.

18. Stephen Herbert, *Stamping out racism in football*, This briefing provides background to the issue of racism in Scottish football and on the role of the 'Show Racism the Red Card' campaign, for a Member's debate in the Chamber on Tuesday 18 May 2004, on motion S2M-1214 in the name of Bill Butler MSP, Scottish Parliament Information Centre (SPICe), 3.

19. Stephen Herbert, "Stamping out racism in football," 4.

20. European Commission, DG Education & Culture, Studies on Education and Sport, *Sport and Multiculturalism*, Final Report, (A Report by PMP in partnership with the Institute of Sport and Leisure Policy Loughborough University, August 2004), 23.

21. European Commission, DG Education & Culture, Studies on Education and Sport, "Sport and Multiculturalism," Appendix C, 7.

Chapter Seven

European Union response to racism

One of the core principles of the European Union (EU), ever since the Single European Act (1987), concerns the right of EU citizens to mobility. Key to the smooth process of EU integration, therefore, is the issue of nationality; however, what is essential to assimilation is also fundamental to the doctrine of nationalism. Hence, the matter of nationality is central to this study, given that racial discrimination often reflects extreme forms of nationalism and associated stereotypes. According to the 'Acquisition and Loss of Nationality: Policies and Trends in 15 European States' report, produced by the Institute for European Integration Research Austrian Academy of Sciences and based on the results of the EU project on 'The Acquisition of Nationality in EU Member States: Rules, Practices and Quantitative Developments,' the subject of nationality defines the relationship between individuals and a given state. Within a EU context, nationality confers certain rights, in addition to those usually provided by the state, including the right to move and reside within any of the member states. EU citizenship, therefore, becomes all the more important when considering the naturalization of individuals from third countries and, in general, the immigration policies of member states. Apparently, naturalization is a valuable component of integration, intended to facilitate the settling of immigrants. Refugees and asylum seekers, for example, may require a new nationality, merely to ensure protection of their rights by another state, also supported by the Geneva Convention and the European Convention of Nationality (1997). However, the sheer number of naturalized immigrants and their increasing mobility has caused a rising tide of discontent among certain sections of the member states' populations.

While the 2003 European Social Survey indicated that 79 percent of the respondents experienced no problems regarding ethnic minorities, nearly half of them were skeptical towards multiculturalism. The results of the 2003 Eurobarometer revealed a similar view, taking into account that 60 percent of the respondents in the EU-15 expressed concerns with regard to diversity; however, the percentage was considerably lower in the new member states (42 percent). Hence, in an attempt to assess the impact of ethnic minority communities on the European Union, the European Monitoring Centre on Racism and Xenophobia (EUMC) published a series of reports concerning the Europeans' attitude towards these ethnic minority groups. The report on the *'Majorities' attitudes towards minorities in European Union Member States'* indicated that people in Austria and Germany opposed multiculturalism (with Greece and Italy closing in); expressed resistance to multicultural society (including Belgium, Greece, Sweden, Denmark, Spain and Portugal, Britain and the Netherlands); believed that the limits to multicultural society had been reached (plus all members apart from the Nordic states); were against civil rights, similar to those of legal residents, being granted to legal immigrants (together with Belgium and Great Britain); and favored policies regarding the repatriation of legal immigrants, particularly when unemployed, (in addition to Portugal, Greece, Ireland, Italy, Spain and France). The report also revealed that those to oppose multiculturalism and granting civil rights to legal immigrants, as well as those who believed that multiculturalism had reached its limits and favored repatriation policies, were people who stopped their education before or at the age of eighteen; had low income; were of old age; unskilled and skilled manual workers, as well as the unemployed; lived in rural areas; and supported right-wing political parties.

The EUMC report on the *'Majorities' attitudes towards minorities in (former) Candidate Countries of the European Union'* indicated that people in Cyprus and Latvia expressed resistance to multiculturalism (together with Estonia, the Czech Republic and Lithuania); believed that the limits to multicultural society had been reached (including Estonia, the Czech Republic, Hungary and Malta); were against civil rights being granted to legal immigrants (as well as Estonia, Hungary, Slovenia, Slovakia, the Czech Republic and Malta); and favored policies regarding the repatriation of legal immigrants (plus Malta and Turkey). The report also revealed that those to oppose multiculturalism and granting civil rights to legal immigrants, as well as those who believed that multiculturalism had reached its limits and favored repatriation policies, were usually people who stopped their education before or at the age of twenty-one, although those who finished before or at the age of fourteen showed less resistance to multiculturalism; unskilled manual workers and, to a lesser extent, skilled manual workers, self-employed people and routine nonmanual workers; lived in rural areas; did not attend religious services; had low income; and were of old age. However, these views were not as rigid and widespread as is the EU-15.

Finally, the EUMC report on the *'Majorities' attitudes towards minorities in Western and Eastern European Societies'* indicated that the Europeans showed much resistance to immigrants (particularly in Greece, Hungary, Portugal, Finland, Britain, Luxembourg and Austria), asylum seekers (with Britain, Belgium, the Netherlands, former East Germany, Hungary and Slovenia leading the group) and diversity (Portugal, Greece, Poland, the Czech Republic and Slovenia scoring higher); favored ethnic distance (Italy, Greece, the Czech Republic, Slovenia and Hungary) and the repatriation of criminal migrants (Portugal, Italy, Greece, former East Germany, Poland, the Czech Republic and Hungary); and perceived migrants as a threat to society (Greece, the Czech Republic, Hungary, former East Germany and Slovenia). Resistance to migrants, asylum seekers and diversity, as well as radical views on ethnic distance and migrants posing a threat to society were more often shared by people who stopped their education early, skilled and unskilled manual workers, retired or disabled, of old age, lived in rural areas, attended religious services, supported right-wing political parties and had low income.

Evidently, the member states are not always as hospitable a place for immigrants, as the levels of development of these civilized European societies may suggest, despite the well publicized endeavors of the EU to facilitate integration and promote cultural diversity and equality. Certain sections of the populations of the states that make up the EU are obviously reluctant to endorse multiculturalism, even though the majority of these countries have accommodated ethnic minority groups for more that a century. It is imperative, therefore, to assess all relevant causes that may account for the Europeans' attitude towards minorities.

DISCRIMINATION IN POLITICAL DISCOURSE

The rise of nationalism throughout Europe at the turn of the century obliged, in March 2005, the European Commission against Racism and Intolerance (ECRI) to adopt a Declaration—along the lines of the *Charter of European Political Parties for a Non-racist Society* (February 1998)—that condemned the use of racist, anti-Semitic and xenophobic elements in political discourse and encouraged the adoption of relevant policies and measures by the member states of the Council of Europe to combat discrimination. For instance, the German *Nationaldemokratische Partei Deutschlands* has often expressed racist and anti-Semitic views when making reference to Turkish immigrants, the EU candidacy of Turkey and Israel's military operations at the expense of the Palestinians. The *Nationaldemokratische Partei Deutschlands* had also opposed the extension of EU membership to Central and Eastern European countries, as had the Austrian *Freiheitliche Partei Österreichs*, which also voiced concerns with regard to immigration. The *Dansk Folkeparti* and the *Democracia Nacional*, in Denmark and Spain respectively, are known for their xenophobic views—as are *Alleanza Nazionale* and *Lega Nord* in Italy—and maintain links with other right-wing parties in Europe, such as the *Vlaams Blok* in Belgium, the French *Front National* and the Swedish *Ny Demokraterna*. In the case of France, extreme right-wing parties tend to associate immigration with insecurity or economic crises and oppose Turkey's bid for membership with the EU, due to their resistance to

Islamism. However, Euro-skeptic parties exploit the issue of xenophobia as well. The *Mouvement pour la France* focused its electoral campaign on the issues of Turkey's EU candidacy, immigration and Christianity. Nonetheless, its leadership never accused the Arabs openly for the tragic events of 11 September 2001, unlike Robert Kilroy-Silk, leader of the *UK Independence Party*. Although less frequently, government parties too have expressed xenophobic views (e.g., Luxemburg, Sweden, the Netherlands, Denmark and Switzerland) and anti-Semitic rhetoric in European and national elections (e.g., Belgium, France and Hungary).

In Europe, extreme right-wing parties relate their ideology to nationalism, xenophobia, resistance to immigration and anticommunism, thus breeding racism and discrimination, while immigrants are blamed for unemployment and crime in society. The revival of extreme right-wing groups is better illustrated through renewed neo-Nazi violence in Germany, the strong presence of the *Front National* in France, the electoral success of Vladimir Zhirinovsky in Russia, the participation of *Alleanza Nazionale* and the *Slovak National Party* in the Italian and Slovakian governments respectively, as well as the electoral successes of the *Freiheitliche Partei Österreichs*, the *People's Party* in Switzerland and the *Vlaams Blok*. Paradoxically, Austria and Switzerland have low levels of unemployment, thus the state of economy does not account for the increase of support for extreme right-wing parties; in Spain and Portugal support for the extreme right is limited, even though both countries suffer from unemployment; and, similarly, unemployment in Belgium is higher in Wallonia, but the extreme right enjoys support in the region of Flanders. In Central and Eastern Europe, following the collapse of communism, the national identities that had long been oppressed found a novel way of expression through nationalistic parties, such as the *Serbian Radical Party*, the *Republicans* in the Czech Republic, the *Confederation for an Independent Poland*, the *Romanian National Unity Party*, the *Slovak National Party* and the *Justice and Life Party* in Hungary. Although extreme right-wing parties in Central and Eastern Europe share similarities with their Western counterparts, as regards racism, xenophobia and anti-Semitism, the former often physically abuse ethnic minorities and never fail to declare their separatist aspirations. The atrocities in former Yugoslavia are a prime example of ethnic intolerance, with Latvia, Estonia and Hungary denying their ethnic minorities access to power and equal rights. Anti-Semitism is also gaining support, even though Jewish communities in this part of Europe are insignificant in terms of numbers.

Still, with few exceptions, the electoral success of the extreme right in Europe is limited. The *Freiheitliche Partei Österreichs* became more xenophobic when immigrants reached the gates of Austria after the end of the Cold War period and witnessed a considerable increase in electoral success reaching more than 20 percent at national level and exceeding 25 percent at European Parliament elections. Its grand achievement, nevertheless, was the 1999 federal elections, when it amassed nearly 30 percent of the popular vote—an unprecedented phenomenon in modern European politics—thus forcing the EU to impose sanctions upon the newly formed Austrian government. Likewise, the *Front National* in France became a force to be reckoned in the 1990s, as it surpassed the 10 percent threshold to achieve parliamentary representation. The *Front National* promotes ethnocentric values and draws its support from blue-collar workers and the petty bourgeoisie. However, in January 1999, Bruno Mégret, the General Delegate of the party, left the *Front National* and formed the *Mouvement national*, subsequently renamed *Mouvement national républicain*, thus diminishing the prospects of the extreme right to increase its popularity. Both parties focus on immigration and the integration of non-Europeans, demand the return of foreigners to their countries of origin and aspire to the principle of 'priority for French citizens' (*Préférence nationale*), thus questioning the issue of foreigners being granted civil rights. The *List Pim Fortuyn* party in the Netherlands, the *British National Party*, the *Dansk Folkeparti*, the *Norwegian Progress Party*, the *League of Polish Families*, *LAOS* in Greece, the *Slovene National Party*, the Latvian *Fatherland and Freedom Party* and the *Ny Demokraterna* have also enjoyed electoral success, albeit of minor significance. The *Nationaldemokratische Partei Deutschlands* and the *Republikaner* in Germany, and the *Movimento Sociale-Fiamma Tricolore, Alleanza Nazionale* and *Lega Nord* in Italy have all witnessed a decline in support; Spain, Estonia, Lithuania, Malta and Portugal have considerably smaller extreme right-wing parties; whereas in Cyprus, Finland, Ireland and Luxembourg, such extreme right groups are virtually absent from the political spectrum.

Given the relatively strong presence of extreme right-wing groups in Europe, the Parliamentary Assembly of the Council of Europe issued Resolution 1345 (2003), *Racist, xenophobic and intolerant discourse in politics*, which specified that:

"4. The Assembly is itself a body of democratically elected national representatives and as such is profoundly and immediately concerned with the preservation and promotion of political freedoms and pluralism. It therefore supports without reservation full protection of the rights contained in Articles 10 and 11 of the ECHR, concerning the freedoms of expression and of assembly and association, without which pluralist democratic political activity would be impossible.

5. The Assembly observes, however, that Articles 10 and 11 are not absolute rights but qualified rights, the enjoyment of which may be limited by competing public interests, amongst which are the prevention of disorder, the protection of morals and the protection of the rights of others. In particular, this allows for limitation of these rights and freedoms when they are exercised in such a way as to cause, incite, promote, advocate, encourage or justify racism, xenophobia or intolerance. The Assembly recalls the relevant jurisprudence of the European Court of Human Rights, and notes with approval the guidance on these matters given by the European Commission for Democracy through Law

(Venice Commission) in its 'Guidelines on Prohibition and Dissolution of Political Parties and Analogous Measures' and by the European Commission
against Racism and Intolerance (ECRI) in its General Policy Recommendation
No. 7 on national legislation to combat racism and racial discrimination.

8. The Assembly recalls its own previous work, in particular Recommendations
1222 (1993) on the fight against racism, xenophobia and intolerance, 1275
(1995) on the fight against racism, xenophobia, anti-Semitism and intolerance,
1438 (2000) on the threat posed to democracy by extremist parties and movements in Europe and 1543 (2001) on racism and xenophobia in cyberspace,
along with Resolution 1308 (2002) on restrictions on political parties in the
Council of Europe member states. The Assembly also recalls the work of the
European Parliament concerning racism, intolerance and xenophobia, in particular its reports on countering racism, xenophobia and intolerance in the
European Union and in the candidate countries. It further recalls the positions
of the United Nations Commission on Human Rights in its Resolutions
2002/39, 2001/43 and 2000/40, of the United Nations General Assembly in its
Resolution 55/82 and of the Secretary General of the United Nations in his
Note A/53/269."[1]

Naturally, the EU places huge emphasis upon democracy and equality, so to
facilitate the process of integration, while at the same time it promotes and de-
fends cultural diversity. In this respect, the Council of Europe underlined in
Resolution 1344 the threat posed to democracy by extremist parties and movements in Europe and made explicitly clear that "Extremism, whatever its nature,
is a form of political activity that overtly or covertly rejects the principles of
parliamentary democracy, and very often bases its ideology and its political
practices and conduct on intolerance, exclusion, xenophobia, anti-Semitism and
ultranationalism."[2] Along the same line of reason, having realized the grave
threat that Nazism posed to social harmony, the Parliamentary Assembly of the
Council of Europe issued, on 19 December 2005, Doc. 10766, *Combating the
resurrection of nazi ideology*, which stipulated that:

"8. Modern Europe has been conceived as a total rejection of the nazi ideas and
principles, with the aim to exclude that such horrendous crimes as those committed by the nazi regime in the name of 'racial superiority' may ever be repeated. The Council of Europe, as the oldest European political organisation
aimed at protecting and furthering democracy, human rights and the rule of
law, has a special responsibility in preventing the resurgence of the nazi ideology.

10. The Assembly is particularly concerned as regards:
10.3. the use of nazi symbols such as the fascist 'swastika,' flag, uniform, etc.,
and others with clear indication to them;

11. Furthermore, the Assembly is worried by political and social phenomena which, while making no direct reference to the nazi regime, should be seen in the light of its ideology, such as:

11.1 the growing number of manifestations of racial, ethnic and religious intolerance in daily life, including, inter alia, desecration of Jewish cemeteries and attacks on religious sites;

11.2. attempts to create, through the media, a negative perception of some ethnic or religious groups;

11.3. growing support for political parties and movements with a xenophobic agenda.

12. Moreover, the Assembly is worried that such manifestations do not always receive enough attention and response on behalf of the political leaders and that public opinion seems now more receptive to racist, xenophobic and extremist ideas.

13. In this connection, the Assembly deems it necessary to recall that Hitler's ideas, outrageous as they look today, found sympathy and support in many European countries.

14. The Assembly believes that it is urgent to step up coordinated action in order to resist efforts aiming at revitalising nazi ideology, to fight xenophobia, intolerance and hatred based on racial and ethnic grounds, political and religious extremism and all forms of totalitarian action. The Council of Europe must play the leading role in this process.

15. In this context, the Assembly welcomes the relevant activities already conducted by various Council of Europe bodies, in particular by the European Commission against Racism and Intolerance (ECRI), but believes that, in order to bring about concrete results, these activities need to be reoriented to include a wider involvement of society.

21. An increase in the number and membership of extremist and xenophobic groups has been observed in several European countries, such as Spain, Austria, Germany, Russia, the Czech Republic and many others.

32. Europe has gone a long way towards integration based on cultural pluralism. The manifestations of the neo-Nazi movement across Europe and the support enjoyed by political parties with xenophobic programmes reflect a dangerous tendency to reject integration, which runs counter to the European tradition. More and more Europeans support the view that the multicultural model is a thing of the past and favour a strengthening of the national element. In a large number of European countries, there has been a sharp decline in tolerance toward immigrants and an increase in support for the expulsion of legal migrants. Islamophobia has been on the rise since the terrorist acts in the United States, and especially after those in Madrid and London."[3]

There is no doubt that the EU is, indeed, much concerned with the racist, xenophobic and extremist views that ethnocentric nationalist fervor has generated across the continent. After all, the revival of radical political ideologies has already jeopardized the relatively smooth process of European integration. The majority of EU member states have already implemented tight immigration policies, while the extreme right appears willing to sacrifice basic human liberties for the cause of internal security. In general, the political implications of racism are detrimental to the core policies of the EU.

RACISM IN EUROPE

The EUMC report on *Racist Violence in 15 EU Member States* indicated that the majority of European states have effective mechanisms in place for the collection of information related to racist incidents and discrimination, which in some cases may shed light into the nature of race-related crimes or the perpetrators, whereas a few countries have no official records of relevant data (Greece, Italy and Portugal).

Austria
Although the Austrian coalition government, led by *Freiheitliche Partei Österreichs*, passed an Asylum Act (May 2003) that certainly did not favor immigrants and asylum seekers, there is hardly any evidence to support that racism is related to political groupings, particularly the *Freiheitliche Partei Österreichs* and its supporters, since relevant official statistics and legal extreme right-wing parties do not exist.

Belgium
The support that the *Vlaams Blok* enjoys somehow reflects the relatively high percentage of Belgians showing intolerance towards immigrants (25 percent, whereas the EU-15 mean is 14 percent). As is usually the case between different parts of a country, Flanders (rural area) experiences higher levels of intolerance towards foreigners than Wallonia (urban area). Even though both regions have extreme right-wing parties, the *Front National* and the *Vlaams Blok* in Wallonia and Flanders respectively, only the latter can claim a significant role in politics. What accounts for this discrepancy is that while Wallonia can claim much experience with immigration—stretching over a period of more than a century and having almost completed the immigrants' integration—the region of Flanders, at the same time, was suffering from emigration, whereas the phenomenon of immigration is fairly recent in the area. Furthermore, the *Vlaams Blok* was initially established to serve the separatist ambitions of the people in Flanders and has only just turned its attention to foreigners, primarily for electoral purposes, while it is surely not as fragmented a party as the *Front National* and, most sig-

nificantly, is widely supported by manual workers, in other words those that feel more threatened by the presence of immigrants in the country.

Denmark

In Denmark, racist incidents have been largely influenced by the September 11 terrorist acts, the continuous conflict in the Middle East and, surprisingly, elections at national and local level. As a matter of fact, race crimes against the Muslim communities increased dramatically, according to a March 2002 report that was produced by the *Committee on the Elimination of all Forms of Racial Discrimination*. In the elections of 2001, some two months after the tragic events in the United States, the right-wing *Dansk Folkeparti* (Danish People's Party) became part of a coalition government that intended to implement strict immigration and assimilation policies. Those measures reflected the views of the Danish people who considered immigrants as a problem, since Islam, in particular, was perceived as a threat to Danish society. During the 1980s, immigrants were often attacked by extreme right groups such as the Green Jackets (*Grönjakkerne*), who were later on replaced by the skinhead movement and, today, by much smaller neo-Nazi groups, such as Combat 18.

Finland

Asylum seekers have also reached Finland, among them people from Iran, Iraq, Somalia and former Yugoslavia. The local Swedish minority, the remains of Sweden's long lasting rule of Finland, relishes the preferential treatment of the authorities. All parties signed the Charter of the European Political Parties for a Non-Racist Society; however, extreme right parties have been relatively successful in recent elections. The electoral outcome of 2003 indicated that the True Finns party ranked fifth in terms of votes, even though it never hesitated airing its racist and xenophobic views. Another two new extreme right parties that contested the same elections are 'Finland Arises—People Unite' and the 'Blue and White Party,' equally racist and xenophobic, which were largely unsuccessful, but their emergence alone is alarming enough.

France

Even though the French Republic maintains values that pertain to the principle of equality of treatment before law—regardless of ethnic origin—racist incidents were increased, particularly acts of anti-Semitism, perhaps because of the 11 September 2001 events and the tension in the Middle East. Growing support for the *Front National* seems to have coincided with some disturbing racist and xenophobic views, not to mention the debates that surrounded the wearing of headscarves by Muslims as a religious symbol. Not surprisingly, anti-Semitic views were more common among a section of right-wing supporters, known as '*droite gaulliste*' and a fraction of Catholics. The *Commission Nationale Consultative des Droits de l'Homme* noted in 2002 that 62 percent of racist incidents related to anti-Semitism. Nevertheless, while most racist incidents were associated with the extreme right in the mid-1990s (68 percent in 1994), figures decreased significantly (14 percent in 2001 and 9 percent in 2002) and anti-Semitic acts were often instigated by North African youth—though no related official data is available.

Germany
Due to Germany's dishonorable Nazi past, the collection of data that denote the ethnic background of people is prohibited and, as a result, is limited to nationality alone. Most certainly, such an unorthodox measure can only hinder the identification of the origins of all those who fall victims of racial abuse. At least, the German State monitors the activities of extreme right-wing groups and parties associated with extremism, xenophobia and anti-Semitism. Nevertheless, despite the high levels of racist crime in the early 1990s, numbers have been decreasing ever since, though this is most probably related to Germany's new data collection mechanism. Evidently, the vast majority of racist incidents occur in the eastern part of the country, which has been experiencing high levels of unemployment ever since the fall of communism; however, a significant number of incidents are not always considered by the authorities as racist acts, while others remain unreported. Regardless, nearly half of racist acts are directed against foreigners, with some 50 percent being asylum seekers, while those that are often targeted are people of African, Turkish and Vietnamese origins, as well as gypsies.

Greece
The Greeks witnessed the first waves of immigrants in the 1990s. This sudden, more or less, influx of foreigners dominated the political agenda of LAOS (Popular Orthodox Alarm) and Proti Grammi (Front Line). Despite the largely unsuccessful campaign of LAOS in the 2004 elections, the party succeeded in electing one Member of the European Parliament in the same year, whereas the Front Line's support is only marginal. On the whole, from all ethnic groups, Albanians are more likely to suffer from racial discrimination.

Ireland
Ireland has long suffered from emigration, given the numbers of Irish people that left the island in search of a better future elsewhere, usually nearby Britain or the more distant United States. Today, the same country is recognized as a destination for immigrants, primarily of Islamic background, due to the growth of Ireland's economy in the 1990s. Even though Ireland is nowadays coming to terms with the complex issues that stem from immigration, religious diversity, for one, is certainly nothing new to the authorities, given the awkward relationship between the Catholic and Protestant communities. Although racist incidents in Ireland are seemingly rare, oddly enough, both official and unofficial data suggest otherwise. However, this disparity may simply reflect the improved data collecting method that police authorities have adopted.

Italy

Italy's extreme right-wing parties relish more support in the north, where the *Lega Nord, Forza Italia* and *Alleanza Nazionale* succeeded altogether in commanding a considerable part of the electorate at the turn of the century, which saw all three become part of a government coalition. These extreme right parties, together with neo-fascist and neo-Nazi formations, such as the *Movimento Sociale-Fiamma Tricolore, Forza Nuova* and *Fronte Sociale Nazionale*, never fail to project xenophobic views, with *Forza Nuova* being the most prominent representative of racism, anti-Semitism and anti-Islamism in Italian political discourse. Taking into account the fact that relatively few governments ever applied effective policies that concerned the issue of immigration, relevant laws depend for the most part on EU legislation. Therefore, the more or less predictable problems that stem from controversial issues like immigration remain unresolved, while the parties that once comprised an extreme right coalition at government level still focus their campaigns on immigration in order to maintain the necessary political support. It is noteworthy that opposition to ethnic diversity is not high up the *Lega Nord* agenda, rather it seems to serve its separatist views well.

Luxemburg

An astonishing 86 percent of the population is made up of foreign nationals with EU citizenship, while the largest minority concerns the Portuguese. Extreme right parties are absent from Luxemburg's political spectrum, considering that the National Movement, founded in 1989, was dissolved in 1996. Moreover, the main political parties of Luxemburg signed in 1998 the Charter of the European Political Parties for a Non-Racist Society.

Netherlands

In the Netherlands, increasing support for extreme right-wing parties and their electoral success, as in the case of the *List Pim Fortuyn* party, coincided with an increase in race-related crimes. Despite the otherwise limited appeal of such parties to the public, extreme right groups were often responsible for racist incidents. As a matter of fact, the House of Representatives revealed in the *Report on Ethnic Minority Integration Policy for 2003* that considerable numbers of Dutch people had rather negative views with regard to multiculturalism, even though the same report also indicated a continuous decline in the prejudiced attitude of the majority towards ethnic minority groups in the 1991–2002 period. Sadly, the murder of filmmaker Theo van Gogh in November 2004 instigated a number of racist incidents at the expense of the Muslim community, merely because the aggressor had Islamic origins. Interestingly, the murder of Pim Fortuyn in May 2002 was believed to have been committed by a member of the Muslim community, due to Fortuyn's racist views, until it was realized that it was a white Dutchman. Nevertheless, the National Discrimination Expertise Centre recorded twenty incidents (out of 198) related to the extreme right in 2001 and only eight (out of 242) in 2002, even though the Dutch Monitoring Centre on Racism and Xenophobia recorded, in 2002, twelve racist incidents (out of 264) related to extreme right groups.

Portugal

Extreme right-wing parties in Portugal have only managed to attract limited support, with the *Nationalist Renovator Party* being the prime political formation responsible for both generating xenophobia and targeting immigrants. As a result, integration remains in the realm of whatever government is in power. Moreover, given that Portuguese legislation prohibits the collection of data on ethnicity and that certain constitutional and legal guarantees exist for the protection of basic human rights, people in Portugal share the view that their society is free of racism.

Spain

While the Portuguese believe that racism is absent from their society, the Spanish people seem more intolerant towards immigrants. In Spain, the number of crimes related to racism is increasing, often committed by extreme right-wing groups, while immigration features frequently as the main cause of race-related crime. Although the negative image of immigration in the media is probably superfluous, the March 2004 train bombings in Madrid certainly gave it yet another dimension—anti-Islamism. The extreme right, however, does not bear much political significance, in terms of support, apart from *Plataforma por Cataluña*, yet at regional level. In an attempt to address these issues, the socialist government currently in power intended to put into effect the Law on Aliens, thus allowing the legalization of irregular immigrants. Not surprisingly, the report made reference to the November 2004 friendly football match between England and Spain in Madrid and even stressed that football stadiums provide extreme right groups with the opportunity to recruit new members. All in all, there are no significant extreme right groups in Spain, however, participation in such movements is constantly increasing and so is the involvement of these extremist groups in racist incidents.

Sweden

In Sweden, racist incidents are more commonly witnessed in the southern part of the country. As in other countries, immigration again is ascribed a negative image in the media, as immigration is often considered as the principal cause of crime. It is worthy of note that the fact that the number of racist acts in Sweden exceeds that of any other Scandinavian country, with black people and non-Europeans being the likely victims. Although the Swedish Security Police make a point of arguing that these incidents are not in any way related to a particular ideology or organization, some studies have revealed a strong connection between the increase of youth unemployment on one hand and the arrival of asylum seekers and the spread of racial violence on the other. As a matter of fact, evidence suggests that members of certain extreme right groups, in particular the *Nationalsocialistisk Front* (National Socialist Front) and the *Nationell Ungdom* (National Youth), are often responsible for committing race-related offences. In this respect, Sweden's police authorities revealed that in 2002 only 15.4 percent of all racist incidents and 17.6 percent of anti-Semitic acts were related to the extreme right. Nevertheless, in the following year the number of racist incidents instigated by extreme right groups amounted to 18.1 percent, whereas the figure denoting anti-Semitic acts had also increased to an alarming 23.4 percent.

United Kingdom

Although the support that the *British National Party* enjoys is clearly marginal, the May 2003 local elections indicated an increase of support in the north of England and the West Midlands, though it may be related to the heated debates on asylum seekers and the 2001 riots between youth of different ethnic backgrounds. Not surprisingly, the 2000 British Crime Survey stressed that members of ethnic minorities were more likely to fall victims of racially motivated crimes by white Britons. At the same time, a EUMC report, The Impact of 7 July 2005 London Bomb Attacks on Muslim Communities in the EU, underlined the impact of international terrorism, since it delivered a massive blow to the very foundations of social harmony. In the aftermath of the London bombings, in July 2005, the British government announced that any acts of vengeance against the Muslim community would be severely treated by the authorities; yet an increase in racist incidents was, indeed, noted. Even though the media's initial response was to discourage people from resorting to violence against the Muslim population, their attitude soon changed when it was realized that the perpetrators were British-born, thus producing the necessary grounds for reports and debates on issues concerning integration, immigration policies and Islamic fundamentalism. A survey conducted by the BBC revealed that 62 percent of the respondents claimed that multiculturalism was positive, though 32 percent believed that it was a threat to British culture and 54 percent argued that parts of Britain had changed significantly—to worse—due to immigration. At the same time, the Muslim respondents felt proud when British teams performed well in international competitions (89 percent), agreed with non-Muslims that assimilation policies were necessary and stressed that foreigners who encourage terrorist activities should be deported (74 percent).

The authors of the *Racist Violence in 15 EU Member States* report concluded that some of the causes that encourage racist conduct are global conflicts, a colonial or fascist past of the country in question and immigration policies. Interestingly, though one hypothesis would surely suggest that racist incidents, by and large, take place in societies that include large ethnic minority communities, the phenomenon of anti-Semitism proves otherwise, given the small Jewish communities throughout the continent.

* * *

Another EUMC report, *Migrants' Experiences of Racism and Xenophobia in 12 EU Member States*, published in May 2006, revealed equally disturbing facts, as regards the 'perceived discrimination by different respondent groups.'

Austria
In Austria, among 861 interviewees from ethnic minorities, discriminatory experiences were by far most widespread among respondents with African background (50 percent), whereas considerably lower rates were revealed in the case of migrants from Bosnia (18 percent) and Turkey (14 percent). According to the Austrian study, one-fifth of the respondents who experienced discrimination reported those incidents to the police.

Belgium
In Belgium, among 756 interviewees from ethnic minorities, 56 percent of respondents with Chinese background, 29 percent Congolese, 28 percent Turkish and 26 percent Moroccan felt that they had been discriminated against under different conditions because of their foreign background. According to the Belgian study, a quarter of the respondents who experienced discrimination reported those incidents to the police.

France
In France, among 312 interviewees from ethnic minorities, 30 percent of Central African respondents and 24 percent of respondents with Maghrebi background felt that they had been discriminated against because of their foreign background. According to the French study, 27 percent of Central African respondents and 15 percent Maghrebi reported that they had experienced discrimination at least once to the police.

Germany
In Germany, among 819 interviewees from ethnic minorities, 35 percent of Black respondents, 13 percent Turkish, 12 percent Yugoslavs and 7 percent Italians felt that they had been discriminated against under different conditions because of their foreign background. According to the German study, one-fifth of the respondents who experienced discrimination reported those incidents to public authorities.

Greece
In Greece, among 858 interviewees from ethnic minorities, 34 percent of immigrants from the former Soviet Union, 32 percent Romanians, 31 percent Albanians and 21 percent Arabs felt that they had been discriminated against under different conditions because of their foreign background. According to the Greek study, only 2 percent of the respondents who experienced discrimination reported those incidents to public authorities.

Ireland

In Ireland, among 1089 interviewees from ethnic minorities, 22 percent of 'Black and Other South/Central African' respondents, 14 percent Eastern Europeans, 12 percent Asians and 10 percent North Africans felt that they had been discriminated against under different conditions because of their 'ethnic/national origin.' According to the Irish study, discrimination was relatively often reported to authorities. More than one-fifth of the people who experienced discrimination in the context of racist violence or crime made a report to the police.

Italy

In Italy, among 388 interviewees from ethnic minorities, 35 percent of respondents with Senegalese background, 30 percent Moroccans, 28 percent Peruvians, 26 percent Albanians and 14 percent Philippinas felt that they had been discriminated against under different conditions because of their foreign background. According to the Italian study, discrimination is rarely reported to the police.

Luxemburg

In Luxemburg, among 1400 interviewees from ethnic minorities, 13 percent of migrants from Cape Verde, 10 percent from former Yugoslavia and 8 percent Belgians and Portuguese alike felt that they had been discriminated against under different conditions because of their foreign background. According to Luxemburg's study, the groups that were more likely to suffer from discrimination were also likely to report those incidents to public authorities more often.

Netherlands

In the Netherlands, among 794 interviewees from ethnic minorities, migrants from Turkey were mostly discriminated against, whereas migrants from Indonesia were clearly those who experienced discrimination least often. According to the Dutch study, 10 percent of the respondents who experienced discrimination reported those incidents to the police.

Portugal

In Portugal, among 1619 interviewees from ethnic minorities, all migrant groups shared similar rates of discrimination (around 20 percent) with migrants from Ukraine scoring 20 percent and migrants from Guinea-Bissauan registering 24 percent.

Spain

In Spain, among 668 interviewees from ethnic minorities, Moroccan migrants were most discriminated against, followed by migrants from Ecuador. Colombian experienced the least discrimination. According to the Spanish study, only 1 percent of the respondents who experienced discrimination reported those incidents to public authorities.

United Kingdom
In the case of the United Kingdom, none of the seven groups of respondents
(Black African, Black Caribbean, 'Black Other' and migrants of Indian, Paki-
stani or Middle Eastern descent) produced information regarding discrimination.
According to the UK study, 37 percent of the respondents who experienced dis-
crimination reported those incidents to public authorities.

ANTI-RACISM LEGISLATION

The *European Convention for the Protection of Human Rights and Fundamental Freedoms* of the Council of Europe, implemented in 1953, was rather
weak in addressing issues related to racist offences, although Article 14 made
explicit reference to racial discrimination. As it happens, the Convention simply
concerned violations of rights and freedoms committed by States, while the
European Court of Human Rights could only take into consideration matters
related to racist violence, if subject to a course of action, or lack of it, taken by a
State. In contrast, the *Framework Convention for the Protection of National
Minorities* of the Council of Europe (1998) was the first legally binding European Convention that specifically provided for the protection of national minorities. The Convention's impact, nevertheless, was limited, given that certain
member states failed to ratify the Convention at the outset, while it also fell
short of providing a definition of 'national minority.' The apparent lack of substance, eventually, prompted the ECRI to adopt General Policy Recommendation No. 7 on *National Legislation to Combat Racism and Racial Discrimination*
(2002). The General Policy Recommendation remedied the deficiency of the
previous Convention effectively, by suggesting that action be taken at national
level to address racial discrimination and xenophobia, but failed to attain legal
status and thus was not a binding instrument. Relevant pieces of legislation, at
EU level, include the *Joint Action to Combat Racism and Xenophobia* (1996),
the *Racial Equality Directive* 2000/43/EC and the *Employment Equality Directive* 2000/78/EC, though the last two are subject to interpretation at the level of
individual member states. It should be noted that Article 13 of the EC Treaty
and Article 29 of the EU Treaty together form the necessary basis for the development and application of the instruments mentioned above.

* * *

The Commission for Racial Equality and the Minority Policy Group published,
in March 2002, the *Combating Racial and Ethnic Discrimination: Taking the
European legislative Agenda Further* report, intended to produce an insight on
antidiscrimination legislation in Europe. According to the report, the Amsterdam
Treaty (1999) gave the EU legal powers to adopt laws against racism, given that
during the 1990s there was "an apparent rise in (violent) racism across Europe;

the growth in support for parties of the extreme right-wing; a perceived need to 'balance' the restrictive effects of EU immigration and asylum policies with measures to promote the integration of third-country nationals; and the identification of significant discrimination against certain national minorities in many of the EU applicant states." The Treaty endorsed Article 13 that "provided a legal competence for the EU Council to take 'appropriate measures to combat discrimination based on sex, racial or ethnic origin, religion or belief, disability, age or sexual orientation"[4] and amended Article 29 of the EU Treaty to enable all pertinent actors within the European police and judicial cooperation scheme to prevent and combat racism. Among the proposals submitted by the European Commission to battle discrimination was the *Racial Equality Directive* (2000). The Vienna Declaration of 1993, as adopted by the Council of Europe, addressed issues of racial discrimination, xenophobia, anti-Semitism and intolerance, influenced by the outbreak of ethnic conflict in the Balkans and membership with the Council of Europe being extended to former communist European countries. The Vienna Declaration produced the necessary grounds for the establishment of the ECRI within the Council of Europe, which sought "the establishment of an independent right to nondiscrimination"[5] that was characteristically absent from the provisions of the European Convention on Human Rights (ECHR).

Even though the *Racial Equality Directive* prohibits discrimination on grounds of 'racial or ethnic origin,' neither term is defined in the directive or in any of the related documents. Some member states were concerned with the use of the term 'racial origin' as it implied that "biologically separate 'races' exist in humanity"; others argued that the exclusion of the term could "create potential loopholes in the law." To this end, an agreement was reached when Recital 6 was added to the preamble of the *Racial Equality Directive*, which stipulates that "the European Union rejects theories which attempt to determine the existence of separate human races. The use of the term "racial origin" in this Directive does not imply an acceptance of such theories." Moreover, the *Racial Equality Directive* fails to provide protection concerning discrimination related to either religion or nationality, with Article 3(2) specifying that "This Directive does not cover difference of treatment based on nationality and is without prejudice to provisions and conditions relating to the entry into and residence of third country nationals and stateless persons on the territory of Member States, and to any treatment which arises from the legal status of the third country nationals and stateless persons concerned."[6] Article 1(1) of Protocol 12 of the ECHR states that "The enjoyment of any right set forth by law shall be secured without discrimination on any ground such as sex, race, colour, language, religion, political or other opinion, national or social origin, association with a national minority, property, birth or other status."[7] Protocol 12 protects against all forms of discrimination, such as those based on race, color, religion and national origin. Moreover, "Article 2(4) of both directives stresses that 'an instruction to discriminate against persons on grounds of racial or ethnic origin, or religion or belief, will amount to unlawful discrimination. This will be particularly useful in tackling discrimination via third parties."[8]

Furthermore, it was at the European Conference against racism (Strasbourg, October 2000), when the need to strengthen the powers of the ECRI was realized. As a result, the Committee of Ministers adopted a new Statute for ECRI (June 2002), which established its role as the leading institution in the struggle against racial discrimination. The powers of the ECRI were enhanced following a meeting of the Council of Europe (Warsaw, Third Summit, May 2005), where the Heads of State and Government of the member states of the Council of Europe provided the means with which the ECRI would cooperate with national authorities and institutions to promote those policies and measures deemed necessary to combat discrimination related to racial, religious and linguistic issues, as well as to national or ethnic origin. Based on the European Council Directive 2000/43/EC, member states of the EU are required to set up national bodies to preserve the equal treatment of all persons regardless of racial or ethnic origin. Likewise, ECRI's General Policy Recommendation No. 7 argued, in Chapter V on 'Common Provisions,' for the significance of such specialized bodies in implementing national legislation to combat racial discrimination.

* * *

The Home Office produced in April 2002 a study, *Tackling racial equality: international comparisons*, which produced an account of the various measures employed by different states to combat racial discrimination and compared the approach of the United Kingdom to that in other countries. The report stressed that the history of different European countries dictates, to an extent, their approach to racism. Countries that suffered most from Nazism (e.g., Austria, Germany and Italy) have adopted a more radical approach, such as prohibiting extremist groups, the display of Nazi symbols and holocaust denial, while others focused on legal instruments to address discrimination (e.g., Britain, Ireland, the Netherlands and Sweden). On the whole, European countries differ in their approach to the issue of racism, given that some consider race-related incidents as "a general criminal offence, or as a general offence with increased penalties for racial motivation. The third way is to have specific racially motivated offences. Several countries have a mixture of offences in all three categories. The advantage of treating racial violence as a general offence is that it is not necessary to prove a racial motivation for an attack, the evidence for which is difficult to obtain. However, having specific offences or enhanced penalties for racist motivation sends a clear signal that such crimes are particularly serious and unacceptable."[9] Still, the main obstacle in combating racial discrimination effectively relates to the fact that few only countries keep records of ethnicity data (e.g., Britain and the Netherlands). And even when such data becomes available in other countries too, they generally concern nationality, thus excluding immigrants that have acquired the nationality of the host country. Taking into account the potential impact of racial discrimination on community cohesion, it is fundamental that governments address the issue effectively, by disseminating anti-racism information and initiating relevant campaigns. The Home Office report mentioned a number of such projects in Europe, made reference to certain governments' endeavors to provide immigrants with equal opportunities in employment and underlined the significance of education in promoting cultural diversity and tolerance. The report concluded that

> "European countries are the weakest in making specific provisions to tackle racial discrimination. Their legal arrangements are incoherent, with a mixture of civil and criminal laws, or labour codes, and a variety of enforcement mechanisms. In countries that rely on criminal codes for preventing discrimination, the law is little used because of the higher burden of proof needed. Most have no explicit provision for positive action, and some countries have no provision for individuals to bring cases. Ireland, Norway, Sweden, the Netherlands, and the UK are exceptions, as there is one civil statute (sometimes two, if employment is treated separately), and an enforcement body—although with a variety of powers and assistance available. The Netherlands and Northern Ireland also impose positive obligations on employers. Member states of the EU will, however, improve on this when the 2000 Race Discrimination Directive is implemented. In contrast, and undoubtedly as a result of experience of Nazism and fascism, several European countries have specific laws on hate speech and against specified groups. Many European countries too have concentrated their efforts into promoting the benefits of immigration and diversity, and into encouraging tolerance. However, there is confusion about terminology and difficulties about obtaining factual data to identify differences of access and to monitor progress. This reflects their relatively recent experiences of immigration and ethnic diversity. The exceptions again are mainly Britain and the Netherlands, which have the longest experience of implementing policies to prevent racism and discrimination and to promote diversity."[10]

For the record, the report also mentioned that England and Wales were the only European nations that prohibited racist chanting at football matches.

* * *

The International Centre for Migration Policy Development produced in 2004, on behalf of the EUMC, the *Migrants, minorities and legislation* report, which assessed the legal instruments against discrimination available in the EU member states. The focal point of the report was the implementation of the Racial Equality Directive in the EU-15. Among all member states, only Austria, Belgium, Denmark, France, the Netherlands, Portugal, Sweden and the United Kingdom succeeded in fulfilling the task in an appropriate manner. On the contrary, Finland, Germany, Greece, Ireland, Italy, Luxemburg and Spain were in the process of transposing their legislation.

The Equal Treatment Act, *Gleichbehandlungsgesetz* (1979), as well as the Federal Equal Treatment Act, *Bundes-Gleichbehandlungsgesetz* (1993), in Austria, were both revised to accommodate the needs of the Racial Equality Directive. A general antidiscrimination law was adopted in Belgium, on 12 December 2002, which provides protection against all forms of discrimination, in line with Article 13 of the Treaty of Amsterdam and the Racial Equality Directive. The new law produces the necessary grounds for the Centre for Equal Opportunities and Opposition against Racism to take legal action against racial discrimination. The Danish government transposed the Racial Equality Directive through Act No. 411 (June 2002), set up the Danish Centre for International Studies and Human Rights and revised the Act on Equal Treatment appropriately so to provide guarantees against discrimination related to racial and ethnic origins (July 2003). The parliament in France passed an Anti-Discrimination Bill (November 2001) intended to combat discrimination of all forms. The Netherlands became the first EU member state to have an antidiscrimination law in place, when the Equal Treatment Act, *Algemene wet gelijke behandeling*, was passed in 1994, which was amended to incorporate the Racial Equality Directive. In Portugal, Law 134/99 (1999) was adopted to provide guarantees against racial and ethnic discrimination, following the rationale of the International Convention on the Elimination of all forms of Racial Discrimination, and was amended to serve the purpose of the Racial Equality Directive. The Swedish government proposed in 2001 measures to combat racial discrimination and xenophobia and, by 2002, a Committee of Inquiry was set up to monitor the application of antidiscrimination legislation. Finally, in the United Kingdom the Race Relations Act (1976) was revised to allow for the implementation of the Racial Equality Directive. The government also founded the Commission for Equalities and Human Rights (November 2003), in line with Article 13 of the EC Treaty, whereas the Anti-Terrorism, Crime and Security Act (2001) amended the Public Order Act (1986) to deliver more severe sentences.

* * *

The ECRI, in cooperation with the Minority Policy Group, published a report on *The implementation of European anti-discrimination legislation: work in progress—The implementation of the Racial Equality Directive (2000/43/EC) and the Employment Equality Directive (2000/78/EC) as it relates to religion and belief in 15 EU Member States*. The *Racial Equality Directive* and the *Employment Equality Directive* were due to be completed by July and December 2003 respectively. The only countries that respected the deadlines were Portugal and Sweden.

Austria
Austria ratified in 1972 the International Convention on the Elimination of All Forms of Racial Discrimination, which is the cornerstone of all legislation related

to antidiscrimination that, today, penalizes incitement to racial hatred and discrimination. The Federal Constitution in Article 7 makes reference to the equal treatment of all Austrian nationals, but based on Article 1 of the International Convention on the Elimination of All Forms of Racial Discrimination, the Constitutional Court made a ruling that extends the right to equal treatment to non-nationals. Moreover, the terms 'race and ethnic origin' were replaced in the constitution by the term 'ethnic belonging' (*ethnische Zugehörigkeit*), given that '*Rasse*,' race, was severely abused in Nazi Germany. However, institutions devoted to antidiscrimination lack the necessary independence that would produce, perhaps, better results, since the relevant law that discussed the likely constitutional protection of these bodies met strong resistance in the parliament by the opposition.

Belgium

In Belgium, the usual victims of discrimination originate from the sub-Saharan Africa (countries like Rwanda and the Democratic Republic of Congo) and North Africa. Those that belong to the second group of immigrants arrived in Belgium during the 1960s, when the country was in need of low-skilled labor. The main obstacle, nevertheless, in collecting the necessary information on the ethnic background of people who have been discriminated against, is much related to the fact that the majority of those immigrants have acquired Belgian nationality. Therefore, the increase in crime, due to Islamophobia after 9/11, is not accurately reflected in statistical information. To combat racism, Belgium makes good use of the Council of Europe's *Convention for the Protection of Human Rights and Fundamental Freedoms* (Article 14), the United Nation's (UN) *International Covenant on Civil and Political Rights* (Article 26), the UN *International Convention on the Elimination of all Forms of Racial Discrimination* (March 1966), the Moureaux Law and the Constitution. The latter provides the necessary guarantees to safeguard the equality of all Belgians before law, the principle of nondiscrimination (Articles 10 and 11) and also stipulates that foreign nationals, too, enjoy the same rights and freedoms, though with some exceptions. The main institution that addresses the issue of racial discrimination in Belgium, founded in 1993, is the Centre for Equal Opportunities and Opposition to Racism (*Centre pour l'égalité des chances et la lutte contre le racisme*). The Centre promotes human values, opposes discrimination and has the capacity to take legal action, under certain conditions, against racist offenders.

Denmark

As in the case of Belgium, most immigrants arrived in Denmark during the 1960s, when the local industry was in need of labor. However, the oil crises of the 1970s brought about massive unemployment, forcing the Danish Government to ban immigration in November 1973. The number of foreigners, nevertheless, was never decreased. On the contrary, those immigrants that opted to prolong their stay in Denmark—terrified at the prospect of being denied re-admission once they exited the country—were joined by their family members, as the Danish Aliens Act dictates so, asylum seekers coming from regions marred by conflict and, of course, EU nationals. When the Danish Peoples Party was included in the government, after the 2001 elections, it actively sought the abolition of institutions related to antidiscrimination, such as the Board for Ethnic Equality and the Documentation and Advisory Centre on Racial Discrimination. The Danish Peoples Party, which seems to include a number of members that hold racist views, felt so strong about the abolition of all such institutions that it did not hesitate to demand that the matter was suitably resolved, in return for voting in favor of the Danish State financial budget for the year 2002. Eventually, the Board for Ethnic Equality was abolished, whereas financial assistance to the Documentation and Advisory Centre on Racial Discrimination was halted. What remained to provide the essential guarantees against discrimination, were the Danish Constitutional Act and the International Convention on the Elimination of All Forms of Racial Discrimination, ratified in 1971. However, in line with Act No. 411 of 6 June 2002, which established the Danish Centre for International Studies and Human Rights, the Institute of Human Rights, according to Article 13 of the Act, was set up.

Finland

Finland's main ethnic groups concern Estonians, Russians, Somalis, Swedes and people from former Yugoslavia, while national minorities include the Jewish, Roma, Russian and Tatar people, as well as the indigenous Sámi people. Nevertheless, the overall number of immigrants is considerably low. The prime legal instruments to protect against discrimination are the Constitution, the Equality Act and the Penal Code.

France

Ethnic minority communities in France are made up, predominantly, by Europeans originating from as diverse countries as the Baltic States, Italy, Portugal, Romania, Russia, Spain and Turkey, and Africans (Maghreb and sub-Saharan Africa). In general, people from these ethnic backgrounds have benefited from integration policies that provide for equal treatment. Naturalization has contributed immensely to integration; even so, some groups are discriminated against, such as the Turkish, Maghreb and African communities, not to mention the offspring of immigrants or else the 'second generation' migrants and the Jewish community. On the whole, French legislation provides the necessary guarantees against discrimination, like the preamble of the Constitution (October 1946), the Constitution of the Fifth Republic (October 1958) and the Declaration of the Rights of Man and of the Citizen (August 1789), whereas the Penal Code protects the equality of all people (Article 187-1) and the Lellouche Law (February 2003) concerns penalties for racist, anti-Semitic and xenophobic acts. Yet some religious issues come into conflict with French legislation, for example, Law No. 2004-228 (March 2004) prohibited in educational institutions, at all levels, the use of symbols and distinctive clothing that could reveal people's religious convictions.

Germany

To combat all forms of discrimination, the German government has established a number of foundations devoted to the struggle against racism and xenophobia, such as the 'Forum against Racism' (1998) and the 'Alliance for Democracy and Tolerance against Extremism and Violence' (2000). Germany has ratified the International Convention on the Elimination of All Forms of Racial Discrimination (1969), the European Charter for Regional or Minority Languages (1998) and the International Labor Organization Convention 111 (1961), but not Protocol No.12 of the Convention for the Protection of Human Rights and Fundamental Freedom. The European Framework Convention for the Protection of Minorities entered into force in 1998. Within Criminal Law, there are the Laws for the Protection of Youth contain prohibitions to spreading materials that are potentially inciting racial hatred buttressed by criminal sanctions; however, in Civil Law there is no special antidiscrimination legislation regarding discrimination on the base of race and ethnic origin. Finally, Article 3.3 of Basic Law and the Federal Constitutional Court provide for respect and equal treatment of all religions, since religion constitutes an integral part of the rights protected by the constitution. However, there has been growing debate with regard to the core values of Christianity and its importance to the German people, given the emphasis put on Islamic symbols, similarly to France.

Greece

The only ethnic minorities that reside in Greece are Turkish, Pomaks and Roma. The European Convention on Human Rights and the International Covenant on Civil and Political Rights are the main legal instruments against discrimination, together with Article 5 (2.a) of the Greek Constitution. As for anti-racism legislation, Law 927/1979 was introduced in 1979, amended by Law 1419/1984 and Law 2910/2001).

Ireland

Religious divisions of Ireland appear to dominate all other forms of discrimination. In this respect, the Irish Constitution (1937) recognized, first and foremost, the role of the Holy Catholic Apostolic and Roman Church in society and, then, the Church of Ireland, the Presbyterian Church, the Methodist Church, the Religious Society of Friends, Jewish congregations and other religions that existed at the time of its adoption. Today, these subcategories have been removed from the Constitution, due to the 1972 referendum.

Italy

Just as immigration is a relatively new aspect of Italian society, equally novel is the issue of antidiscrimination legislation. Legislation related to antidiscrimination, therefore, is scarce, apart from the Italian Constitution (1948). The constitution stipulates that all citizens 'are equal before the law without distinction of gender, race, language, religion, political opinions, personal and social conditions.' However, the legal protection of freedom of religion remains relatively poor. Moreover, the Muslim community maintains no official relationship with the Italian State, which is certainly a cause for concern given the rise of Islamophobia. Regardless, racism in Italian society exists and the ethnic groups that are more likely to fall victims of racial discrimination concern Albanians, Muslims and Africans.

Luxemburg

The population of Luxemburg includes some 38 percent of foreigners, the larger groups regarding Italians and Portuguese. Luxemburg has ratified the European Convention on Human Rights, the European Convention on Human Rights and the International Convention on the Elimination of all forms of Racial Discrimination, the main legal instruments against discrimination together with the Constitution.

Netherlands

In the Netherlands, immigrants mainly originate from Surinam and Morocco. Other ethnic groups concern people from the Dutch Antilles, which is still part of the Kingdom of the Netherlands, Indonesia, Italy, Portugal, Spain, Turkey and Yugoslavia. The Constitution, the International Convention on the Elimination of All Forms of Racial Discrimination and the Criminal Code are the main legal sources that provide guarantees against discrimination. In terms of religion, Article 23 of the constitution includes provisions for the establishment of schools devoted to the needs of distinct religious groups. Considering that Catholic, Protestant and Jewish schools already exist, it is probable that Islamic schools may soon follow, even though it is questionable whether it would contribute to the integration of the Muslim community.

Portugal

Immigration in Portugal is a rather unusual phenomenon, as it includes expatriates who decided to return from France, Germany, Latin America, South Africa and the United States, once democracy was restored in 1974. They were joined by citizens of former colonies such as Angola, Cape Verde, Guinea-Bissau, Mozambique, São Tomé and Princípe, and Timor, with the majority opting to adopt the Portuguese nationality. More recent trends of immigration involve Moldavians, Romanians and Ukrainians. Furthermore, the constitution and the International Convention on the Elimination of All Forms of Racial Discrimination are the main legal instruments against discrimination, while Law No. 134/99 introduced new measures to combat racism.

Spain

The main instrument against discrimination in Spain is the Constitution (1978), which dictates in Article 14 that "Spaniards are equal before the law and may not in any way be discriminated against on account of birth, race, sex, religion, opinion or any other condition or personal or social circumstance." Article 13 stresses that "aliens shall enjoy in Spain the public freedoms guaranteed by this Title, under the terms established by treaties and the law," while Article 9 urges public authorities "to promote conditions that ensure that the freedom and equality of individuals and of the groups that they form are real and effective; to remove obstacles that impede or hamper the fulfillment of such freedom and equality; and to facilitate the participation of all citizens in political, economic, cultural and social life."[11] Like Portugal, Spain is a non-confessional state.

Sweden

The Swedish Constitution and the European Convention on Human Rights are the main legal instruments against discrimination.

United Kingdom

The United Kingdom has antidiscrimination legislation in place since 1965. The Race Relations Act (amended in 200), in particular, urges all public authorities to defend and promote racial equality.

* * *

The ECRI also produces country-by-country reports that evaluate the attempts of the member states of the Council of Europe in addressing the issue of racial discrimination. These reports are primarily concerned with the implementation of EU antidiscrimination legislation intended to promote integration and social cohesion, as well as underline the values of cultural diversity. Building upon previous country reports, all making a number of recommendations with regard to the application and development of relevant legal instruments, the ECRI monitors the success and effectiveness of the member states. For the purpose of this study, it is imperative to focus on the legislation of those countries that have suffered most from racial discrimination in football, namely France, Germany, Italy, Spain and the United Kingdom.

France

According to the third report on France, as of June 2004, Protocol No. 12 to the European Convention on Human Rights and the International Convention on the Protection of the Rights of All Migrant Workers and Members of their Families (July 2003), had not been signed or ratified. The government signed only the Convention on Cyber-crime (November 2001) and its Additional Protocol (January 2003), both on the subject of the criminalization of racist and xenophobic acts committed through computer systems, whereas the law of 16 November

2001, which concerned the fight against racial discrimination on grounds of physical appearance and surname, was strengthened. Despite the legal instruments at the disposal of French authorities, intended to combat racial discrimination, the National Advisory Committee on human rights revealed that in 2003 some 72 percent of all race-related incidents were related to anti-Semitism, even though the number of incidents committed by individuals who associated with the extreme right remained constant.

Germany

According to the third report on Germany, as of December 2003, Protocol No. 12 to the ECHR, the European Convention on the Legal Status of Migrant Workers (1977) and the European Convention on Nationality (February 2002), had all been signed, though not ratified. Germany had also signed the Additional Protocol to the Convention on Cyber-crime (January 2003) and expressed her intension to sign the Revised European Social Charter and the European Convention for the Participation of Foreigners in Public Life at Local Level, though not the provisions of Chapter C that concerned the eligibility and voting rights of foreign residents. Moreover, Germany implemented Article 14 of the International Convention on the Elimination of All Forms of Racial Discrimination in September 2001, which made possible the filing of petitions to the Committee for the Elimination of Racial Discrimination, but failed to sign the International Convention on the Protection of the Rights of All Migrant Workers and Members of their Families. Most importantly, Germany modified the Nationality Law (January 2000) to allow non-citizens to acquire the German nationality through more relaxed legal procedures; yet non-citizens are first required to renounce their former nationality, whereas the children of immigrants born in Germany ought to choose one nationality before they reach the age of twenty-three. In light of these developments, the ECRI asked German authorities to review the issue of dual nationality. It is worthy of note that immigrants from Turkey find it difficult to give up their Turkish nationality, even though some 40 percent of the immigrants that belonged to this ethnic group were naturalized. Nevertheless, ever since the new law was put into effect, naturalizations increased by 56 percent per year. Germany, too, witnessed a sudden increase in racial discrimination, given the impact of Islamophobia—following the tragic events of September 11—and the size of the Muslim community (some 3,200,000 resided in the country). As regards the involvement of the extreme right in racist incidents, the Federal Office for the Defense of the Constitution revealed that although the number of extremists was in decline since 1998, race-related violent acts had increased—more often witnessed in East Germany. Hence, in an attempt to minimize the impact of extreme right groups on integration, the German authorities called the *Nationaldemokratische Partei Deutschlands* unconstitutional. As it happens, the Constitutional Court "blocked the banning of the NPD on grounds that the Government's case rested on the actions of NPD members who had been shown to be agents of the German intelligence service."[12]

Italy

According to the third report on Italy, as of December 2005, racist, xenophobic and anti-Semitic acts were rarely witnessed. Not surprisingly, such incidents were more likely to take place in the northern and central parts of Italy (53 percent and 40 percent respectively and only 7 percent in the south during 2004). It is noteworthy, however, that race-related acts were not always reported or were treated as ordinary criminal offences. Equally significant is the fact that in the post-September 11 period, Muslims in Italy attracted the attention of the media and were often related to Islamic fundamentalism and/or terrorism during public debates. The report also stressed that race-related incidents often occurred during football matches and that the Italian authorities intended to eliminate racism from football by establishing specialized bodies. More precisely, Italy urged the police authorities to cooperate with supporters' organizations, while the Ministry of the Interior and the Italian football governing bodies expressed their determination to impose fines and even suspend football matches.

Spain

According to the third report on Spain, as of June 2005, Article 14 of the Spanish Constitution grants citizens the right to equality before law, yet its application is limited to Spaniards. As far as racism in Spain is concerned, the 11 September 2001 events made Muslim communities, particularly Moroccans, extremely vulnerable to race-related violence; however, the Madrid bombings (March 2004) did not bring about hostility towards the Muslim community, though people from this background were reportedly more frequently discriminated against. The ECRI noted that people in Spain have low levels of awareness about racism and discrimination, while other groups that are usually victimized concern immigrants from North Africa, sub-Saharan Africa and Latin America. The report also made reference to racist incidents during football matches, often related to extremist groups. In general, Spanish football authorities have done little to address the problem effectively. Yet the Spanish football governing bodies signed on March 2005 a Protocol that produced the necessary grounds for the adoption of measures intended to eliminate racism from football, endorsed by the majority of professional clubs. The Observatory for Racism and Violence in Sports, founded on December 2004, is currently monitoring the process of implementation of the Protocol.

United Kingdom

According to the third report on the United Kingdom, as of December 2004, Part III of the Public Order Act (1986) was limited to providing protection against incitement to racial hatred. When the ECRI stressed the need to develop legal instruments concerned with incitement to hatred against religious groups, the government announced plans to introduce such legislation. Scottish legislation, in contrast, includes provisions against both racially and religiously motivated offences, ever since the implementation of the Criminal Justice Act 2003 (June

2003). Likewise, the Criminal Justice (No. 2) Order 2004, in Northern Ireland, introduced provisions that take into account racial and religious motivation, thus equipping courts with the necessary tools to deliver the appropriate judgment. Finally, the Race Relations (Amendment) Act 2000, in England, focuses on eliminating discrimination and promoting equal opportunities. As in the case of other West European countries, one of the mains causes of racial discrimination in Britain is much related to Islamophobia, which is often linked to the public's negative perceptions of Islam, also extended over the issue of terrorism. The phenomenon of anti-Semitism, on the other hand, has also increased in the UK, usually reflecting events in the Middle East. Moreover, ECRI noted an increase in hate crimes against ethnic minority groups in Northern Ireland, principally, due to sectarianism, often involving right-wing extremist groups. The ECRI, nevertheless, also noted that following the interracial riots of 2001 in northern England, the UK developed a strategy concerning community cohesion, which was implemented when the Community Cohesion and Race Equality Strategy was launched in January 2005.

All in all, incitement to racial hatred and discrimination is prohibited in the legislation of all EU-15 member states; however, the legislation of a number of states (e.g., Germany, Greece, Ireland, Luxembourg and the Netherlands) have no provisions for allowing courts to consider cases differently when racial discrimination is identified as a cause and increase the sentence. Notwithstanding the fact that the legal arsenal of the EU-15 seems well equipped on paper, in practice the legal instruments available merely render governments ineffective and their acts insufficient. Hence, twenty-first century Europe is still far from the racism-free environment that EU officials hope to foster. Advocating a Europe founded on cultural diversity and equality surely merits praise, lacking the decisive legal instruments to accomplish the mission is foul play. In football terms, for example, this sort of inefficiency would come close to fielding the best possible XI in Europe without the necessary football kit and have them play on a rough surface. Beyond any shadow of doubt, the performance of the footballers would be severely affected, the more illustrious players included.

FOOTBALL IN THE EU

European bodies have recently developed an intimate relationship with the world of sport, given the overall appeal of athletics to the masses. Apart from the obvious economic gains that would attract the attention of an organization like the Community, the potential contribution of sport to integration adds a wholly different dimension to its very essence. In fact, the Council of Europe stressed that sport is 'an ideal platform for social democracy' and thus, central to the campaign against racial discrimination and xenophobia. With regards to the king of sports, the Council of Europe resolution of 6 December 2001 stipulates that in international football matches involving at least one member state, "Spectators will not be admitted if they are carrying objects that in any way reflect political aims, discrimination, racism or insulting attitudes."[13] Naturally, the European Parliament, too, soon recognized the significance of sport to social inclusion. Members of the European Parliament (MEPs) and the President, Josep Borrell, met on 14 March 2006 to adopt a resolution against racism in football. The resolution received unparalleled support, taking into consideration that a record 423 MEPs were in favor of Europe-wide action. Certainly, the role of Football Against Racism in Europe (FARE) was instrumental in gaining the necessary support of MEPs and, therefore, adopting a resolution that prompts the Union of European Football Associations (UEFA) to endorse those measures deemed crucial to the elimination of racism in football. The president of the European Parliament also stated that football's modern day plague reflected social divisions in Europe, thus the need to combat all forms of racial discrimination and eradicate such an appalling phenomenon from all spheres of life, including football.[14] The declaration, launched on 30 November 2005, praised the contribution of both FARE and UEFA and stated:

"The European Parliament,
– having regard to Rule 116 of its Rules of Procedure,
A. recognising the serious incidents of racism that have occurred in football matches across Europe,
B. whereas one of the objectives pursued by the European Union under Article 13 of the EC Treaty is protection against discrimination based on ethnic origin and nationality,
C. whereas football players, like other workers, have the right to a racism-free working environment, as set down in the case-law of the Court of Justice of the European Communities,
D. whereas football's popularity offers a new opportunity to tackle racism,
1. Strongly condemns all forms of racism at football matches, both on and off the field;
2. Commends the excellent work that organisations such as UEFA and FARE (Football Against Racism in Europe) have done in tackling these problems;
3. Calls on all those with a high profile in football to speak out regularly against racism;
4. Calls on national football associations, leagues, clubs, players' unions and supporters' groups to apply UEFA best practice, such as the UEFA Ten-Point Plan of Action;
5. Calls on UEFA and all other competition organisers in Europe to ensure that referees have the option, according to clear and strict guidelines, of stopping or abandoning matches in the event of serious racist abuse;
6. Calls on UEFA and all other competition organisers in Europe to consider the option of imposing sporting sanctions on national football associations and clubs whose supporters or players commit serious racist offences, including the option of removing persistent offenders from their competitions;

7.   Instructs its President to forward this declaration, together with the names
     of the signatories, to the Council, the Commission, the governments of the
     Member States and UEFA."[15]

Furthermore, MEPs suggested that broadcasting networks interrupt sound or
transmit in black and white, when racist incidents occur, particularly, during the
2006 World Cup in Germany. The proposal came from MEP Claude Moraes,
inspired by the Italian state broadcaster (RAI), which showed football matches
in black and white following a week marred by racist incidents. Regrettably,
neither the European Parliament does, nor UEFA would have the authority to
put into effect such a radical decision.

     However, the king of sports game is not just utilized in terms of integration
or the moral values it promotes. The popularity of the game and its festive character was underlined when the European Commission organized together with
UEFA a football match, on 13 March 2006, between a European all-star team
and Manchester United, at Old Trafford, to celebrate the 50th anniversary of the
European Union. As it happens, the football team that represented the EU comprised three Brazilians, even though Ronaldihno had only just acquired Spanish
citizenship; however, the President of the European Commission, José Manuel
Baroso, emphasized that "It is a positive sign that the EU selection is open to
people who don't have European citizenship."[16] He then added "It is a great way
to mark the 50th Anniversary of the creation of the European Union through the
great game of football. It inspires Europeans in a unique way, through a shared
passion and a language understood by all." In the same context, Michel Platini,
President of UEFA, said "Football brings people together. In a continent so
proud of its cultural diversity, football offers a common language. It helps to
integrate different communities. At its best, our sport conveys some of Europe's
basic values: the rule of law, respect for others, freedom of expression, teamwork and solidarity."[17] Manchester United was selected as the first English football club to take part in European competition half a century ago. For the record,
the home team defeated Europe's XI by four goals to three.

CONCLUSION

     The founding fathers of the European Community aspired to a democratic
environment, derived from human values, for Europe to reemerge from the
ashes of the Second World War, revitalize its economy and prevent future conflicts on the continent. And they were largely successful in laying the foundations for the development of an economic power and maintaining peace among
the member states. However, the arrival of immigrants in Europe gradually
brought about internal divisions that jeopardized the very essence of the Community. The right to mobility might have supported the multicultural identity of
Europe, yet the clashing races highlight the ill-assorted European societies. It

seems that cultural diversity and equality, vital components of European integration, are oftentimes alternated by xenophobia and racial discrimination respectively, consequently promoting extremism. Arguably, the economic, political and social changes that stem from the process of Europeanization account for the divisions that have stained the history of Europe, albeit unintentionally. Ever since the collapse of communism in Central and Eastern Europe and the subsequent rise of nationalism throughout the continent, the extreme right found fertile ground to publicize its radical views and reestablish itself, thus contributing to the resurgence of fascism. In most countries the extreme right enjoys minimal support, though its electoral success in Austria should not be underestimated; however, its mere presence in European politics is probably sufficient to spawn a racist and xenophobic culture.

Evidently, all EU member states mentioned above appear well equipped, theoretically, in terms of the legal instruments available to combat racism. Antidiscrimination legislation, undoubtedly, has the potential to convey meaningful messages to offenders and harness social divisions to produce a well-integrated society. The very concept of the rule of law is fundamental to societies as diverse as Europe's, whereas its practical application has the capacity to contribute to community cohesion, in conjunction with the necessary legal instruments. Nevertheless, forging a cohesive community through vigorous measures, no matter their legal substance, may have adverse effects, since such an approach could shake the foundations of society. Communities comprising ethnic minority groups run the risk of becoming entangled in deep cultural divisions, with irreparable consequences, when the implementation of antidiscrimination legislation is lethargic enough to clearly intimidate those most likely to be racially discriminated against. In this case, legislation must be supported by relevant antiracism campaigns; however, the sheer size of modern European societies constitutes a daunting task. On the contrary, football stadiums may indeed offer a better opportunity to educate people and eradicate racism and xenophobia, particularly, given the spirit of the popular game.

Interestingly, a number of reports devoted to issues like immigration, xenophobia and racial discrimination in the EU, make particular reference to racist incidents at football matches. Obviously, such disturbances are of major concern to European bodies, among them the European Commission, the European Parliament and the European Monitoring Centre on Racism and Xenophobia. While the EUMC collects and, then, disseminates data related to racism and xenophobia with the intention to monitor the behavior of EU member states and their practices, the two supranational institutions—acknowledged for their commitment to further European integration—have had a more pragmatic approach. Their collaboration with the ultimate European football governing body, UEFA, has already contributed to the campaign against racism; nonetheless, their mission is far from accomplished. Although the collective endeavors of all pertinent actors certainly merit credit, they may confront an intricate situation. Given that racism in football is, more often than not, considered as a reflection of social divisions—a phenomenon that has its roots in society—clubs may, therefore, question the association of racial discrimination to football and their anticipated involvement in anti-racism campaigns. Even the prospect of clubs delivering information in connection with offenders or racist incidents, as a general rule, lacks credibility, since most football clubs would strive to escape the 'racist' label. Hence, to rid football of racism surely entails the irrefutable commitment of all interested parties, anyway involved in the game, to take action in concert with the only purpose of combating racism decisively and effectively.

Notes

1. Council of Europe, Parliamentary Assembly, Resolution 1345 (2003), *Racist, xenophobic and intolerant discourse in politics*.

2. Council of Europe, Parliamentary Assembly, Resolution 1344 (2003), *Threat posed to democracy by extremist parties and movements in Europe*.

3. Council of Europe, Parliamentary Assembly, Doc. 10766, *Combating the resurrection of nazi ideology*, Rapporteur: Mr Mikhail Margelov, Russian Federation, European Democrat Group (Political Affairs Committee, 19 December 2005).

4. Isabelle Chopin and Jan Niessen, eds., *Combating Racial and Ethnic Discrimination: Taking the European legislative Agenda Further* (Commission for Racial Equality, Migration Policy Group, Brussels/London, March 2002), 8.

5. Chopin and Niessen, eds., "Combating Racial and Ethnic Discrimination: Taking the European legislative Agenda Further," 11.

6. Chopin and Niessen, eds., "Combating Racial and Ethnic Discrimination: Taking the European legislative Agenda Further," 12.

7. Chopin and Niessen, eds., "Combating Racial and Ethnic Discrimination: Taking the European legislative Agenda Further," 14.

8. Chopin and Niessen, eds., "Combating Racial and Ethnic Discrimination: Taking the European legislative Agenda Further," 16.

9. Mary Coussey, *Tackling racial equality: international comparisons*, Home Office Research Study 238 (Home Office Research, Development and Statistics Directorate, April 2002), vii.

10. Coussey, "Tackling racial equality: international comparisons," 41.

11. Lorenzo Cachón, "Spain," in *The implementation of European anti-discrimination legislation: work in progress, The implementation of the Racial Equality Directive (2000/43/EC) and the Employment Equality Directive (2000/78/EC) as it relates to religion and belief in 15 EU Member States*, Isabelle Chopin, Janet Cormack and Jan Niessen eds., European Commission against Racism and Intolerance (Migration Policy Group, December 2004), 74.

12. European Commission against Racism and Intolerance, CRI (2004) 23, Third Report on Germany, Adopted on 5 December 2003, Strasbourg, 8 June 2004, 32.

13. Council of Europe, *concerning a handbook with recommendations for international police cooperation and measures to prevent and control violence and disturbances in connection with football matches with an international dimension, in which at least*

one Member State is involved, resolution of 6 December 2001 (Official Journal of the European Communities, 24.1.2002), 23.

14. Kick It Out, "Euro MP's join call for action to tackle racism," <http://www.kickitout.org> (13 Mar. 2006).

15. European Parliament, Tackling racism in football, Written declaration of the European Parliament on tackling racism in football (Texts adopted at the sitting of 14 March 2006), 87.

16. Filipe Rufino, "EU kicks off 50th birthday with football match," <http://www.eupolitix.com/EN/News/200703/94aab8f8-da04-4a0c-bf89-f7144387d10e.htm>(12 Mar. 2007).

17. European Commission press release IP-07-313, *Celebration Match: 50 Years in Europe & 50 Years of Europe* (Brussels, 12 March 2007), 1.

Chapter Eight

Conclusion

Looking at a map of Europe may inspire any traveler for it is a continent rich in history and culture, with marvelous architecture and picturesque landscapes. From the ancient Greek and Roman civilizations to modern day, Europe has been in a constant state of flux, which almost certainly accounts for the diversity of the continent. Hence, it is no coincidence that social scientists consider Europe as a vast and well-equipped laboratory, which enables them to conduct exhaustive investigations regardless their subject matter. Europe is an amalgamation of distinct communities with inherently entrenched features that compose a remarkable setting. Above all, it is a mosaic of nations, a medley of races that had to learn how to peacefully coexist with one another, at least, for the purpose of setting up and sustaining the supranational structure that is the European Union. The experiment has been quite successful, but old rivalries have not yet subsided. European Union citizenship is certainly not a panacea, since color, ethnicity and culture persist in maintaining divisions of all forms in society, thus producing the necessary grounds for intolerance to mushroom. It is acknowledged, widely so, that segregation only generates exclusion and discrimination, therefore, racism in European societies comes just about 'naturally.' However, racism in sport is a wholly different matter.

While the game of football is susceptible of alterations (tactical, technical or otherwise), the core principles of the sport dictate that there is no room for discrimination. Sadly, racism has not only infiltrated the world of football, it spread as quickly as an epidemic would, thus condemning the popular game to disparagement and hardship. Racist chants have subjected players and spectators alike to an incongruous cacophony, whereas race-related incidents clearly demonstrate the wickedness of the unprincipled and those who failed to acclimatize to the novel cultural, economic, political and social realities that characterize modern Europe. Although any one of two clubs playing each other may as easily win, draw or lose the match, football can only hope for one result in its endeavor to eliminate racism. Nevertheless, the prospect of defeating racial discrimination is all but gloomy, given that the vast majority of football fans are interested in the game alone and do not share disturbing views. As a matter of fact, football—

by means of its popularity and appeal—has weathered the embarrassment and even thrived on it, sending a powerful message to all envious at heart. Yet it is fundamental that all pertinent actors continue to campaign against racism to facilitate the smooth development of the game.

Racism is no ordinary opponent, certainly not a negligible one. Fascist and communist regimes tolerated discrimination and even encouraged it. Religion exploited the game to emphasize divisions in society and nationalism embraced it to maintain what is often an epic gap between distinct ethnic communities. As a consequence, spectators from ethnic minority backgrounds were physically abused, most likely discouraging them from ever attending a football match again, whereas players have been severely degraded during match-day, thus affecting both their overall performance on the field and their perceptions of the crowd that, supposedly, congregated to applaud their footballing skills and support their club with fervor. Football might have been, in a sense, the very first immigrant in its history, as it traveled the world over mixing with different cultures to allow room for expansion and inviting people from distinct backgrounds to play the game, but certainly succeeded in achieving wide support and recognition. In contrast, today's immigrants, the players in football terms, strive to gain approval or convince their critics of their abilities. Still, charming a football crowd and pledging commitment to the club they play for, so that all players, irrespective of color, religion or ethnicity, relish support from their fans should not prove an arduous task. Displaying their football skills and contributing to the club's success in general, is often deemed sufficient for players to become idolized and earn the necessary respect. For all its obscurity, this particular aspect of racism in football is, theoretically, the least complex to address effectively and conclusively.

Institutional racism, on the other hand, is a far more controversial issue. The promotion of non-whites to the higher echelons of football, whether in managerial or administrative positions, is more often than not hindered by solid walls and glass ceilings. Black players, in particular, often express their frustration for not receiving the attention they deserve, as far as success during their football careers is concerned, given their limited presence—if not exclusion—from non-playing positions. Taking into account the case of England, it is evident that institutional racism epitomizes the grave threat posed by discrimination. The issue of underrepresentation exempted, notwithstanding the magnitude of this matter too, implications pertaining to the perceived lack of organizational skills of all but the whites is shocking enough to shake the foundations of the popular game. Put it simply, that some football players are good for running after a ball, but not managing a club or being an integral part of the game's governing bodies, is undoubtedly beyond comprehension. This dimension of racism, unlike the one discussed earlier, is far more distressing. On this occasion, emphasis is put on human characteristics denoting intelligence and proficiency, rather than biological factors, thus attacking the dignity of all those unable to claim white, European, ancestry. To an extent, this lack of confidence in potential non-white managers and administrators may also reflect the incredibly low levels of participation from ethnic minority communities in football, even though this absurd phenomenon is best attributed to other noninstitutional causes.

European football has claimed unparalleled success at club and national level, therefore, maintaining a high degree of popular interest in football competitions that is followed by an ever-increasing attendance at football matches. However, the color of spectators, and probably that of the game too, remains predominantly white. People from ethnic minority background are, indeed, a rarity today on the terraces, not that they ever enjoyed much higher numbers. Their virtual absence from football stadiums across Europe could only be explained through a long process of intimidation, considering the hostile environment that the activities of groups inclined to the extreme right generated. The small number of individuals that belonged to ethnic minority groups were soon forced to reconsider their interest in football, since the abuse that those football fans suffered during match-days every so often exceeded the 'norm' or else the kind of degradation that football players from a similar background had to endure. Regrettably, those few courageous fans were not only physically abused on the terraces, they were also racially discriminated against in the immediate surroundings of the football stadiums, taking into account the fact that more than a few clubs are based in areas heavily populated by ethnic communities. Under these conditions, it is no surprise that ethnic minority groups resist the desire to take part, at any level, in the beautiful game.

Naturally, the role of anti-racism organizations devoted to football, the impact of both the European Union, as a single political entity, and its member states, and the contribution of football's governing bodies, notably FIFA, UEFA and their affiliated members, is of paramount significance. The necessary cooperation of all pertinent actors in organizing pan-European anti-racism campaigns in conjunction with the implementation of related antidiscrimination legislation, are all indispensable ingredients of the eradicating-racism-from-football recipe. There is much evidence to confirm that their collaboration is well under way, as well as to suggest that this unique partnership has already produced results. Nevertheless, racial discrimination in football continues to distort the decent image of the popular game, therefore, still commanding the attention of all those anyhow involved in the sport. As one might expect, only their concerted action will achieve in defeating the grave threat that has jeopardized football's integrity in a decisive manner. Unless racism in football is not a recently formed a threat as is assumed, but an ominous foe that never ceased to exist. Perhaps, racism in football was so deviously concealed that any endeavor to address it in effect was merely destined to failure.

Indeed, football's governing bodies, players and fans, all became aware of the presence of racial discrimination in the game during the mid-1990s, when the football-related anti-racism organizations that had only just come to life brought the issue to the attention of the authorities. However, it is widely acknowledged that racism was present in football during the 1970s and 1980s as well. At the same time, nevertheless, hooliganism was of major concern to Europeans, thus keeping authorities everywhere engrossed in violence and disorder in and around football stadiums. It is quite possible that hooliganism cast a shadow over racism, thus deceiving FIFA, UEFA and the national football associations. Particularly since ignoring racist incidents almost made sense, in view of the manifold issues that stemmed from hooliganism. Any narrow-minded football official would most probably agree that a few insults in racist language now and then are harmless enough to take no notice of, unlike the more 'physical' hooliganism. What's more, it appears that racist incidents were often mistaken for hooligans' acts, in which case the authorities' lack of response to racially aggravated offences is, perhaps, commonsensical. In contrast, racial discrimination is nowadays treated more efficiently, principally, due to its evident capacity to strike at the foundations of multicultural societies. Hence, it is crucial that all pertinent actors realize that racism in football requires their undivided attention and resolve or else the beautiful game will never succeed in restoring its status, even though anti-racism campaigns have already produced encouraging results.

As it happens, football and education share some vital features, as regards their impact on community cohesion and integration. Just as sport has the capacity to promote integration and bridge the apparent gap that separates people from different cultural backgrounds or ethnic groups, education serves the purpose of enlightening people and raising awareness about racial discrimination, by emphasizing the distinctive qualities of cultural diversity. Manifestly, a combination of antidiscrimination legislation, anti-racism campaigns and relevant disciplinary measures may have already produced the desired effects, however, it is definite that education constitutes a significant partner in the campaign against racism, taking into account the fact that educational schemes can only strengthen the nature and scope of any such activities. In fact, quite a number of anti-racism organizations devoted to the sport have successfully mixed football with education, thus providing youngsters with the opportunity to learn that all humans are equal, while having fun at the same time. With no doubt, educating football fans about the merits of multiculturalism is, indeed, a first concrete step toward eradicating racism from football, but much more is anticipated from the same direction. Given that racism is a societal problem, the essence of education will be fully realized once it addresses effectively people of all ages and backgrounds. It is imperative that education is employed, therefore, to counteract the subversive influence of racial discrimination in society, rather than depending solely on national and football's authorities. Besides, the same threat that currently undermines the image of football, also questions key ideas that education endeavors to promote, such as ethical principles, moral values and respect. As a consequence, it is fundamental that football and education form a common, formidable, front, aiming at eliminating racism once and for all.

Yet the most sinister aspect of racial discrimination is people denying that racism exists. It may well be a defense mechanism to assure oneself that all parts of society are in order and fit perfectly well, nevertheless, this polemic is utterly unethical and serves only those that turn a blind eye to an alarming phenomenon. Undoubtedly, to deny that racism exists in football is scandalous enough to encourage the amplification of the problem, if racist offenders interpret the response of authorities as lacking in character and determination. This is precisely the case, more or less, in countries like Cyprus, Scotland and Spain, as well as in several Eastern European nations. Taking seriously into account that no society even comes close to utopia, it may be sound to argue that discrimination of all forms will persist for as long as it feeds on intolerance and, especially, ignorance.

As a final remark, contemplating the likely opposition from some readers to the occasional use of judgmental language and emotional adjectives, it is necessary to make known our intent. While any reader would identify with the critical position that is being advanced, as regards racism and intolerance in European football, strong language—as already illustrated in previous chapters, though from a much different perspective—is more often than not purposeful. The comment on Jean-Marie Le Pen in chapter 6 or the one succinctly describing Paolo Di Canio's attitude in chapter 4, for example, serve one particular cause alone. Such rhetoric simply reflects the need to remind the reader, as well as emphasize, that racist speech and acts are beyond any shadow of doubt shocking and shameful. Racism and intolerance are two phenomena not to be taken lightly; they should be publicly condemned instead. In this respect, it is a moral obligation to combat discrimination of all forms and promote a more cultured sense of identity within the one race that is humans.

APPENDIX

ECRI DECLARATION ON THE USE OF RACIST, ANTI-SEMITIC AND XENOPHOBIC ELEMENTS IN POLITICAL DISCOURSE
(adopted on 17 March 2005)

The European Commission against Racism and Intolerance (ECRI), being firmly convinced that tolerance and pluralism are at the foundation of genuinely democratic societies and that diversity considerably enriches these societies:
— Condemns the use of racist, anti-Semitic and xenophobic elements in political discourse
— Stresses that such discourse is ethically unacceptable
— Recalls Europe's history, which shows that political discourse that promotes religious, ethnic or cultural prejudice and hatred considerably threatens social peace and political stability and inevitably leads to suffering for entire populations
— Is alarmed at the consequences that this type of discourse is having on the general climate of public opinion in Europe
— Is deeply concerned that the use of racist, antisemitic and xenophobic political discourse is no longer confined to extremist political parties, but is increasingly infecting mainstream political parties, at the risk of legitimising and trivialising this type of discourse
— Notes with serious concern that this type of discourse conveys prejudices and stereotypes in respect of non-citizens and minority groups and strengthens the racist and xenophobic content of debates on immigration and asylum
— Notes with serious concern that this type of discourse often conveys a distorted image of Islam, intended to portray this religion as a threat, and that antisemitism continues to be encouraged, openly or in a coded manner, by certain political leaders and parties. ECRI deplores the fact that, as a result of the use of racist, antisemitic and xenophobic political discourse:
— Ill considered measures which impact disproportionately on particular groups or affect the latter's effective enjoyment of human rights are being adopted
— The long-term cohesion of society is damaged
— Racial discrimination gains ground
— Racist violence is encouraged.
Faced with this situation, ECRI stresses that political parties can play an essential role in combating racism, by shaping and guiding public opinion in a positive fashion.
It suggests the following practical measures:
— Self-regulatory measures, which can be taken by political parties or national parliaments
— The signature and implementation by European political parties of the Charter of European Political Parties for a Non-Racist Society which encourages a responsible attitude towards problems of racism, whether it concerns the actual organisation of the parties, or their activities in the political arena
— Effective implementation of criminal law provisions against racist offences (including those establishing racist motivation as an aggravating circumstance) and racial discrimination, which are applicable to all individuals
— The adoption and implementation of provisions penalising the leadership of any group that promotes racism, as well as support for such groups and participation in their activities

— The establishment of an obligation to suppress public financing of organisations which promote racism, including public financing of political parties ECRI calls on political parties to formulate a clear political message in favour of diversity in European societies. ECRI calls above all for courageous and effective political leadership, which respects and promotes human rights.

CHARTER OF EUROPEAN POLITICAL PARTIES FOR A NON-RACIST SOCIETY
(Utrecht, 28 February 1998)

We, the democratic political parties of Europe,

Having regard to the international human rights instruments signed and ratified by our European Union Member States, in particular to the United Nations Convention on the Elimination of All Forms of Racial Discrimination,

Having regard to article 1 of this Convention, which defines racial discrimination as ". . . any distinction, exclusion, restriction or preference based on race, colour, descent or national or ethnic origin which has the purpose or effect of nullifying or impairing the recognition, enjoyment or exercise on an equal footing of human rights and fundamental freedoms in the political, economic, social, cultural of any other field of public life . . .",

Having regard to the preamble to the Single European Act in which the Member States of the European Community declare to work together to promote democracy on the basis of the fundamental rights recognised in the constitutions and laws of the Member States, in the European Convention for the Protection of Human Rights and Fundamental Freedoms and the European Social Charter,

Having regard to the Treaty of Amsterdam which enables the European Community to ". . . take appropriate action to combat discrimination based on . . . racial or ethnic origin, religion or belief . . ." and facilitates police and judicial cooperation in the framework of the European Union in preventing and combating racism and xenophobia,

Recognising that the fundamental rights as enshrined in the international human rights instruments signed and ratified by the EU member states include the right to free and uninhibited political speech and debate,

Mindful that according to these same international human rights instruments one's political freedoms are not absolute in view of the equally fundamental right to be protected against racial discrimination and that therefore political freedoms cannot be allowed to be abused to exploit, cause or initiate prejudice on the grounds of race, colour, ethnic origin or nationality or for the purpose of seeking to gain the sympathy of the electorate for prejudice on such grounds,

Being aware of the special tasks and responsibilities of political parties as actors in a democratic political process, defending, articulating and bearing witness to the basic principles of a democratic society; providing a platform for discussion on issues where there may be differences of opinion, integrating different views into the process of political decision making, thereby enabling society to solve conflicts of interest and of opinion between various social groups through dialogue rather than through opting out and conflict; selecting representatives at various levels for active participation in the political process,

Convinced that free use of one's political rights can and must go hand in hand with firmly upholding the principle of non-discrimination and is inherent in the democratic process itself,

Being convinced furthermore that representation of ethnic minority groups in the political process is properly an integral part of the democratic process, since political parties are or should strive to be a reflection of society,

Commit ourselves to adhere to the following specific principles of good practice:

— To defend basic human rights and democratic principles and to reject all forms of racist violence, incitement to racial hatred and harassment and any form of racial discrimination.

— To refuse to display, to publish or to have published, to distribute or to endorse in any way views and positions which stir up or invite, or may reason-able be expected to stir up or to invite prejudices, hostility or division between people of different ethnic or national origins or religious beliefs, and to deal firmly with any racist sentiments and behaviour within its own ranks.

— To deal responsibly and fairly with sensitive topics relating to such groups and to avoid their stigmatization.

— To refrain from any form of political alliance or cooperation at all levels with any political party, which incites or attempts to stir up racial or ethnic prejudices and racial hatred.

— To strive for the fair representation of the above mentioned groups at all levels of the parties with a special responsibility for the party leadership to stimulate and support the recruitment of candidates from these groups for political functions as well as membership,

And further pledge to take appropriate action to ensure that all persons who work for or associate themselves in any way with any of our election campaigns or other activities will be aware of and at all times act in accordance with the above principles.

ECRI GENERAL POLICY RECOMMENDATION No. 8,
ON COMBATING RACISM WHILE FIGHTING TERRORISM

The European Commission against Racism and Intolerance:

Having regard to the European Convention on Human Rights, and in particular to its Article 14;

Having regard to Protocol N° 12 to the European Convention on Human Rights;

Having regard to the International Covenant on Civil and Political Rights, and in particular to its Articles 2, 4 (1), 20 (2) and 26;

Having regard to the Convention relating to the Status of Refugees and the Protocol relating to the Status of Refugees;

Having regard to the Guidelines of the Committee of Ministers of the Council of Europe on human rights and the fight against terrorism;

Recalling the Declaration adopted by ECRI at its 26th plenary meeting (Strasbourg 11-14 December 2001);

Recalling ECRI General Policy Recommendation No.7 on national legislation to combat racism and racial discrimination and ECRI General Policy Recommendation No.5 on combating intolerance and discrimination against Muslims;

Recalling the Convention on cyber-crime and its additional Protocol concerning the criminalisation of acts of a racist and xenophobic nature committed through computer systems as well as ECRI General Policy Recommendation N° 6 on combating the dissemination of racist, xenophobic and anti-Semitic material via the Internet;

Recalling the European Convention on the Suppression of Terrorism, the Protocol amending the European Convention on the Suppression of Terrorism and other international instruments against terrorism, notably those adopted in the framework of the United Nations;

Firmly condemning terrorism, which is an extreme form of intolerance;

Stressing that terrorism is incompatible with and threatens the values of freedom, democracy, justice, the rule of law and human rights, particularly the right to life;

Considering that it is therefore the duty of the State to fight against terrorism;

Stressing that the response to the threat of terrorism should not itself encroach upon the very values of freedom, democracy, justice, the rule of law, human rights and humanitarian law that it aims to safeguard, nor should it in any way weaken the protection and promotion of these values;

Stressing in particular that the fight against terrorism should not become a pretext under which racism, racial discrimination and intolerance are allowed to flourish;

Stressing in this respect the responsibility of the State not only to abstain from actions directly or indirectly conducive to racism, racial discrimination and intolerance, but also to ensure a firm reaction of public institutions, including both preventive and repressive measures, to cases where racism, racial discrimination and intolerance result from the actions of individuals and organisations;

Noting that the fight against terrorism engaged by the member States of the Council of Europe since the events of 11 September 2001 has in some cases resulted in the adoption of directly or indirectly discriminatory legislation or regulations, notably on grounds of nationality, national or ethnic origin and religion and, more often, in discriminatory practices by public authorities;

Noting that terrorist acts, and, in some cases, the fight against terrorism have also resulted in increased levels of racist prejudice and racial discrimination by individuals and organisations;

Stressing in this context the particular responsibility of political parties, opinion leaders and the media not to resort to racist or racially discriminatory activities or expressions;

Noting that, as a result of the fight against terrorism engaged since the events of 11 September 2001, certain groups of persons, notably Arabs, Jews, Muslims, certain asylum seekers, refugees and immigrants, certain visible minorities and persons perceived as belonging to such groups, have become particularly vulnerable to racism and/or to racial discrimination across many fields of public life including education, employment, housing, access to goods and services, access to public places and freedom of movement;

Noting the increasing difficulties experienced by asylum seekers in accessing the asylum procedures of the member States of the Council of Europe and the progressive erosion of refugee protection as a result of restrictive legal measures and practices connected with the fight against terrorism;

Stressing the responsibility of the member States of the Council of Europe to ensure that the fight against terrorism does not have a negative impact on any minority group;

Recalling the pressing need for States to favour integration of their diverse populations as a mutual process that can help to prevent the racist or racially discriminatory response of society to the climate generated by the fight against terrorism;

Convinced that dialogue, including on culture and religion, between the different segments of society, as well as education in diversity contribute to combating racism while fighting terrorism;

Convinced that thorough respect of human rights, including the right to be free from racism and racial discrimination, can prevent situations in which terrorism may gain ground;

Recommends to the governments of member States:

- to take all adequate measures, especially through international co-operation, to fight against terrorism as an extreme form of intolerance in full conformity with international human rights law, and to support the victims of terrorism and to show solidarity towards the States that are targets of terrorism;

- to review legislation and regulations adopted in connection with the fight against terrorism to ensure that these do not discriminate directly or indirectly against persons or groups of persons, notably on grounds of "race", colour, language, religion, nationality or national or ethnic origin, and to abrogate any such discriminatory legislation;

- to refrain from adopting new legislation and regulations in connection with the fight against terrorism that discriminate directly or indirectly against persons or groups of persons, notably on grounds of "race", colour, language, religion, nationality or national or ethnic origin;

- to ensure that legislation and regulations, including legislation and regulations adopted in connection with the fight against terrorism, are implemented at national and local levels in a manner that does not discriminate against persons or groups of persons, notably on grounds of actual or supposed "race", colour, language, religion, nationality, national or ethnic origin;

- to pay particular attention to guaranteeing in a non discriminatory way the freedoms of association, expression, religion and movement and to ensuring that no discrimination ensues from legislation and regulations—or their implementation—notably governing the following areas:

- checks carried out by law enforcement officials within the countries and by border control personnel

- administrative and pre-trial detention
- conditions of detention
- fair trial, criminal procedure
- protection of personal data
- protection of private and family life
- expulsion, extradition, deportation and the principle of *non-refoulement*
- issuing of visas
- residence and work permits and family reunification
- acquisition and revocation of citizenship;

- to ensure that their national legislation expressly includes the right not to be subject to racial discrimination among the rights from which no derogation may be made even in time of emergency;

- to ensure that the right to seek asylum and the principle of *non-refoulement* are thoroughly respected in all cases and without discrimination, notably on grounds of country of origin;

- to pay particular attention in this respect to the need to ensure access to the asylum procedure and a fair mechanism for the examination of the claims that safeguards basic procedural rights;

- to ensure that adequate national legislation is in force to combat racism and racial discrimination and that it is effectively implemented, especially in the fields of education, employment, housing, access to goods and services, access to public places and freedom of movement;

- to ensure that adequate national legislation is in force to combat racially motivated crimes, racist expression and racist organisations and that it is effectively implemented;

- to draw inspiration, in the context of ensuring that legislation in the areas mentioned above is adequate, from ECRI General Policy Recommendation No.7 on national legislation to combat racism and racial discrimination;

- to ensure that relevant national legislation applies also to racist offences committed via the Internet and to prosecute those responsible for these kinds of offences;

- to ensure the existence and functioning of an independent specialised body to combat racism and racial discrimination competent, *inter alia*, in assisting victims in bringing complaints of racism and racial discrimination that may arise as a result of the fight against terrorism;

- to encourage debate within the media profession on the image that they convey of minority groups in connection with the fight against terrorism and on the particular responsibility of the media professions, in this connection, to avoid perpetuating prejudices and spreading biased information;

- to support the positive role the media can play in promoting mutual respect and countering racist stereotypes and prejudices;

- to encourage integration of their diverse populations as a mutual process and ensure equal rights and opportunities for all individuals;

- to introduce into the school curricula, at all levels, education in diversity and on the need to combat intolerance, racist stereotypes and prejudices, and raise the awareness of public officials and the general public on these subjects;

- to support dialogue and promote joint activities, including on culture and religion, among the different segments of society on the local and national levels in order to counter racist stereotypes and prejudices.

ECRI GENERAL POLICY RECOMMENDATION NO. 9,
ON THE FIGHT AGAINST ANTISEMITISM

The European Commission against Racism and Intolerance (ECRI):

Having regard to Article 14 of the European Convention on Human Rights;

Having regard to Protocol No. 12 to the European Convention on Human Rights, which contains a general clause prohibiting discrimination;

Having regard to the case law of the European Court of Human Rights and recalling that the Court held that disputing the existence of crimes against humanity committed under the National-Socialist regime was one of the most severe forms of racial defamation and of incitement to hatred of Jews and that the denial of such crimes against humanity and the justification of a pro-Nazi policy could not be allowed to enjoy the protection afforded by Article 10 of the European Convention on Human Rights;

Having regard to the Additional Protocol to the Convention on Cyber-crime concerning criminalization of acts of a racist or xenophobic nature committed through computer systems;

Recalling ECRI's General Policy Recommendation No. 1 on combating racism, xenophobia, anti-Semitism and intolerance and ECRI's General Policy Recommendation No. 2 on specialised bodies to combat racism, xenophobia, antisemitism and intolerance at national level;

Recalling also ECRI's General Policy Recommendation No. 7 on national legislation to combat racism and racial discrimination, which contains the key elements of appropriate legal measures in combating racism and racial discrimination effectively;

Bearing in mind the Declaration of Concern and Intent on "Antisemitism in Europe today" adopted on 27 March 2000 by the participants in the Strasbourg "Consultation on Antisemitism in Europe today", convened by the Secretary General of the Council of Europe;

Having regard to Recommendation (2001) 15 of the Committee of Ministers to member States on history teaching in twenty-first century Europe, which was confirmed by Ministers of Education at the ministerial seminar held in Strasbourg in October 2002;

Recalling the principles contained in the Charter of European political parties for a non-racist society;

Taking note of the conclusions of the OSCE Conferences on Antisemitism held in Vienna on 19-20 June 2003 and in Berlin on 28-29 April 2004;

Recalling the work of the European Union in combating racism and discrimination and taking note of the conclusions of the seminar on "Europe against antisemitism, for a Union of Diversity" organised in Brussels on 19 February 2004;

Recalling that the legacy of Europe's history is a duty to remember the past by remaining vigilant and actively opposing any manifestations of racism, xenophobia, antisemitism and intolerance;

Paying homage to the memory of the victims of the systematic persecution and extermination of Jews in the Shoah, as well as of the other victims of policies of racist persecution and extermination during the Second World War;

Paying homage to the Jewish victims of killings and systematic persecution under totalitarian regimes following the Second World War, as well as other victims of these policies;

Stressing in this respect that the Council of Europe was precisely founded in order to defend and promote common and just values—in particular the protection and promotion of human rights—around which Europe was rebuilt after the horrors of the Second World War;

Recalling that combating racism, xenophobia, antisemitism and intolerance is rooted in and forms part of the protection and promotion of human rights;

Profoundly convinced that combating antisemitism, while requiring actions taking into account its specificities, is an integral and intrinsic component of the fight against racism;

Stressing that antisemitism has persisted for centuries across Europe;

Observing the current increase of antisemitism in many European countries, and stressing that this increase is also characterised by new manifestations of antisemitism;

Noting that these manifestations have often closely followed contemporary world developments such as the situation in the Middle East;

Underlining that these manifestations are not exclusively the actions of marginal or radical groups, but are often mainstream phenomena, including in schools, that are becoming increasingly perceived as commonplace occurrences;

Observing the frequent use of symbols from the Nazi era and references to the Shoah in current manifestations of antisemitism;

Stressing that these manifestations originate in different social groups and different sectors of society;

Observing that the victims of racism and exclusion in some European societies, themselves sometimes become perpetrators of antisemitism;

Noting that in a number of countries, antisemitism, including in its new forms, continues to be promoted, openly or in a coded manner, by some political parties and leaders, including not only extremist parties, but also certain mainstream parties;

Believing that an adequate response to these phenomena can only be developed through the concerted efforts of all relevant actors in European societies, including representatives of different communities, religious leaders, civil society organisations and other key institutions;

Stressing that efforts to counter antisemitism should include the thorough implementation of legal provisions against racism and racial discrimination in respect of all perpetrators and for the benefit of all victims, with special emphasis on the provisions against incitement to racial violence, hatred and discrimination;

Convinced furthermore that these efforts should also include the promotion of dialogue and cooperation between the different segments of society on the local and national levels, including dialogue and cooperation between different cultural, ethnic and religious communities;

Emphasising strongly the role of education in the promotion of tolerance and respect for human rights, thereby against antisemitism;

Recommends that the governments of the member States:

− give a high priority to the fight against antisemitism, taking all necessary measures to combat all of its manifestations, regardless of their origin;

− ensure that actions aimed at countering antisemitism are consistently given their due place amongst actions aimed at countering racism;

− ensure that the fight against antisemitism is carried out at all administrative levels (national, regional, local) and facilitate the involvement of a wide range of actors from different sectors of society (political, legal, economic, social, religious, educational) in these efforts;

− enact legislation aimed at combating antisemitism taking into account ECRI's suggestions in its General Policy Recommendation No. 7 on national legislation to combat racism and racial discrimination;

– ensure that the law provides that, for all criminal offences, racist motivation constitutes an aggravating circumstance, and that such motivation covers antisemitic motivation;
– ensure that criminal law in the field of combating racism covers antisemitism and penalises the following antisemitic acts when committed intentionally:
a. public incitement to violence, hatred or discrimination against a person or a grouping of persons on the grounds of their Jewish identity or origin;
b. public insults and defamation of a person or a grouping of persons on the grounds of their actual or presumed Jewish identity or origin;
c. threats against a person or a grouping of persons on the grounds of their actual or presumed Jewish identity or origin;
d. the public expression, with an anti-Semitic aim, of an ideology which depreciates or denigrates a grouping of persons on the grounds of their Jewish identity or origin;
e. the public denial, trivialisation, justification or condoning of the Shoah;
f. the public denial, trivialisation, justification or condoning, with an antisemitic aim, of crimes of genocide, crimes against humanity or war crimes committed against persons on the grounds of their Jewish identity or origin;
g. the public dissemination or public distribution, or the production or storage aimed at public dissemination or public distribution, with an antisemitic aim, of written, pictorial or other material containing manifestations covered by points a), b), c), d), e), f) above;
h. desecration and profanation, with an antisemitic aim, of Jewish property and monuments;
i. the creation or the leadership of a group which promotes antisemitism; support for such a group (such as providing financing to the group, providing for other material needs, producing or obtaining documents); participation in its activities with the intention of contributing to the offences covered by points a), b), c), d), e), f), g), h) above;
– ensure that criminal legislation covers anti-Semitic crimes committed via the internet, satellite television and other modern means of information and communication;
– ensure that the law provides for an obligation to suppress public financing of organisations, which promote antisemitism, including political parties;
– ensure that the law provides for the possibility of disbanding organisations that promote antisemitism;
– take the appropriate measures to ensure that legislation aimed at preventing and sanctioning antisemitism is effectively implemented;
– offer targeted training to persons involved at all levels of the criminal justice system— police, prosecutors, judges—with a view to increasing knowledge about antisemitic crimes and how such acts can be effectively prosecuted;
– take steps to encourage victims of anti-Semitic acts to come forward with complaints of antisemitic acts, and put in place an effective system of data collection to thoroughly monitor the follow-up given to such complaints;
– establish and support the functioning of an independent specialised body along the lines set out in ECRI's General Policy Recommendation No. 2 on Specialised bodies to combat racism, xenophobia, antisemitism and intolerance at national level, and ensure that the actions carried out by this organ cover all forms of antisemitism;
– introduce anti-racist education into the school curriculum at all levels and in an integrated manner, including content that builds awareness about antisemitism, its occurrences through centuries and the importance of combating its various manifestations, ensuring that teachers are provided with the necessary training;

– promote learning about Jewish history as well as about the positive contribution of Jewish persons, communities and culture to European societies;

– promote learning about the Shoah, and the developments leading up to it, within schools and ensure that teachers are adequately trained in order to address this issue in a manner whereby children also reflect upon current dangers and how the recurrence of such an event can be prevented;

– promote learning and research into the killings and systematic persecution of Jewish and other persons under totalitarian regimes following the Second World War;

– where antisemitic acts take place in a school context, ensure that, through targeted training and materials, school directors, teachers and other personnel are adequately prepared to effectively address this problem;

– encourage debate within the media professions on their role in fighting antisemitism, and on the particular responsibility of media professionals to seek to, in this connection, report on all world events in a manner that avoids perpetuating prejudices;

– support the positive role the media can play in promoting mutual respect and countering antisemitic stereotypes and prejudices;

– support and encourage research projects and independent monitoring of manifestations of antisemitism;

– support the activities of non-governmental organisations, which play an important role in fighting antisemitism, promoting appreciation of diversity, and developing dialogue and common anti-racist actions between different cultural, ethnic and religious communities;

– take the necessary measures to ensure that the freedom of religion is fully guaranteed, and that public institutions make provision in their everyday practice for the reasonable accommodation of cultural and other requirements;

– support dialogue between different religious communities at local and national levels in order to counter racist stereotypes and prejudices, including through providing financing and establishing institutional fora for multi-faith dialogue;

– ensure that religious leaders at all levels avoid fueling antisemitism, and encourage religious leaders to take responsibility for the teachings spread at the grassroots level;

– encourage political actors and opinion leaders to take a firm public stand against antisemitism, regularly speaking out against its various manifestations, including all its contemporary forms, and making clear that antisemitism will not be tolerated.

WRITTEN DECLARATION OF THE EUROPEAN PARLIAMENT ON TACKLING RACISM IN FOOTBALL
Texts adopted at the sitting of Tuesday 14 March 2006

The European Parliament,

–   having regard to Rule 116 of its Rules of Procedure,

A.   recognising the serious incidents of racism that have occurred in football matches across Europe,

B.   whereas one of the objectives pursued by the European Union under Article 13 of the EC Treaty is protection against discrimination based on ethnic origin and nationality,

C.   whereas football players, like other workers, have the right to a racism-free working environment, as set down in the case-law of the Court of Justice of the European Communities,

D.   whereas football's popularity offers a new opportunity to tackle racism,

1.   Strongly condemns all forms of racism at football matches, both on and off the field;

2.   Commends the excellent work that organisations such as UEFA and FARE (Football Against Racism in Europe) have done in tackling these problems;

3.   Calls on all those with a high profile in football to speak out regularly against racism;

4.   Calls on national football associations, leagues, clubs, players' unions and supporters' groups to apply UEFA best practice, such as the UEFA Ten-Point Plan of Action;

5.   Calls on UEFA and all other competition organisers in Europe to ensure that referees have the option, according to clear and strict guidelines, of stopping or abandoning matches in the event of serious racist abuse;

6.   Calls on UEFA and all other competition organisers in Europe to consider the option of imposing sporting sanctions on national football associations and clubs whose supporters or players commit serious racist offences, including the option of removing persistent offenders from their competitions;

7.   Instructs its President to forward this declaration, together with the names of the signatories, to the Council, the Commission, the governments of the Member States and UEFA.

KICK IT OUT
Campaign Action by Clubs

The campaign calls on clubs to take the following steps:
to issue a statement saying that the club will not tolerate racism, spelling out the action it will take against those engaged in indecent or racist chanting. The statement should be printed in all match programmes and displayed permanently and prominently around the ground
make public address announcements condemning racist chanting at matches
make it a condition for season ticket holders that they do not take part in this or other forms of offensive behaviour
take action to prevent the sale of racist literature inside and around the ground
take disciplinary action against players who engage in racial abuse
contact other clubs to make sure they understand the club's policy on racism
encourage a common strategy between stewards and police for dealing with abusive behaviour
remove all racist graffiti from the ground as a matter of urgency
adopt an equal opportunities policy in relation to employment and service provision.

FIFA EXTRAORDINARY CONGRESS
Resolution
(Buenos Aires, 7 July 2001)

The Extraordinary Congress of FIFA, meeting in Buenos Aires on 7 July 2001, according to the Statutes of FIFA, and representing all National Associations and Continental Confederations united in football's world governing body;

having considered the term "racism" in the current context to apply primarily to acts of discrimination based above all, but not exclusively, upon differences between human individuals on the basis of skin colour and ethnic origin;

having noted with deep concern the current infiltration of racist elements into football stadiums and other activities connected with football;

having analysed the worthy efforts taken to combat this unwelcome trend by football administration at various levels (clubs, leagues, national associations, etc.) and by non-governmental organisations in the fight against racism having reiterated the constant need within football and in the community at large for programmes aimed at educating people of all ages and of all social classes (but especially children and young people) about the evils of racism and the benefits of social inclusion;

having acknowledged the need for football administrators and groups to co-operate with governmental authorities at all levels, the police and other civil authorities, educational bodies and others, to take action that is appropriate, forceful and effective, the Extraordinary Congress, following the declaration against racism adopted by the FIFA Executive Committee in March 2000, and following the FIFA Conference Against Racism in Football held in Buenos Aires on 6 July 2001,

requires all persons involved directly or indirectly with the sport of football at all levels and in all countries to join a concerted action to exchange information and experiences in order to combat effectively and conclusively all manifestations of racism within the game, by denouncing and sanctioning all persons indulging in racism in any form;

calls upon all governments and civil authorities at all levels to co-operate fully with the game's authorities and to give unqualified support to these efforts requires football authorities to give greater support to social groupings in introducing educational programmes and establishing a dialogue with known racism offenders for a better understanding of their motives;

requires all organisers of football matches to impose regulations that refuse admission to football grounds to any persons indulging in, or suspected of intending to indulge in acts of racism or related violence, and to ban all articles that convey any message of a racist content in words or in symbols;

requires competition organisers to appoint observers for sensitive matches in order to monitor and report manifestations of racism in any form;

requires stadium stewards to co-operate with police forces to act swiftly and decisively to apprehend and to eject immediately any persons violating such regulations;

requires match organisers to take the necessary effective measures to ban any such offenders from attending further matches;

requires football fans to support organisers and civil authorities in identifying and removing racist elements from spectator areas;

requires clubs to foster a spirit of social inclusion among players by ensuring that they treat team-mates, opponents, referees, officials, spectators and all other persons, whether connected with the game or not, with respect and without discrimination as to their ethnic origin;

requires team coaches and club officials to impose effective punishments upon players in their charge who indulge in or condone any form of racist behaviour, either on the field of play or in their public or private lives;

requires all football bodies at all levels to ensure racial equality in the employment, appointment and election of individuals in all areas of activity and to work with ethnic groups to involve them more closely in football activities;

requires referees to be more vigilant with regard to gestures or verbal offences of a racist nature between players and/or coaches and/or the public, and to take immediate action to punish offenders and to report such incidents clearly and fully;

requires the media to strongly condemn all acts of racist behaviour or declarations by any persons or groups, and to refrain from reporting such behaviour or declarations in a manner that may serve to provoke confrontation, and calls upon football websites (including those of clubs and national associations) to incorporate prominent anti-racism messages on their home-pages;

requires all members of the worldwide football community to take every opportunity to maximise the social impact of football to encourage social inclusion and the elimination of racism in society;

requires all Confederations to monitor all activities relating to the fight against racism in football and to report regularly to the FIFA Executive Committee.

FACTBOX ON FARE

1996 Four football-based anti-racist projects, in Sheffield, London, Bologna and Dortmund receive European Commission (EC) funding

1997 As part of the "European Year against Racism", various football projects are sponsored by the EC

1999 (February) Establishment of the FARE network and passing of a FARE plan of action in Vienna

2000 (June) Official launch of FARE in the European Parliament in Brussels before the EURO 2000 finals

2001 (April) First FARE Action Week against Racism and Discrimination in European Football with 50 events in 9 countries

2001 (July) FARE representatives speak at the FIFA Conference against Racism in Buenos Aires

2001 (August) UEFA award their charity cheque of 1 Million Swiss Francs to FARE; FARE becomes a member of the UEFA charity portfolio

2002 (April) Second FARE Action Week with 100 events in 17 countries

2002 (October) Third FARE Action Week with more than 300 events in 18 countries

2002 (September) Start of a two-year antidiscrimination project co-funded by the EC

2002 (November) FARE receives the "Free Your Mind Award" at the MTV Europe Music Awards in Barcelona

2003 (March) The conference "Unite against Racism" hosted by Chelsea FC is jointly organized by UEFA, FARE and the English FA

2003 (October) Some 400 initiatives in 24 countries join the 4th FARE Action Week FARE receives the 'Jean Kahn Award' of the European Monitoring Centre on Racism and Xenophobia (EUMC)

2004 (June) FARE at UEFA EURO 2004 in Portugal

2004 (October) With hundreds of initiatives—including all 32 Champions League teams—in 33 European countries the 5th FARE Action Week has been Europe's biggest antiracism campaign in football so far

2005 (April) FARE networking conference in Bratislava

RACIAL EQUALITY STANDARD FOR PROFESSIONAL CLUBS
Awarded by Kick It Out

The Racial Equality Standard for Professional Football Clubs sets out a series of measures in a framework document to encourage and support the development of racial equality practice at professional clubs. Developed by Kick It Out, with the support of football's governing bodies, and from source materials including Sporting Equal's Achieving Racial Equality: A Standard for Sport, the Standard will formalise a club's commitment to ensure spectators, players, managers, and administrative staff can work within an environment free of discrimination, and encourage community accessibility. The Standard is based on three levels of achievement and covers three main areas of activity at each level. Achievement in the three levels of activity will be supported by relevant evidence and verified by an independent accreditation panel.

Preliminary: The club will have demonstrated a commitment to racial equality by producing a written equal opportunities policy and a race equality action plan for all areas of activity. The plan will be monitored. The plan will include an assessment of the club's current supporter base, community development targets and clear guidelines for dealing with abuse. Intermediate: The club will have demonstrated clear improvements in services as a result of monitoring, consulted local ethnic minority communities and implemented its action plan. The club will be able to show clear evidence of the implementation of an equal opportunities policy. Advanced: The club will be an exemplar in the way it encourages the participation of ethnic minorities at all levels, and areas of activity, as employees, supporters and of community outreach.

LIST OF KEY OBJECTIVES—PRELIMINARY LEVEL

STADIUMS AND OUTREACH

Use all available means within the stadium to disseminate the clubs anti-racism stance, including the display of highly visual notices, a perimeter advertising board, regular and varied notices in match-day programmes, and regular and varied public address announcements;

Make it a clear condition for season ticket holders not to engage in racial abuse or harassment;

Ensure a clear policy on reporting, collating and dealing with incidents of racial abuse, chanting or harassment within the stadium;

Publicise, and encourage reporting to, Kick It Out's incident reporting line (0800 169 9414);

Monitor all complaints received of abuse/harassment inside your stadium, action taken to deal with them, and any particular problem issues;

Collect information on the current average number of ethnic minority fans;

Collect information on the numbers of ethnic minority participants in all outreach activities including those of the football in the community programme and Academy/youth development centre;

Hold an anti-racism day of action;

POLICY AND PLANNING

Make a clear public commitment to achieving racial equality at the club;

Develop a racial equality action plan or objectives to work alongside existing strategies, with appropriate targets for achievement;

Develop a written Equal Opportunities Policy with guidelines for action;

Ensure local ethnic minority communities are aware of your stated commitment;

Nominate a senior member of the staff team to take a lead on the development and implementation of racial equality measures at the club;

ADMINISTRATION AND MANAGEMENT

Obtain approval for the racial equality action plan from the Chief Executive Officer or Director;

Obtain approval for Equal Opportunities Policy with delivery proposals;

Collect information on the ethnic origin, age, sex and disability of those involved in all areas of management, coaching, administration and employment at the club (you are not required to include match-day only staff or playing staff under the age of 16);

Assess the race equality training needs of all staff involved in the development, delivery of services and management of your organization;

LIST OF KEY OBJECTIVES—INTERMEDIATE LEVEL

STADIUMS AND OUTREACH

Develop anti-racism resource materials:

Using findings from audit exercise to ensure all services (including ticketing and merchandise) are marketed effectively to groups under-represented on match-days;

Consider using positive images of ethnic minorities in promotional and marketing materials at your club;

Use the participation audit to develop a community development action plan to target any gaps in contact with local ethnic minority communities;

Develop a specific scheme with external partners to target ethnic minority communities;

Hold more detailed anti-racism days of action with more activities:

Develop a rolling training plan to ensure all stewards undertake module 7 of the Stewards Training package (2003);

Promote the use of ethnic minority role models;

POLICY AND PLANNING

Develop a working group of appropriate partners (including representation from ethnic minority groups, and fans) to look at issues of racial equality at your club and to give support to implement the standard;

Set up a consultation process with key partners/stakeholders, including for example ethnic minority staff, fans and local community groups;

Review previous racial equality action plan and set specific, achievable and measurable targets within all programmes:

Promote your club as one that is working to achieve racial equality targets:

ADMINISTRATION AND MANAGEMENT

Collect information on the ethnic origin, age, sex and disability of those involved in match-day roles such as stewards and catering staff;

Review impact of Equal Opportunities Policy;

Consider developing a specific recruitment or training programme to bridge any gaps there may be in representation from ethnic minorities following above and audit of staff at all levels;

Include racial equality objectives in staff job descriptions and work programmes in each area of activity;

Provide racial equality training for key directors, administrative staff, and coaches;

Redress specific problems of under-representation from ethnic minorities in areas of playing and coaching, eg. the development of black coaches, schemes to spot young Asian footballers;

LIST OF KEY OBJECTIVES—ADVANCED LEVEL
STADIUMS AND OUTREACH
Organise detailed anti-racism days of action;
Draw up a plan for ongoing initiatives with ethnic minority communities including representation at community events;
Actively encourage community use of your stadium to ensure familiarity by ethnic minority community groups;
Undertake regular monitoring of number of supporters from ethnic minority communities;
Set targets for the number of ethnic minorities to be attracted to stadiums;
POLICY AND PLANNING
Develop an ongoing review process to ensure all racial equality policies are effectively and regularly reviewed;
Ensure that all staff have received training in racial equality issues;
Publicise and promote your achievements as a club who have made significant gains in taking forward anti-racist policies and practices;
ADMINISTRATION AND MANAGEMENT
Look at ways to encourage/attract people from ethnic minority groups that are under-represented in your club as employees, coaches, in the Academy/ Youth Development Centre, etc;
Provide appropriate support for individuals from ethnic minorities to achieve their full potential within your organization;
Undertake ongoing monitoring of your equal opportunities policy;
ACCREDITATION PROCESS
To gain each level of the Racial Equality Standard. clubs will need to submit a portfolio of evidence to illustrate how they have met the objectives in the three areas of activity.
EXAMPLES OF BEST PRACTICE
Support for clubs from Kick It Out
Kick It Out will provide guidance and support for all professional clubs who are working on the Racial Equality Standard.
A Development Officer has been employed to work with clubs on an on-going basis to help provide ideas about how clubs can meet each of the objectives and examples of good practice from within football and other industries.
Good Practice Guide
An information pack has been designed to accompany each of the three levels of the Standard to help support clubs through the process.
The pack details what evidence can be submitted to meet the objectives and sets out some examples of best practice and suggested methods of working. This may be helpful to clubs to build long-term foundations for sustainable club and community activity.
Clubs will need to record, collate, verify and analyse all evidence to provide an assessment of the achievements and progress they have made.
Valid sources of evidence will include:
• Audit forms/monitoring information
• Publicity materials
• Correspondence with community groups
• Minutes of meetings/consultations
• Correspondence with management
• Photographs of signs/perimeter boards/public signing of charter

The evidence will be submitted to an independent accreditation panel chaired by Lord Herman Ouseley, with members experienced in the field of race and equality, organisational development and sports administration. A panel member will case manage each club during the accreditation process. This will ensure the evidence is independently assessed and additional support requirements are identified. The award is valid for three years in the expectation that clubs will be aspiring to the next level of achievement. If after three years the next level has not been achieved, the club will be asked to re-submit evidence to maintain the existing level. Clubs that are successful will be awarded a kite mark for each level for use on official documents.

UEFA

TO THE MEMBERS OF FIFA
Circular no. 1026
Zurich, 28 March 2006
GS/pmu-mjo
Revision of article 55 of the FIFA Disciplinary Code: Non-discrimination

Dear Sir or Madam,

FIFA has always taken its role in combating discrimination of any kind very seriously. Despite this fact, there has been a surge in discriminating gestures and language at football matches in recent months. At its meeting on 16 and 17 March 2006, the FIFA Executive Committee therefore decided to take vigorous action against this deplorable trend and to impose harsher sanctions than those hitherto pronounced under article 55 of the FIFA Disciplinary Code (FDC).

Article 55, paragraph 1 therefore now stipulates a match suspension of five matches at every level of football as well as a stadium ban and a minimum fine of CHF 20,000 for any act or expression of a discriminatory and/or contemptuous nature. If an official commits such an offence, the fine will be CHF 30,000.

Furthermore, an association or club will be fined CHF 30,000 if any of its supporters display discriminatory banners or behave in a discriminatory or contemptuous manner during a match. If spectators cannot be identified as supporters of one or the other association or club, the host association or club will be sanctioned accordingly. The stadium ban on offending spectators remains at least two years (par. 3).

The new provision in par. 4 stipulates that if any player, official or spectator behaving in a discriminatory or contemptuous manner can be attributed to a certain team, three points will automatically be deducted from that team for the first offence. In the case of a second offence, six points will be deducted, and after a further offence, the team will be relegated. In the case of matches played without points being awarded, the team in question will be disqualified.

The confederations and associations are obliged to incorporate the provisions of this article in their disciplinary code and statutes and to enforce the sanctions stipulated. Any association fails to comply with this article will be excluded from international football for two years (par. 5).

The amended article 55 FDC takes effect immediately and the new, complete wording is enclosed for your information.

You are therefore kindly requested to take note of the amendments and to pass them on to your members. The amendments to article 55 FDC must also be enforced within the association.

Yours faithfully,

FEDERATION INTERNATIONALE
DE FOOTBALL ASSOCIATION
Urs Linsi
General Secretary

FARE ACTION WEEK AGAINST RACISM 2006

Europe/UEFA
17 October 2006:
The "UEFA Champions League", will kick-off the 7th Action Week. Europe's top football stars will help to spread the message too as they stand united against racism. All 32 teams taking part in the UEFA Champions League will show their opposition to racism as part of UEFA's contribution to the FARE Action Week. Activities will include the captains of all the teams wearing Unite Against Racism armbands, player-escort children sporting Unite Against Racism T-shirts, announcements being made to fans in stadiums over the loudspeaker calling for opposition to all forms of racism, and Unite Against Racism adverts being placed in match day programmes as well as the official UEFA Champions League magazine Champions.
17.10., Steaua Bucharest—Real Madrid, Dynamo Kiev—Olympique Lyon, Celtic Glasgow—Benfica Lisbon, Manchester United—FC Copenhagen, CSKA Moscow—Arsenal London, FC Porto—Hamburger SV, RSC Anderlecht—AC Milan, OSC Lille—AEK Athens
18.10., FC Chelsea—FC Barcelona, Werder Bremen—Levski Sofia, Inter Milan—Spartak Moscow, Sporting Lisbon—Bayern Munich, Galatasaray Istanbul—PSV Eindhoven, Girondins Bordeaux—FC Liverpool, Olympiakos Pireaus—AS Roma, Valencia—Schachtjor Donezk

Africa
17 October 2006:
Congo's organisation LISPED (Ligue Sportive pour la Promotion et la defence des droits de l'Homme) presents the Action Week activities (like an interethnic tournament and a meeting with schools) in a Press Conference with media and institutions.
19 October 2006:
First day of Interethnic Tournament organised in Ashaiman (Ghana) by association Ashaiman Against Racism. The participants will be teams from Ghana refugees' camp.
19 October 2006:
LISPED (Ligue Sportive pour la Promotion et la defence des droits de l'Homme) organizes in Kinshasa a tournament among several ethnic groups, volunteer and refugees, to strike public opinion and fight against the discriminations existing in Congo.
20 October 2006:
LISPED (Ligue Sportive pour la Promotion et la defence des droits de l'Homme) organizes in Kinshasa a meeting with the tournament participants where to present FARE activities, the aim is to create an equivalent net in Africa.
21 October 2006:
Second day of Interethnic Tournament organised in Ashaiman (Ghana) by association Ashaiman Against Racism. The participants will be teams from Ghana refugees' camp.
30 October 2006:
For the last Action Week Day LISPED (Ligue Sportive pour la Promotion et la defence des droits de l'Homme) organizes a meeting with kids of several schools, to give an antiracist message to the teams of National Football League.

Armenia
21 October 2006:
The NGO "Youth for Democracy" will run a youth tournament with four teams in Yerevan. All the teams will be mixed (refugees, ethnic minorities and locals). On the following day there will be a video workshop and a discussion with the children and their parents, led by the research centre "Prospectus".

Austria
20 October 2006:
Wiener Sportklubs' fan club "FreundInnen der Friedhofstribüne" will organise the following actions for the third league home match versus Admira II: an auction of the kick-off (with Ute Bock who consults refugees) on www.sportclubplatz.com; the team enters the stadium with banners from FARE and the association of Ute Bock; a tombola and fundraising actions in the stadium; invitation from Ute Bock and her "fosterlings" for the match, talk with the stadium speaker; web banners on www.wienersportclub.com, www.wienersportclubplatz.com, www.friedhofstribuene.at; info desks of the association of Ute Bock; articles about Ute Bocks' projects in the stadium newspaper.
21 October 2006:
The women club "Mädchen und Frauenfußballverein 23" will produce rain jackets with the logos of FARE and Frauenfußballverein. Additionally they will distribute flyers and posters, which broach the issue of racism and sexism within football, during their home match versus Altenmarkt 1b. Before the match will start, they will show a banner with an anti-racist slogan to the spectators.
21 October 2006:
The Austrian national football league "Österreichische Bundesliga" will promote the FARE action week during each match of the 13th round of the T-Mobile Bundesliga (21./22.10.) as well as the 14th round of the Red Zac Erste Liga (27.10.) under the motto: "Show the red card to racism!" All teams and their accompanying children will show red cards to racism in the stadium. Also the adjudicators will get involved and will wear FairPlay logos on their tricots. For the match Red Bull Salzburg versus FK Austria Vienna fans will prepare an anti-racist choreography. The highlight of the stadium actions will be the reading of anti-racist statements by players of each team. Furthermore the anti-racist spot, which was produced by pay-TV station Premiere and the Austrian national football league, by FARE partner "FairPlay-vidc", will be screened on the video screens of the stadiums. FairPlay-vidc will distribute 17.000 fanzines, which were produced in cooperation with the football magazine "ballesterer fm". It contains the statements of fans from Austria, Italy, Spain, France, Denmark, Germany, Czech Republic and Switzerland.
21 October 2006:
Fan club "Blau-Weiss Fans gegen Rassismus" will produce stickers for the regional league home match Blau-Weiß Linz versus Feldkirchen. The players of Blau-Weiß Linz will warm-up in FARE t-shirts and will present an anti-racism banner before the kick-off. Furthermore the fan club will organise in cooperation with the "Österreichisches Dokumentationsarchiv" and the Berlin group "Reihe antifaschistischer Texte" a workshop about rightist extremist codes in Austrian and German fan scenes for fans, supporters and social workers.
21 October 2006:
The amateur clubs "Prater SV" and "SC Triester" will warm-up in anti-racism T-shirts. Both clubs participate since years in the FARE action week.

22 October 2006:
The national women's league club "ASK Erlaa" will show at the matches of all of its teams the red card to racism and will present their new key fobs with the FARE logo. They will also promote their anti-racism matches on posters and in the programme magazine.

22 October 2006:
The recently founded migrants' club "New African Football Academy" will meet the Jewish club "Maccabi Vienna" for a league match. Players of both teams will show the red card to racism. The home team will warm-up in FARE t-shirts and distribute information on FARE and racism within football.

25 October 2006:
The club "FC Wacker Innsbruck" and the fan club "Verrückte Köpfe '91" will organise a closing event for the CD-project "Eine Stadt-Ein Verein: FC Wacker Innsbruck, Eine Halbzeit für Burkina Faso". They will present the documentary "Sold Out" and all facts of the CD project. The invitation will call for asylum seekers, bands and DJs from Africa.

26 October 2006:
The migrants' and fugitive club "FC Sans Papier—Die Bunten" will organise two anti-racism days accompanying their matches versus H-Toron (26.10.) and Vienna International (28.10.). The invitation will call explicitly for people, who are affected by racism and discrimination.

27 October 2006:
The college of higher education "Fachhochschule Kärnten für Soziale Arbeit" will do a project with the second league club FC Kärnten. As a highlight there will be an anti-racism match versus FC Gratkorn in the framework of the FARE AW. Additionally to the actions, which will be done by all second league teams, players of FC Kärnten will warm-up in T-shirts with the slogan "Show the red card to racism!". The club will invite the children of an SOS Kinderdorf for the match. An anti-racism workshop for them will be prepared and afterwards they will accompany the players to the football ground before the kick-off. Furthermore choreography by the fan club "Amigos" will be shown.

28 October 2006:
The amateur club "ASV Roter Stern Innsbruck" will organise an indoor match for 16 clubs (African, Serbian, Croatian, Bosnian and Latin American communities, fan clubs from FC Tirol).

28 October 2006:
The amateur club "SGP Mieminger Plateau" fights against the discrimination of their migrant players from Turkey and will show the red card to racism at their home match versus Scharnitz.

28 October 2006:
The migrant club "Etsan Vienna Türkgücü SKV" will warm-up in FARE t-shirts before their home match versus ESV Südost.

28 October 2006:
The amateur club "SV Rasenspieler Wolfersberg" will warm-up in anti-racism t-shirts and distribute FairPlay magazines at their home match versus Florio.

3 November 2006:
Das Spiel Flavia Solva I—SV Frauental I im Römerstadion Leibnitz über Initiative des Präsidentes des Steirischen Fußballverbandes Dr. Gerhard Kapl und Schiedsrichterobmann Franz Roschitz, der Vereine "Flavia Solva" und "Frauental" unter

das Motto "Fußball gegen Rassismus" gestellt und es wird vor Beginn des Spieles ein entsprechendes Zeichen gesetzt.

Azerbaijan
21 October 2006:
The NGO "Ganja Voluntary Public Union" will organise a tournament until 28.10. under the motto "Football Against Discrimination in Azerbaijan". The aim of the tournament is the fight against discrimination, breaking up stereotypes and the empowerment and of girls and young women.
22 October 2006:
The "League for Intercultural Cooperation" in partnership with the Association of Football Federations of Azerbaijan will hold anti-racism events at three league matches: 22.10. Inter vs. Ganjlarbirliyi, 23.10. Garabagh vs. Olimpik, 28.10. Neftchi vs. Karvan, where the players will show racism the red card and call for tolerance. 3500 flyers will be distributed.

Belarus
17 October 2006:
The youth association "Next Stop—New Life" will organise a photo exhibition in the Palace of Arts on the subject of "Sports against Racism". The second event will be a tournament in Minsk with fans from several ethnic minorities. The photo exhibition will be also shown in the stadium.

Belgium
10 October 2006:
Starting with a press conference the "Centre for Equal Opportunities and Opposition Towards Racism" will organise a two week campaign to fight racism and monkey chanting in Belgian football. Elements are activities in the stadiums, a media campaign and an anti-racism charter to be signed by the clubs. Partners in this campaign are the Belgian FA, all professional clubs, the fan federation, the players union Sporta, five ministries and media. A TV-spot will be show during the football broadcasts and 80000 posters will be printed. The activities in the stadiums will consist of the presentation of banners, fan action with posters, choreographies and photographs.

Bulgaria
17 October 2006:
The "Youth Centre Haskovo" will organise a seminar "Sport and especially football as a way to get people together closer and fight against racism", distribute flyers and information materials and organise a youth football tournament for mixed teams.
17 October 2006:
The "St. Cyril and Methodius High School of Humanities" will organise a four school football tournament for 14-15 years old youths incl. matches for girls teams and a training session with players from first league club PFC Botev Plovdiv. Additionally there will be a poster and picture competition. The finals will be on 22.10.
21 October 2006:
The campaign that will be organized by "People to People International" at the American University will start with a multimedia presentation and a series of lectures and workshops on the issue of racism. The campaign will reach to its peak with a football match between the team of the Roma minority of Blagoevgrad and the students of the

university. The university team will be selected from the students with different backgrounds so that the match realises its main purpose of kicking out Racism from Football. Before the beginning of the match starts Hristo Stoichkov is appointed to hold a speech. After the match there will be a march of the players and spectators to the University Campus through the city in order to inform the city residents about the activity and will continue with "Movie Nights" where different documentaries and movies on racism will be shown.

Croatia
17 October 2006:
The youth organisation "Step Ahead" will organise a press conference and present a series of educational video materials and during the action week. The indoor soccer championship with 40 participating teams will see them showing the red card to racism and ethnic discrimination.
17 October 2006:
The "Centre for Peace Studies" cooperates with the Croatian Football Association and plans to place boards against racism, homophobia and neo-Nazism in Croatian stadiums.
24 October 2006:
The "SDR Roma" will organise a football tournament for Roma teams from the Balkans until 26.10.

Cyprus
28 October 2006:
The "Cyprus Footballers Association" in cooperation with Cyprus College will present anti-racism banners at league matches. First league club Apollon Limassol will join the FARE AW at the match against Akritas.

Czech Republic
21 October 2006:
The "Fanproject Liberec" from the champion Slovan Liberec will join the FARE AW for the first time at the home match against Plzen. Together with the fans they will create an anti-racist choreography and dedicated pages in the match day programme.
22 October 2006:
The "Bohemians Prague Ultras" will produce big banners with the slogans "United Colours of Bohemka" and "Bohemka Against Racism" for the home match against Usti nad Labem in the second league.
Denmark
21 October 2006:
The fan club "Bröndby Fans Mod Racisme" will distribute leaflets and anti-racism stickers at the away match in the first league against Horsens.

Finland
24 October 2006:
"Atlantis FC", a second league club, will organise a mixed anti-racist indoor tournament for academy players and migrant youths.
28 October 2006:
"FIMU", a Finnish multicultural sports organisation, will organise a futsal tournament

under motto "Football for Tolerance, against Racism and Violence", involving the Finnish FA, referees, police and migrants.

28 October 2006:

The sports organisation "Liikkukaa!org" will organise a "Respect"-game between Brazilian football players and migrants. Before the match the captains and coaches will read statements against racism and anti-racism posters will be distributed, followed by a round table discussion after the match.

30 October 2006:

The "Mondial Stars", a team consisting mainly of migrants from Africa, will play a friendly match against a team of referees to promote intercultural respect.

Former Yugoslav Republic of Macedonia

17 October 2006:

The "Macedonian Center for Culture and Development" will organise a joint press conference with the Macedonian FA and the other participants of the FARE AW in Macedonia. In all matches of the first league the players will show banners with the logo "racism and nationalism out of the game" and red cards with the same slogan. The MCCD will have several presentations in live TV shows and will distribute anti-racist materials and flyers to fan groups.

20 October 2006:

"YMCA Macedonia" will organise the "Together on the playground against racism!" indoor tournament for eight teams with players with mixed religious and ethnical background. The teams come mainly from NGOs dealing with sport and minority issues and refugees teams. This is traditional tournament will be organised for the fourth time during the FARE AW.

20 October 2006:

The "National Roma Centrum" in Kumanovo will organise a football tournament with teams from Roma, Albanian and Macedonian communities. Before the tournament there will be a parade through the city with a banner saying "The game is same for all".

20 October 2006:

The daily educative centre for children and youths "Organisation of Women of Sv. Nikole" will organise a 5-a-side football tournament with 12 teams, the groups are going to be mixed from different sexes and different ethnic groups (Macedonians, Vlavs, Turks, Serbs, Roma) of the age from 15 to 25 years. T-shirts with the FARE logo and flags for the participants will be produced. The purpose of the activities is the establishment of mixed groups, without ethnic, national and religious prejudices mutual friendship in this two days tournament.

22 October 2006:

The "Youth Forum Bitola" will produce and distribute t-shirts with anti-racist messages among the different ethnic groups (Macedonians, Roma, Turks, Albanians). In cooperation with FC Pelister a press conference with players and club managers will be held to inform on the campaign and activities during the football match. An anti-racist flag will be produced and given to the supporters of the club. The players will wear anti-racist t-shirts and will be accompanied from children of different ethnic groups (mainly Roma) onto the pitch.

22 October 2006:

The "Union of Students of the Philological Faculty" will dedicate the matches of their football team in the university league to anti-racism. The will display anti-racism banner, produce leaflets and play with special jerseys with the FARE logo.

23 October 2006:
The NGO "Council for Prevention of Juvenile Delinquency" in Kavadarci, where a mixed population of Macedonians and Roma citizens is living, will invite youths from both communities to renew the old football field; and thus to contribute to improving the sport capacities in the city and to encourage the local young people to participate in sports. The participants will take part in a football tournament played on this field. The aim is that through working and playing football together the youths will get closer with each other regardless of their different ethnic background.
25 October 2006:
The "European House" in Skopje will distribute bilingual leaflets at a football match between Vardar, which is a team mainly consisting of Macedonians, and Baskimi, which is a team mainly consisting of Albanians.
28 October 2006:
The aim of "MKD Prokultura" is the inclusion of women and girls especially from ethnic minorities and will organise a football tournament. This will be first tournament for girls in Skopje.

France
17 October 2006:
From 26.9.-6.11. the anti-discrimination organisation and FARE partner "LICRA" will organise and coordinate several events in France during the AW. Departments in various cities will hold tournament, meetings and conferences:
26.9.-31.10., LICRA Suresnes, starting with a public meeting and a conference and a movie projection on racism and violence in sports, this will be followed in October in elementary schools.
4.10., LICRA Bordeaux, futsal tournaments organised by high schools in Gironde, during these tournaments anti-racist statements will be read, prizes will be awarded and debates will be organised.
11.10., LICRA Vanves, meeting to raise awareness of young football players of the sports football club of Vanves on racism.
21.10., LICRA Levallois, friendly football tournament with eight teams from the local area of Levallois, one girl at least in each team.
29.10., Cantal's district and LICRA Cantal-Quercy, distribution of t-shirts or arm-bands to all football players of the region with logos of LICRA and anti-racism slogans.
6.11., LICRA Dunkerque, multi sports tournament (football, basketball, volleyball, handball) in a high school.
LICRA Lyon and UCPA, meeting in a leisure centre (UCPA centre) in Lyon, the activities with the children will be presented in the centre around the subject of racism, incl. film projection, prevention, posters etc.
21 October 2006:
Eight Members (in Sochaux, Rennes, Metz, Valence, Clermont, Bordeaux, Cannes, Liège (Bel), Lausanne (Sui)) of the network "Réseau Supporter de Resistance Antiraciste" will display banners against racism, the activities will differ from choreographies, t-shirts and discussions.
22 October 2006:
The regional football league "LAFA" will organise two football matches during the AW with teams composed of players mostly from ethnic minorities. Before the games the

players will warm up with t-shirts against racism and show anti-racism banners, the captains will read an anti-racist statement and leaflets will be distributed to the fans.
22 October 2006:
"Ultras Marseille" will display the banner "Fight Fascism—Fight Racism" at the top league match Olympique Marseille—Olympique Lyon.
27 October 2006:
"SOS Racisme" will organise a friendly football tournament to promote tolerance and to promote the "living together".
28 October 2006:
In cooperation with "LICRA" fans from Paris St-Germain will show racism the red card at the home match against Rennes.

Georgia
21 October 2006:
The NGO "Human Rights and Humanitarian Law Centre Themis" will organise a tournament for youth teams from minorities' schools and other institutions in Tbilisi. It is planned to invite professional football players to discuss the issues of discrimination and tolerance in football.

Germany
14 October 2006:
The "Supporters Crew" from the amateurs' club RSV Göttingen 05 will organise an anti-racism day in cooperation with the club. The team will use special tricots with the slogan "RSV Göttingen 05 against Racism". In the fan area there will be a banner which says "Everybody is welcome in our place—Against intolerance within Football and Elsewhere". On the day of the match print materials, containing the programme, will be distributed. The match day programme will inform about the day as well as the stadium speaker during the match. Local anti-racism groups will organise information desks. After the match, there will be an auction of the special tricots. The money raised shall support local groups.
15 October 2006:
"Jugendtreff St.Hedwig Paderborn" will produce special banners with anti-racist slogans for the second league match SC Paderborn 07 vs Tus Koblenz.
17 October 2006:
The fan group "FCKFANS-gegen-Rassismus" from 1. FC Kaiserslautern will raise awareness for the topics of racism and discrimination in the stadiums. A special focus on the two topics will be featured in the fanzine "Weiß der Teufel", which will report on e.g. an event of the association of Sinti and Roma Rheinland-Pfalz, an interview with the author of the book "Der Betze unterm Hakenkreuz", etc. The fanzine contains a sticker with the slogan "Yes to hell—No to Racism".
17 October 2006:
The migrant-organisation "Forum Afrika" will organise a couple of football matches and school workshops in Gelsenkirchen.
17 October 2006:
The "Schalker Fan-Initiative" will cooperate with "The Point", an institution in Gelsenkirchen to support AIDS-prevention which is also a meeting point for young gays and lesbians. Together they will create posters which will show homosexual teenagers wearing football shirts with anti-discrimination slogans.

17 October 2006:
The women team from "Türkiyemspor Berlin" will produce sports wear with the FARE logo, playing matches involving women and girls from migrant families.
17 October 2006:
Amateur club "SV Surwold" will produce tricots with an imprint of the FARE logo. The aim of this action is to solidarise with migrant players and to deliver the message to young people that everybody is equal, no matter what skin colour.
17 October 2006:
"FSC Dynamo Windrad" will arrange banners around the football ground, which is used by many—also migrant—teams. The banners will show the slogan "Football against Racism in Europe" in different languages.
19 October 2006:
"1. FC Lokomotive Leipzig" will produce stickers and posters which will be distributed in the stadium and the town.
20 October 2006:
In cooperation with the German FA and the German Football League FARE partner "Dem Ball egal" will organise a joint anti-racism weekend, 20-23 October, under the motto "Football is multicoloured" at all 36 matches from the Bundesliga to the third leagues. A short anti-racism clip featuring well-known German actor Peter Lohmeyer ("The Miracle of Berne") will be shown at all grounds with video screens. At each game both teams will be accompanied onto the pitch by children wearing Dem Ball egal T-shirts. The players will hold up red cards with the message "Show Racism the Red Card". At the same time as many fans as possible will be encouraged to join in by holding up A6 size red cards placed on seats and handed out at the entrance to terraced stands before the game. These cards will contain information on the Action Week and useful web links, etc. The intention is for them to be used again rather than simply being thrown away. The stadium announcer will inform the crowd about FARE and the Action Week by reading out a pre-prepared statement. The match programme will contain a half-page article on the event. The activities will be publicised via all DFB/DFL media (website, etc.) as well as the broadcasting and written media.
20 October 2006:
The group "Supporters Club Düsseldorf" will organise a couple of projects during the action week: on 19.10. there will be a film screening that deals with the topic "Homosexuality and Football" in cooperation with Café Bunte Bilder. On 21.10. there will be a commented photo exhibition in the stadium and the choreography "Fortuna loves all colours" in cooperation with Ultras Düsseldorf and a banner at the match of the third league match Fortuna Dusseldorf versus 1. FC Berlin. On 23.10. there will be a discussion with female and male Fortuna fans dealing with the topic "Women and Football".
21 October 2006:
Before the Bundesleila match Borussia Dortmund vs VFL Bochum young female fans of both clubs will meet and play football. They will present banners with the slogans: "Borussen Playgirls gegen Rassismus" and "Bochum Wildcats gegen Rassismus". The action will be supported by the fan projects of Dortmund and Bochum.
21 October 2006:
The fan club "Das Rote Berlin" from Hannover 96 will organise a discussion, that takes place after the national league match Schalke 04 vs Hannover 96. For the discussion, players from lower leagues, who are affected from racism, will be invited. Afterwards a

video, showing an interview with Gerald Asamoah, who was playing for both clubs, will be presented.

21 October 2006:

The gay fan club "Hertha Junxx" from Hertha BSC will create a banner for the home match against Borussia Mönchengladbach, voting tool on website is installed to determine the slogan for the banner. Additionally, new scarves will be produced.

21 October 2006:

"Fanprojekt Dresden" will produce anti-racism banners, flyers and stickers for the third league match Dynamo Dresden vs Werder Bremen II.

22 October 2006:

For the Bundesleague match FC Sachsen Leipzig vs FC Eilenburg, the fan initiative "Wir sind Ade!" will organise a couple of actions. The players will present red cards against racism to demonstrate their fans that the team is international and does not accept racism and discrimination. A leading image for an anti-racism campaign will be produced where players and supporters show red cards with the slogan "Show racism the red card!" in the national language of each player. The pictures will be used for postcards and posters. Shortly before the match will start, an anti-racism banner will be carried on the ground, surrounded by the flags of the players' different nations. Additionally CDs from the FARE partner "Dem Ball ist egal, wer ihn tritt" will be distributed at the stadium entrance.

24 October 2006:

The aim of fanclub "Filmstadt Inferno 99" from Babelsberg 03 is the networking with Ukrainian Fans of Arsenal Kiev. To reach this it will organise a choreography and a stickers distribution for the DFB-match versus Vfb Stuttgart and at Arsenal Kiev.

28 October 2006:

The "Dresdner SC Fanprojekt" will produce for the home match against Dynamo Dresden II two posters with anti-racism designs. Additionally there will be an emphasis on the FARE AW in the fanzines that will be produced before and after the activity. The will produce anti-racist t-shirts and sticker and a Croatian player from DSC will hold a short speech before the match.

28 October 2006:

For the home match of FC St. Pauli versus Borussia Mönchengladbach II 22 children from football project "Kiezkick—Fußball der Kulturen" will be invited. This project is organised by the "Fanladen St. Pauli" in cooperation with FC St. Pauli and several social organisations of the district. The Children from 7–12 years are all living in Hamburg's district St. Pauli and come mainly from migrant families. Once a week the boys and girls come to the open football training, sometimes there are children from 14 different countries. The children will wear t-shirts with the slogan and logo of "KiezKick—Fußball der Kulturen" and accompany the players on the field. During half-time the children will carry an anti-racism-banner over the field together with Fanladen-workers.

"Fanladen", "Ultras St. Pauli" and the club will start a solidarity campaign for a German label whose anti-Nazi symbols had been forbidden a the public prosecutors office. The will produce two-pole banners with the forbidden symbols and wall paper in front. Additionally the club will distribute 10000 stickers "against right-extremism". The club will send out a press statement against this forbiddance. The sticker "FC St. Pauli gegen Rechts" is the most successful merchandising product with more than 2 million stickers sold since 10 years.

As third element the "Ultras St. Pauli" will make choreography at the beginning of the second with big banners to welcome refugees in the stadium.
29 October 2006:
"Fanprojekt Hannover" will organise an action day for the women's team from Hannover 96. Brochures and buttons with the topics "Women and Football" will be distributed. On the cover of the brochure the migrant players of Hannover 96 carry a FARE banner. The slogan for the picture is: "Frauen für mehr Toleranz und weniger Diskiminierung im Fußball". The brochure will also contain information about FARE and the Frauenfußballverein network as well as interviews with players concerning the topics racism, sexism and xenophobia within football.

Greece
13 October 2006:
"Euroscience Greek Regional Section" will organise internet competitions for Greeks and migrants: participants (8-16 years old youths) who have to create players cards with biographical notes, images and videos with the help of a pattern, the cards will be published on the website, voting tool selects the best card; announcement with posters.
26 October 2006:
The "Organisation of Youth & Sports" of the municipality of Athens will organise a tournament for schools with a high percentage of minorities and migrants.
26 October 2006:
"Research Institute for the Development and Promotion of Digital Access" is a Greek non profit organization that has developed the project www.e-filathlos.gr. Its a Greek portal trying to connect all fans against violence and ethnic discrimination. On 26.10. they will participate together with the "Organisation of Youth and Sports" of the municipality of Athens in a tournament for schools with a high percentage of minorities and migrants. "E-filathlos" will participate with t-shirts against violence and red cards with the motto "red card on violence" for the kids. In addition they are planning to give commemorative diplomas to all the children that will participate in the tournament.
27 October 2006:
The sports newspaper "Sportday" will host a conference on "Football fights racism" with representatives from the Greek ministry for sports, the European Parliament, UEFA, the Greek Football Federation and professional football players.

Hungary
21 October 2006:
The "Mahatma Gandhi Human Rights Organisation" will organise two anti-racism events with MTK Budapest (vs. Fehérvár on 27. 10.) and Ferencvaros TC on 29. 10.
21 October 2006:
The "Győzelemert Simon Gyerekfoci" will hold an anti-discrimination day at Ferencvaros stadium with a training session and a competition for youths (11-14 years old).
28 October 2006:
The "Hungarian Players Association" will organise a common campaign in the first league. The players will wear anti-racism t-shirts for warm up, tannoy announcements will be made and two children (boys and girls with Hungarian or ethnic minority background) will present a FARE banner at line up. Before Kick off the players will throw

the t-shirts to the fans as the children will kick a white and a black ball to the tribunes.

Ireland
3 October 2006:
First league club "Galway United" will help launch the anti-racism venture "Show Racism the Red Card" at Galway City Museum, which is serving as a forerunner for the FARE AW. This third regional project of "Show Racism the Red Card Ireland" is supported by the PFAI, Galway City Partnership, Galway City Council and the Irish Rugby Player Union. 3000 posters, showing the Galway United squad with the anti-racist slogan in eight languages, will be distributed.

11 October 2006:
Starting with the European Championship qualifier against the Czech Republic where a kids game prior to kick off took place, the newly formed "Football Intercultural Advisory Group" (Football Association of Ireland, Sport Against racism in Ireland, Show Racism the Red Card Ireland, Department of Justice, Equality and Law Reform, National Consultative Committee on Racism and Interculturalism) will promote a fortnight of action. In the first league the players will t-shirts for warm up. Grassroots are also encouraged and supported to organise small events.

25 October 2006:
"Sport Against Racism in Ireland" will organise the workshop "Levelling the playing fields in football" with the keynote speakers: Des Tomlinson (intercultural officer, Irish FA), Michael Boyd (Irish FA), Dr. Anne Bourke (University College Dublin).

Israel
4 November 2006:
The NGO "New Israel Fund" will organise that hundred youngsters will parade on the pitch wearing "Let's Kick Racism Out of Israeli Football" t-shirts along with the two teams at the match Beitar Jerusalem vs. Maccabi Haifa.

Italy
3 October 2006:
Presentation in Rome of the books "Black Italian" (history of black athletes who dress the Italian colours) by Mauro Valeri.
Valeri published in 2005 "La Razza in campo" (a history of the black revolution in football) and the new book is his ideal continuation. Black Italians is the name gaved to the Italians migrant in Australia and United States; Mauro Valeri takes this term to tell about all the people who live in Italy since many years, even if they've got different cultural roots and often for this reason they are discriminated.

12 October 2006:
Attacco Antirazzista, is an evening happening against racism organised by RazzismoSTOP, YaBasta! and fans group from Venice.
From 19,00 to 21,00 debate on the topic: changing course. Mistakes and trickery in the struggle against racism in football, with representative of Football Federation, Venezia club and the participation of migrant community from Venice. There'll be a performance of a Senegal band.

15 October 2006:
During the match SSC Venezia vs Pavia ultras from Venice will distribute 2.700 copies of

the book Attacco Antirazzista (Antiracist Attack) a monitoring on racism and antiracism in the Italian football.

20 October 2006:

The Polisportiva Antirazzista Assata Shakur Ancona in cooperation with U.I.S.P Ancona, Ambasciata dei Diritti, Circolo Africa, Radio Arancia Network e Radio Conero, organise the happening "Antiracist Place" with the presentation of a video reportage on the experience of the migrants in Marche; presentation of the book "Black Italians" by Mauro Valeri; presentation of the FARE experiences, of migrant athletes and ultras.

21 October 2006:

The Polisportiva Antirazzista Assata Shakur Ancona in cooperation with U.I.S.P Ancona organise at the Stadio del Conero from 13,00 a tournament among Africa, South America, journalists and Polisportiva Assata Shakur

21 October 2006:

The Ultras "Cinghiali del Casale" support Action Week 2006 with the creation of a new tricot for their amateur team, SCD Frassineto. The tricot—with FARE logo and an antiracist motto—will be presented in the match against "Terre del Monferrato" and it will become the official shirt of the team during the championship.

22 October 2006:

UISP Varese organise from 14,00 to 24,00 a street football tournament with fans and children of schools. During the tournament there will be spaces for presenting the video of the Mondiali Antirazzisti and stories of people who participated during the Mondiali

22 October 2006:

In Italian Serie D match N.Campobasso—Nernese, the campobasso ultras "Smoked Head '86" will expose a banner with the slogan "1 day the return, 364 the struggle. No Racism" and another from the Celta Vigo fan (Celterras '87): "Nom ao Racismo".

22 October 2006:

Cooperativa Cantiere Giovani—Frattamaggiore (NA) organises at 17.00 in the structure of Sporting Club Tropical Calcetto, Via Dante Alighieri, Grumo Nevano (Na) a four team multi ethnic tournament against racism, with the delivery of informative materials. At 21.00 there will be a party with prize-giving and music (a Piazza Cirillo, Grumo Nevano-NA) in synergy with the presentation of project "Nuvole" (a project with strong multi cultural contents).

24 October 2006:

UISP Varese organises a public assembly with Varese schools on the topic: a difficult journey in the football world, with the exposition of materials relished by the young. During the day the former player Paolo Sollier speaks about the topic

26 October 2006:

A new webspace for antiracism in UISP site called "Antirazzisti Mondiali. Many tactics, an only team". The site will bring a new national campaign concerning sport against racism that want to present several projects and activities (called tactics) made in Italy and in Europe. The aim is to leave from local to build an antiracist globality increasing activities through communication.

26 October 2006:

UISP Emilia-Romagna organises in Bologna at 11,30 and in Modena at 20,00 the presentation of the book Black Italians by Mauro Valeri. Among the participants: the author, athletes, representatives of the Municipality, Region and Progetto Ultrà/FARE.

27 October 2006:

UISP Roma organises at the Juvenile Prison of Rome a tournament among a teams of the prison, a multiethnic team of the University of Sport and the team of Quartaccio (a district of Rome). During the match the young will realised a banner on the topic of antiracism. Finally, there will be a discussion on the topic among the young and representatives of FARE.

29 October 2006:

Ultras Group Brigate Rosso Blu 1984-Civitanova Marche in the match Civitanovese-Castelfrettese (Italy's Eccellenza Championship) will show antiracist banners and they will create antiracist coreographies and they will give informative materials about AW and Mondiali Antirazzisti. In this match they will invite at stadium some foreign communities.

4 November 2006:

The "Scuola Calcio Primavera" (affiliate to the professionist team Salernitana—Serie C1) joins in Action Week with a subscription (signed by all partecipants to 15edition of amateur tournament Campionato Provinciale CSA.in—rofeo Ottica De Cusatis) of a RETE fare agreement and against racism document. The final aim is to involve all football realities of Salerrno.

5 November 2006:

Ultras Ancona will create at stadium an antiracist choreography for the football match Ancona-Gallipoli.

12 November 2006:

Polisportiva Zelig, UISP Reggio Emilia and Istoreco organizes in Reggio Emilia a sports-cultural manifestation called "I Colori di Reggio": football tournaments, multiethnic market, music and more. For this tournament teams of migrants, volunteer associations, cooperatives etc are invited.

Luxembourg

20 October 2006:

The "Commissariat du Gouvernement aux Etrangers" will organise the conference "Discrimination in football and sports" for sport professionals and volunteer, officials, fans, youth sport associations, youth centres; starting with a sports programme for youths (5-a-side, street ball, volleyball, running for diversity), refreshments, round tables (situation in Luxembourg, positions of ministries, FLF, COSL, European experts). A participating migrant NGO will organise a party after the conference.

Malta

20 October 2006:

The "Malta Football Association" will organise anti-racism events in the first league where a banner saying "Not to racism" will be displayed and players will warm up in FARE t-shirts.

Moldova

28 October 2006:

Fatima, a NGO of African migrants, aims to promote tolerance and friendship in Moldavian football and will organise matches between ethnic minority teams, refugees and youths on the second weekend of the FARE AW. Also a discussion will be organised, an anti-racist slogan will be presented on public transports.

Netherlands
17 October 2006:
The "Vissert Hooft Lyceum" will organise an international school project "The ball is round" (Netherlands, Romania, France) with several elements: exhibition called "Sports and fairplay" with leaflets and posters produced by the pupils; digital forum with tasks in a webpage called E-Sports, girls football matches and women football; film & discussionson violence, xenophobia + discrimination; each participating school will make a short video with pupils interviewed after watching the film.
25 October 2006:
Ehredivisie club "PSV Eindhoven" will hold an anti-racism day at the home match against Sparta Rotterdam. The match day programme will feature a special on the fight against racism. The line up kids wear special t-shirts and the captain will read an anti-racism message. On the video screen an anti-racism spot will be shown before kick off. The players of both teams and the referees will present a big banner with the text "Unite against racism".

Norway
22 October 2006:
The anti-racism campaign "Gi rasisme rodt kort" at the Norwegian Peoples Aid will coordinate activities at seven first league matches where all teams will show red card to racism before the match in cooperation with the Norwegian players union (NISO).

Poland
14 October 2006:
"Fundacja dla Wolnosci" will organise a football tournament for eight teams (refugees from West Africa, Chechnya and Vietnam and Polish school teams), a drawing workshop with professional designers, an exhibition on the second where the drawings will be presented and discussed.
15 October 2006:
FARE partner "Never Again Association" coordinated the activities in Poland and will organise several events in Warsaw:
15.10., refugee football tournament
18.10., gospel concert officially opening the Action Week in Warsaw
21.10., football match Poland—Chechnya, with a group of refugees from Chechnya, plus side events
21.10., Polish-African theatre performance on the theme of Football Against Racism in cooperation with the "Migratory Theatre International Foundation"
25.10., street-art action on the subject of Football Against Racism
26.10., football match between Legia Warszawa and a multi-racial Polish team
27.10., social event with multi-cultural music
16 October 2006:
The "Union of the Unemployed OZB" will hold a seminar and discussion plus a Roma music concert with cooperation of local media.
17 October 2006:
"Stowarzyszenie GTW" will conduct a series of educational activities.
17 October 2006:
"Stowarzyszenie Aktywnosci Spoleczney Mlyn" will organise a discussion and football match with migrants.

17 October 2006:
"Sports club Warta Sieradz" will hold meetings with Black players and organise a football game.
17 October 2006:
Throughout the FARE AW "Stowarzyszenie Lepszy Swiat" will organise a discussion and distribute posters in the city of Poznan.
18 October 2006:
In cooperation with FARE partner "Never Again Association" the "Campaign Against Homophobia" will organise the "Rainbow Cup", a table football tournament in Warsaw. The teams will be mixed, during the tournament films about the problem of tolerance will be shown. The second important event that day will be a "market" where organisations will have a chance to exchange the information and promote their activities among other guests of the event by giving away their brochures. During the event leaflets against discrimination, homophobia and about gender issues will be provided.
18 October 2006:
The "Gimnazjum Zywiec" will organise educational activities with Roma.
19 October 2006:
The sports club "Twierdza" will organise a two days football tournament with the aim to kick against xenophobia, nationalism and stereotypes involving the Ukrainian school in Przemysl, partnership with Ochotnicze Hufce Pracy.
21 October 2006:
"Fundacja MaMa" will organise a discussion and football game with Chechen refugees.
22 October 2006:
"Stowazyszenie Inicjatyw Spolecznych Kulturalny Poznan" will conduct educational activities with first league club Lech Poznan.
24 October 2006:
"Fundacja Kobiet" will organise a football tournament with foreign students in Lodz.

Portugal
17 October 2006:
The "Portuguese Players Union SJPF" will organise a big campaign including actions in the stadiums (players, coaches, referees and ball-pickers will wear anti-racism t-shirts and caps, banners "racismo nao" will be presented), a radio contest, a media campaign in the daily sports papers, a bilingual SJPF magazine, the distribution of badges, a match between footballers and journalists, workshops in schools, the appointment of ambassadors (like Eusébio, Fernando Gomes, Manuel Fernandes, Paulo Sousa and Vítor Baía), a futsal tournament for teams coming from ethnic minorities and migrants and social problematic areas.

Romania
17 October 2006:
The "Pedagogic Lyzeum Sabin Dragoi" will organise a football tournament for mixed teams of youths, parents, teachers. The tournament is followed by a literary competition, a drawing exhibition, a conference on anti-racism, anti-Semitism, and anti-discrimination.
21 October 2006:
The anti-discrimination organisation "CNCD" will organise anti-racism activities at the following first league matches:
21.10., Otelul Galati—Steaua Bucharest

28.10., Rapid Bucharest—CFR Cluj

28.10., Dinamo Bucharest—Politehnica Iasi

At the beginning of the matches the players and the referees will wear t-shirts and banners with the inscription: "Uniti impotriva Discriminarii" (United against Discrimination). Also big posters with specific messages will be exposed at the stadium entrances and flyers will be distributed with the idea to sensitize the fans regarding the negative effects that discrimination can have.

28 October 2006:

The "Initiava Autonoma Craiova" will produce anti-racist posters, leaflets, a banner and t-shirts for the match of Universitatea Craiova against Pandurii Tg. Jiu.

Russia

20 October 2006:

"ETHnICS", a youth group for tolerance in Krasnodar, will organise a friendly mini football match between the mixed teams of foreign and Russian students under the motto "Football for Tolerance!" It will be organised in cooperation the Youth Organisation of the German Community in Russia and Institute of Economics, Law and Arts. Foreign students have become a risk group who is being more and more often attacked by neo-Nazi and skinhead groups in different cities of Russia. Beside information campaigns and help lines, "ETHnICS" has developed a series of activities that are aimed at integrating foreign students into local youth communities to break ice and obtain the safety feeling.

21 October 2006:

The African Union Diaspora Organisation will organise a mini football tournament for minority groups and African teams.

Serbia & Montenegro

17 October 2006:

The "Resource Centre" in Majdanpek will run an information campaign in the local community. At the beginning of the FARE AW there will be a meeting to encourage the schools, football and sport clubs to promote the campaign and to participate actively. Then a tournament for youths will take place where information materials will be distributed and last years banner will be exposed.

21 October 2006:

"FARE Serbia" is going to organise a football tournament for youth teams from clubs and schools incl. ethnic minorities (Hungarian, Romanian, Slovak, Roma, Vlachs) and anti-racism workshops in schools.

At the following first league matches anti-racism activities will take place:

21.10., Smederevo—Vojvodina

28.10., OFK Belgrade—Smedrevo, Mladost Agatin—Red Star

2.11., Partizan—AS Livorno (UEFA Cup)

Leaflets will be distributed at:

21.10., Red Star—OFK Belgrade, Zemun—Banat

28.10., Vojvodina—Zemun

21 October 2006:

The NGO "Youth of Montenegro" will start with a workshop for children from different ethnic origin to talk about racism and discrimination and to prepare flyers and t-shirts. On the next weekend a friendly match will take place at the field of FC Buducnost in Podgorica.

The players will wear t-shirts with anti-racism messages on it. The flyers will be distributed by the volunteers of the organisation.

Slovakia
16 October 2006:
The "Elementary school in Buzica" will run an art competition on the topic "Sport against racism" to create a logo for the project. The best logo will be placed on banners that will be presented at a tournament with four teams from the two schools in Buzica and Nizny Lanec involving the Roma students.
17 October 2006:
The amateur football club "TJ Družstevník Krásno" will start a long term project until January 07 in the FARE AW. They will place a fixed board with an anti-racist slogan on a tribune of the stadium and produce new jerseys with the same slogan to play in the league matches. The Roma population will be offered free tickets for the matches to integrate them into the club.
17 October 2006:
The "Základná škola Zohor" will make lectures for students and discussions on racism. The student will make anti-racist drawings and write essays. The results will be shown in an exhibition in the town hall and football matches will be organised with mixed teams involving the Roma minority.
18 October 2006:
The "College Sahy" will organise a discussion for the students with a local and ex-international football player where the FARE network will be presented and to create ideas for anti-racist logos and slogans for t-shirts. On 28.10. there will be a football match with mixed Slovak and students from the Hungarian minority where the players will wear the self-designed t-shirts.
20 October 2006:
The "Primary school with kindergarden Moravany nad Vahom" will make a walk with the pupils along the "educational path" to a football ground where the children will play and compete in mixed boys & girls teams. The activities there will be a penalty shoot off, a parallel slalom, juggling with the ball and a match. The activities will be accompanied by cultural activities (drawings of children on the asphalt) with topic of coexistence and tolerance between people and a conversation with policemen on the topic of racial attacks. The aim that the children get rid of prejudices and mutual intolerance.
22 October 2006:
The village "Hontianske Tesare", the sports club, the elementary school and kindergarden and the Roma school assistants, will organise a football match of the local team, that consists partly of Roma, connected with other activities like a anti-racist crafts fair.
23 October 2006:
The NGO "Carpe Diem" commenced a survey among the youth of Kosice in September. The purpose of survey is to raise awareness for racism and xenophobia among the youth. Participants of the survey could write down ideas how to fight racism in Kosice. The results of the survey will be announced at the FARE event at the playground of the Carpe Diem Youth Club. The football teams are of various backgrounds (high school students, Roma teams, members of the international youth exchange).
27 October 2006:
The "Slovak Pierre de Coubertin Committee" will organise a multi-national anti-racism tournament in Bratislava for children from 10-12 years. Teams from the Roma and the Hungarian minority are invited, at least two girls have to play in a team. Before the

tournament discussion forums with active top-level athletes, with NGOs (People Against Racism, People In Peril) and with handicapped children and their parents will be organised.

Slovenia
17 October 2006:
The amateur football club "KMN Zvezda Krsko" will create posters with anti-racism and anti-discrimination messages, distribute t-shirts to their opponents in the league and send postcards to the football community in the region.
18 October 2006:
"NK Vanca Vas" is the highest ranked Roma football club in Slovenia and will be the host of a tournament with participants from Slovenia, Croatia and Hungary.
18 October 2006:
The association "Slovene Philanthropy" will organise a tournament in the students arena in Ljubljana. The participants will come from refugees teams from Gambia, Afghanistan, Cameron, from the local women football team and students groups. At the tournament brochures will be distributed.
20 October 2006:
The "Institute of Fair Play and Tolerance in Sport" will organise anti-racism days at all matches of this weekend in the first league in cooperation with the Slovenian FA. The players and the referees will be wearing black & white wristbands. In the past they were used at the friendly football match between national teams of Trinidad & Tobago and Slovenia when all spectators had worn them. The match that will be broadcasted live on TV will see a special protocol before the match: an airplane with long banner ("stop (logo) racism—love (logo) sport") will fly over the stadium. The wristbands will be used also at the matches of the first football league for women. Before matches there will be a press conference and other media activities (interviews, reportage, short articles).
20 October 2006:
The amateur football club "NK Carda Martjanci" will organise five event during the FARE AW where banners, red cards, flyers, FARE t-shirts will be used, interviews with the players will be made and FARE ball with the players signatures will be presented:
20.10., FARE workshop on homophobia, inclusion of girls, racism and discrimination
24.10., U-14 match, NK Carda—NK Triglav Bakovici
26.10., U-12 match, NK Carda—NK Tromejnik
28.10., U-19 match, NK Carda—NK Tisina
29.10., NK Carda—NK Tromejnik

Spain
21 October 2006:
Various associations will participate in a youth event called "Fewer discrimination" (Streetsoccer, Breakdance tournament, intercultural games . . .) organised by "Colectivo de Prevencion e Insercion Andalucia" in Cadiz. The highlight will be the conference "Racism in the European football", with international guests from the Netherlands (R. Spaaij; expert of terrorism, fascism and racism in Europe) and Italy (D. Conti; UISP / FARE), as well as Carles Viñas from Barcelona (who published books and articles about the skinhead movement, racism and violence in football, and Ultra supporter groups).
29 October 2006:
CEPA organise a distribution of anti-racist flyers and stickers, banners against racism and

discrimination in the stadium during Cádiz C.F. vs against Numancia in the second league. CEPA gets support from the local and regional government, Cádiz CF, as well as various supporter groups, institutions and associations.

Switzerland
19 October 2006:
The "Sports Organisation Africa Switzerland" will play friendly matches against Geneva police and Red Cross or UN workers.
28 October 2006:
"Gemeinsam gegen Rassismus", a fan club from Young Boys Bern, will produce a 50 meter long banner for the first league match against FC Zurich. The match day programme will feature an article on the FARE AW and an anti-racism spot will be shown on the video screen. Additionally the fan club plans a choreography and will distribute 20000 postcards with team and FARE logo.

United Kingdom
17 October 2006:
Show Racism the Red Card, now in their 10th year, will be celebrating Action Week with a range of events. See their website for details.
17 October 2006:
Show Racism the Red Card Scotland has over 100 events planned, involving all 42 professional clubs. All professional football sides in the country, will take part in the weekend of action, on October 21/22, as part of FARE's annual protest condemning racism in all forms. 175,000 anti-racist team posters will be distributed during the fortnight. Dundee FC and Dundee United FC were represented at the launch event on 17.10. The Arab Trust were also present at the launch, the Arab Trust giving great support to Show Racism the Red Card initiatives ever since it's introduction to Scotland three years ago. Every school in Scotland will receive a copy of the new SRTRC Scotland video and education pack. The anti-racism workshops, taking place at a number of Learn-direct centres, will be based around Show Racism the Red Card's "A Safe Place" video, which focuses on the treatment of asylum seekers and refugees.
17 October 2006:
Across England and Wales, FARE UK partner Kick It Out, have hundreds of activities planned during Action Week. All 92 clubs will again stand united with campaigners and community groups to send out a clear message against racism and discrimination.
28 October 2006:
FARE partner, Football Unites, Racism Divides hold their Action Week event at Sheffield United FC's home Premiership game against Chelsea. Anti-racist posters, stickers and fanzines will be distributed to fans. A huge choreography against racism will cover an entire stand. During half time, young people from Sheffield's ethnically diverse communities, will demonstrate their football talents which have been aided by Football Unites' coaching schemes. Tannoy announcements will highlight the need for fans to be vigilant against racist abuse.

Route de Genève 46
Case postale
CH-1260 Nyon 2
Tel. +41 22 994 44 44
Fax +41 22 994 44 88
uefa.com

Union des associations
européennes de football

No.71

TO UEFA MEMBER ASSOCIATIONS

For the attention of
the President and the General Secretary

Your reference	Your correspondence of	Our reference	Date
		LASP/stu/gas	22.11.2002

RACISM: Financial Assistance for Anti-Racism Initiatives

Dear Sir or Madam,

As part of the European football family's stand against racism in football, the UEFA Executive Committee, at its meeting in Copenhagen on 8 November, approved a new fund to help member associations organise anti-racism programmes. The scheme of the fund is the following:

- Member associations submit project proposals to UEFA for approval and subsequent financial assistance.

- UEFA makes a contribution of up to CHF 50,000 to cover 50% of the budget of anti-racism activities of member associations.

For the 2002/03 season, this fund will provide 2.6 million Swiss francs for the 52 member associations out of the charity account, financed entirely by fines imposed in UEFA competitions.

UEFA recognises that it has a responsibility to ensure that racism has no place in football. An important part of the sport's success is that it brings together players and spectators from different cultures. Football always has been, and must remain, a game for everyone and a strong force for integration and co-operation.

Allegations of racism in this season's UEFA competitions are at the root of this initiative. The specific incidents are being investigated and, where appropriate, dealt with by the Control and Disciplinary Body. These events remind us all, however, that the problem of racism is a real issue for the European football family and for the image of football in general.

UEFA, working closely with the organisation Football Against Racism in Europe (FARE), has launched a campaign to eliminate racism from football's playing fields and stadiums.

With this initiative UEFA invites all member associations to develop their own programmes to raise awareness and take a stand against racism at national and local level. Campaigns could be conducted in co-operation with leagues and clubs. Member organisations of the FARE network would be available for consultation.

We hope that all elements of the European football family will add a piece to the mosaic against racism, in an effort to eradicate it from our game, both on and off the field.

Please find enclosed further details about financial assistance for anti-racist Initiatives. Applications and/or questions in this respect should be addressed to UEFA's Assistance Programmes unit.

Yours faithfully,

U E F A

Gerhard Aigner
Chief Executive

Enclosure:
- Anti-Racism Project Application Form
- Procedure for financial aid for anti-racism projects

cc (without enclosures)
- UEFA Executive Committee
- UEFA Assistance Programmes Committee
- European members of the FIFA Executive Committee
- FIFA, Zurich

Guidelines for UEFA Member Associations on Anti-Racism Projects

1. Policy
Has your association developed and adopted a written anti-racist policy outlining measures to be taken (such as a code of conduct, national plan of action and distribution of UEFA 10-point plan to clubs) to keep the stadiums free of racism and to promote equal opportunities within your organisation and football structures and through your outreaches?

Indicators
- Approval of anti-racism policy by executive
- Public signing of action plan or code
- Nomination of senior staff to take care of policy implementation

2. Partnership with Targeted Groups
How will you ensure that groups who are potential targets of racism and intolerance (i.e. ethnic and national minorities, immigrants, Jewish community, Roma or refugees) are actively involved in the different stages of the project (planning, implementation, assessment)?

Indicators
- Number of ethnic minorities who will be involved in the different project activities
- Consultation with ethnic minority groups
- Use of positive images of ethnic minorities in your publications

3. Involvement of Fans and Clubs
Does the identity or brand of your campaign or project provide opportunities for active participation and "ownership" by football clubs and fans on the ground?

Indicators
- Ongoing contact with supporter groups, fan projects and/or fan coaches during project implementation
- Number of local football clubs and fan groups participating in the action
- Share of the budget allocated to fan activities

4. Publicity
Have you used available means of communication to publicise your anti-racism stance including the display of visual notices in the stadiums (advertising boards, notices in match day programmes), public address announcements and the publication of anti-racism content in official publications, newsletters, the web-site etc. ?

Indicators
- Appropriate publicity and photographs
- Awareness among spectators and users of FA media

5. Training
Have you thought about providing key actors in your association (referees, match observers, security personal, coaches and football administrators) with anti-racism training to increase their capacity to recognise and challenge racism when it occurs?

Indicators

- Training plan and provision of specific anti-racism training
- Number of key actors and staff involved

6. Expertise in Anti-Racism
Have you approached Non Governmental Organisations (NGOs) experienced in the field of anti-racism in order to seek their support to help you to run your project or campaign more efficiently?

Indicators

- Partnerships with NGOs
- Share of the budget allocated to NGOs

7. Long-Term Process
How will you make sure that the action you are implementing is not a one-off event? Have you considered a follow-up to sustain the project?

Indicators

- Long-term planning
- Planning of resources for follow-up

UEFA CHECKLIST FOR ANTI-RACISM PROJECTS

The checklist below has been developed to help National Associations to plan anti-racism projects, and UEFA to understand the details of projects requesting financial assistance.

Please read the checklist in association with the advice attached to this document and the UEFA/ FARE Good Practice Guide. The checklist should be submitted with the Project Presentation form.

1.   Policy development
(a)   Have you, as an FA, developed a written anti-racism policy, which has been approved by your Executive Committee or Board?

        Yes   ☐
        No   ☐

(b)   Have you sought to raise public awareness of the policy, through for example a public signing or ceremony?

        Yes   ☐
        No   ☐

(c)   Is there a senior member of staff that has been nominated to lead on implementation of the policy?

        Yes   ☐
        Name of member of staff and position:_____
        No   ☐

(d)   Has the UEFA/ FARE Ten-point Plan of Action been sent out to clubs with a request for implementation?

        Yes   ☐
        No   ☐

2.   Scope of the proposed project (multiple answers possible)
(a)   Which of the following problems does your project seek to address?

        Racism and xenophobia   ☐
        Nationalism   ☐
        Anti-Semitism   ☐
        Under-representation of minorities ☐
        Other forms of discrimination   ☐

(b)   Which of the following areas does the project you are developing seek to impact?

        Amateur football   ☐

Professional football   □
Clubs   □
Leagues   □
Youth football   □
Grassroots participation   □
The whole of football   □

(c)   Who are the key audiences for your anti-racism message?

Fans   □
Ethnic minorities and migrants   □
The media   □
Schools and youth   □
The football family   □
Other, please specify _____

3.   Establishing partnerships
(a)   Does your project involve outreach to ethnic minorities or other targeted
        groups?

        Yes   □
        No   □

(b)   If Yes, do you have an estimate of the numbers to be involved?

        Yes   □
        Please give number estimates _____
        No   □

(c)   Have you undertaken any consultation with ethnic minority and migrant groups
        at a regional, national or local level?

        Yes   □
        No   □

(d)   Have you taken steps to ensure widespread ownership of your anti-racism work
        and brand, amongst fans by consulting with supporter groups during the
        development of the project?

        Yes   □
        No   □

(e)   Have you approached non-governmental organisations (NGO's) with
        experience of anti-racism or social work (fan coaching, community relations) to
        support you in the project?

        Yes   □
        No   □

If Yes, please name organisation(s)_____

4.   Publicity
(a)   Are the publicity elements of the 10 point- plan (such as notices in stadiums, pitch side boards, articles in match day programmes) being implemented?

          Yes   ☐
          No   ☐

(b)   Do you intend to use anti-racism content in other official media you have available, such as web-sites, newsletters and other publications?

          Yes   ☐
          No   ☐

5.   Training
(a)   Are there any plans for you offer training in the area of racism and equal opportunities to key actors in football?

          Yes   ☐
          No   ☐

(b)   If Yes, which groups will undertake training?

          Administrative staff   ☐
          Referees   ☐
          Match observers   ☐
          Security staff or police   ☐
          Coaches   ☐
          Players   ☐
          Fans   ☐
          Others, please specify   ☐

6.   Long term planning
(a)   Please state what long-term impact you expect from the project you are planning

_____

_____

(b)   How will you ensure the project you are undertaking is not a one-off event?

_____

_____

(c)   Will you evaluate the success of the project?

          Yes   ☐
          No   ☐

(d)   If Yes how do you propose to evaluate?

          An external evaluation   ☐
          A descriptive evaluation   ☐
          Using press cuttings   ☐
          Photographs   ☐
          Web-site postings and other media   ☐
          Feed back from participants   ☐
          Feedback from fans   ☐
          Feedback from partners   ☐

Selected Bibliography

Agnew, Paddy. *Forza Italia: A Journey in Search of Italy and its Football*, London: Ebury Press, 2006.

Alegi, Peter. *Laduma! Soccer, Politics and Society in South Africa*, South Africa: University of KwaZulu-Natal Press, 2004.

Anastasakis, Othon. "Extreme Right in Europe: A Comparative Study of Recent Trends." *The Hellenic Observatory, The European Institute, London School of Economics & Political Science*. Discussion Paper, No. 3, (November 2000).

Apollon Limassol Football Club vs. Racism, Presentation given to UEFA, 2005/06.

Armstrong, Gary and Richard Giulianotti, eds. *Fear and Loathing in World Football*, New York: Berg Publishers, 2001.

Arnaut, Luis Jose. *"Independent European Sport Review."*

Arzheimer, Kai. "Extreme Right Parties in Germany. An overview." Extreme Right Electorates and Party Success <http://www.politik.uni-mainz.de/ereps/> (2 August 2006).

Asians in Football Forum. *Asians Can Play Football, Another Wasted Decade*, September 2005.

Ayliffe, Daisy. "EU and World Cup: Fighting racism. Paul Elliott's experiences as a player spurred him to become an ambassador in the fight against racism." <http://www.parliament.com> (14 June 2006).

Back, Les, Tim Crabbe and John Solomos. *The Changing Face of Football: Racism, Identity and Multiculture in the English Game*, Oxford and New York: Berg, 2001.

Baldini, Gianfranco. "Extreme Right Parties in Italy. An overview." Extreme Right Electorates and Party Success <http://www.politik.uni-mainz.de/ereps/> (2 August 2006).

Ball, Phil. *Morbo, The Story of Spanish Football*, London: WSC Books, 2003.

———. *White Storm, 100 Years of Real Madrid*, Edinburgh and London: Mainstream Publishing, 2003.

"Barcelona rejoices at UNICEF shirt deal." *International Herald Tribune*, 13 September 2006.

Bauböck, Rainer, Eva Ersbøll, Kees Groenendijk and Harald Waldrauch, eds. "Acquisition and loss of nationality. Policies and trends in 15 European States. Summary and recommendations." Results of the EU-project: *The Acquisition of Nationality in EU Member States: Rules, Practices and Quantitative Developments*. Institute for European Integration Research, Austrian Academy of Sciences, Vienna. (January 2006).

Bjørklund, Tor. "Extreme Right Parties in Scandinavia. An overview." Extreme Right Electorates and Party Success <http://www.politik.uni-mainz.de/ereps/> (2 August 2006).

Bradbury, Steven. "The New Football Communities." Executive Summary. *Sir Norman Chester Centre for Football Research, University of Leicester, UK.* (2001).

Brimson, Dougie. *Kicking Off: Why Hooliganism and Racism are Killing Football*, London, Headline Book Publishing, 2006.

Brimson, Dougie and Eddy Brimson. *Everywhere We Go: Behind the matchday madness*, Headline Review, 2006.

Brown, Adam, ed. *Fanatics! Power, identity and fandom in football*, London and New York: Routledge, 1998.

Bundesliga (DFB) website. *From Keegan to van der Vaart. . .* <http://www.dfb.de> (24 July 2006).

Bündnis Aktiver Fussballfans. "Histories and Activities." <http://aktive-fans.de> (1 November 2006).

———. "The Exhibition." <http://aktive-fans.de> (1 November 2006).

Burney, Elizabeth and Gerry Rose with the assistance of Sandradee Joseph and Rebecca Newby. Institute of Criminology, University of Cambridge. *Racist offences—how is the law working? The implementation of the legislation on racially aggravated offences in the Crime and Disorder Act 1998.* Home Office Research Study 244. Home Office Research, Development and Statistics Directorate, London: Home Office, Crown copyright 2002.

Burns, Jimmy. *Barca, A Peoples Passion*, London: Bloomsbury, 2000.

Campaign Against Racism and Fascism "Are anti-racist football campaigns reaching the grassroots? Soccer's Hidden Racism, Blowing The Whistle." <http://www.carf.demon.co.uk> (6 June 2006).

Carmichael, Fiona and Dennis Thomas. "Does the Best Team Win? An Analysis of Team Performances at EURO 2004." *Football Governance Research Centre, Birkbeck, University of London.* Research Paper No. 2. (2005).

Carnibella, Giovanni, Anne Fox, Kate Fox, Joe McCann, James Marsh and Peter Marsh. "Football violence in Europe." A report to the Amsterdam Group, *The Social Issues Research Centre.* (July 1996).

Carrington, Ben and Ian McDonald, eds. *'Race,' Sport and British Society*, London and New York: Routledge, 2004.

Carter, Elisabeth. "The Extreme Right in Austria. An overview." Extreme Right Electorates and Party Success <http://www.politik.uni-mainz.de/ereps/> (2 August 2006).

Chopin, Isabelle and Jan Niessen, eds. *Combating racial and ethnic discrimination: Taking the European legislative agenda further.* Commission for Racial Equality, Migration Policy Group, Brussels/London, March 2002.

Collins, F. Michael, Ian P. Henry, Barrie Houlihan and James Buller. "Sport and Social Exclusion." A report to the Department for Culture, Media and Sport. *Institute of Sport and Leisure Policy, Loughborough University.* (March 1999).

Connolly, Kevin and Rab MacWilliam. *Fields of Glory, Paths of Gold: The History of European Football*, Edinburgh and London: Mainstream Publishing, 2005.

Council of Europe. "European Convention on spectator violence and misbehaviour at sports events and in particular at football matches." Strasbourg, European Treaty *Series*—No. 120, 19 August 1985.

———. "Threat posed to democracy by extremist parties and movements in Europe." Parliamentary Assembly, Resolution 1344, 2003.

———. "Racist, xenophobic and intolerant discourse in politics." Parliamentary Assembly, Resolution 1345, 2003.

————. "Combating the resurrection of nazi ideology." Report, Political Affairs Committee, Rapporteur: Mr. Mikhail Margelov, Russian Federation, European Democrat Group. Parliamentary, Doc. 10766, 19 December 2005.

Coussey, Mary. *Tackling racial equality: international comparisons.* Home Office Research Study 238. Home Office Research, Development and Statistics Directorate. London: Home Office, Crown copyright, 2002.

Crolley, Liz and David Hand. *Football, Europe and the Press*, London and Portland: Frank Cass Publishers, 2002.

Dimeo, Paul and James Mills, eds. *Soccer in South Asia*, London and Portland: Frank Cass, 2001.

Duke, Vic and Liz Crolley. *Football, Nationality, and the State*, New York: Addison Wesley Longman Publishing Company, 1996.

Eisenberg, Christane, Pierre Lanfranchi, Tony Mason and Alfred Wahl. *The FIFA Centennial Book: 100 Years of Football*, London: Weidenfeld & Nicolson, 2004.

"EU and World Cup: A red card for forced prostitution. Fifa president Sepp Blatter should stop hiding behind legal niceties and publicly condemn forced prostitution, insists Anna Záborská MEP." <http://www.parliament.com> (14 June 2006).

"EU and World Cup: A unique opportunity. The World Cup could be a showcase for promoting anti-racism, tolerance and unity, argues Claude Moraes MEP." <http://www.parliament.com> (14 June 2006).

"EU and World Cup: Champions league. Derby's youth footballers are the winners in a scheme designed to tackle inner city tensions." <http://www.parliament.com> (14 June 2006).

European Commission. Report from the Commission to the Council, with a view to safeguarding current sports structures and maintaining the social function of sport within the Community framework—*The Helsinki Report on Sport*, Brussels, 10 December 1999.

————. Initiative of the Kingdom of Belgium with a view to the adoption of a Council Decision concerning security in connection with football matches with an international dimension, (2001/C 258/06), Official Journal of the European Communities, 15 September 2001.

————. Written question by Glyn Ford (PSE) to the Commission, Subject: Racism in football, 2002.

————. Answer given by Mr Vitorino, on behalf of the Commission, 17 December 2002.

————. Press release. "Celebration Match: 50 Years in Europe & 50 Years of Europe." Brussels, 12 March 2007.

————. Directorate—General Employment, Social Affairs and Equal Opportunities, Discrimination in the European Union, Special Eurobarometer 263/Wave 65.4—TNS Opinion and Social, January 2007.

————. DG Education & Culture. "Studies on Education and Sport, Sport and Multiculturalism." Final Report by PMP in partnership with the Institute of Sport and Leisure Policy, Loughborough University, August 2004.

European Commission against Racism and Intolerance. "The implementation of European anti-discrimination legislation: work in progress. The implementation of the Racial Equality Directive (2000/43/EC) and the Employment Equality Directive (2000/78/EC) as it relates to religion and belief in 15 EU Member States." Isabelle Chopin, Janet Cormack and Jan Niessen (eds.), Migration Policy Group, December 2004.

————. "Examples of good practices: Specialised bodies to combat racism, xenophobia, anti-Semitism and intolerance at national level." January 2006.

————. "Third Report on France." Adopted on 25 June 2004, Strasbourg, 15 February 2005.

————. "Third Report on Germany." Adopted on 5 December 2003, Strasbourg, June 2004.

————. "Third Report on Italy." Adopted on 16 December 2005, Strasbourg, May 2006.

————. "Third Report on Spain." Adopted on 24 June 2005, Strasbourg, February 2006.

————. "Third Report on the United Kingdom." Adopted on 17 December 2004, Strasbourg, June 2005.

————. "General policy recommendation No. 8 on combating racism while fighting terrorism." Adopted on 17 March 2004. Strasbourg, June 2004, Published by the European Commission against Racism and Intolerance, Council of Europe, 2004.

————. "General policy recommendation No. 9 on the fight against anti-Semitism." Adopted on 25 June 2004. Published by the European Commission against Racism and Intolerance, Council of Europe, 2004.

————. "The use of racist, antisemitic and xenophobic elements in political discourse." High-level panel meeting, on the occasion of the International Day for the Elimination of Racial Discrimination, Paris, 21 March 2005, November 2005.

————. "Racism in Rural Areas." Final Report. Dr. Jochen Blaschke and Guillermo Ruiz Torres. Berliner Institut für Vergleichende Sozialforschung Mitglied im Europäinschen Migrationszentrum (in cooperation with Eurofor), 30 November 2002.

————. "Migrants, minorities and legislation: Documenting legal measures and remedies against discrimination in 15 Member States of the European Union." Report submitted by the International Centre for Migration Policy Development (ICMPD) on behalf of the European Monitoring Centre on Racism and Xenophobia (EUMC), Principal authors: Haleh Chahrokh, Wolfgang Klug, Veronika Bilger, Luxembourg: Office for Official Publications of the European Communities, December 2004.

————. "Racist violence in the 15 EU Member States: A comparative overview of findings from the RAXEN National Focal Points Reports 2001–2004." April 2005.

————. "Migrants, minorities and education: Documenting discrimination and integration in 15 Member States of the European Union." Report submitted by Dr Mikael Luciak on EUMC, Luxembourg: Office for Official Publications of the European Communities, 2004.

————. "Overview of theories, hypotheses and results on attitudes of majorities towards minorities." Report 1 for EUMC. Marcel Coenders, Dr. Marcel Lubbers, Prof. Dr. Peer Scheepers University of Nijmegen, Nijmegen Institute for Social and Cultural Research, Department of Social Science Research Methodology, Department of Sociology. April 2003.

————. "Majorities' attitudes towards minorities in European Union Member States, Results from the Standard Eurobarometers 1997-2000-2003." Report 2 for EUMC. Dr. Marcel Coenders, Dr. Marcel Lubbers, Prof. Dr. Peer Scheepers, University of Nijmegen, Nijmegen Institute for Social and Cultural Research, Department of Social Science Research Methodology, Department of Sociology. April 2003.

————. "Majorities' attitudes towards minorities in (former) Candidate Countries of the European Union: Results from the Eurobarometer in Candidate Countries 2003." Report 3 for EUMC. Dr. Marcel Coenders, Dr. Marcel Lubbers, Prof. Peer Scheepers, University of Nijmegen, Nijmegen Institute for Social and Cultural Research, Department of Social Science Research Methodology, Department of Sociology. April 2003.

————. "Majorities' attitudes towards minorities in Western and Eastern European Societies: Results from the European Social Survey 2002–2003." Report 4 for EUMC. Dr. Marcel Coenders, Dr. Marcel Lubbers, Prof. Peer Scheepers, University of Nijmegen, Nijmegen Institute for Social and Cultural Research, Department of Social Science Research Methodology Sociology. April 2003.

————. "Racism, Football and the Internet." On behalf EUMC, by Unione Italiana Sport per Tutti; Comitato regionale Emili-Romagna, Carlo Balestri, Giusi Grasselli, Gerd Dembowski, Stefan Diener, Vienna, April 2002.

————. Working definition of anti-Semitism.

————. Media Release, "Anti-racism in football network FARE win first Jean Kahn Award." Vienna, 30 October 2003.

————. "The impact of 7 July 2005 London Bomb attacks on Muslim communities in the EU." Vienna, November 2005.

————. "Migrants' experiences of racism and xenophobia in 12 EU Member States." Pilot Study. May 2006.

————. "How to combine Integration and Diversities: The challenge of an EU multicultural citizenship." Discussion paper. Marco Martiniello, University of Liège, Vienna 2004.

————. Media Release, "Attitudes towards Migrants and Minorities in Europe, European Monitoring Centre on Racism and Xenophobia releases Eurobarometer and European Social Survey analysis." 15 March 2005.

European Council. Decision of 25 April 2002, concerning security in connection with football matches with an international dimension, (2002/348/JHA), Official Journal of the European Communities, 8 May 2002.

————. Resolution of 6 December 2001, concerning a handbook with recommendations for international police cooperation and measures to prevent and control violence and disturbances in connection with football matches with an international dimension, in which at least one Member State is involved, (2002/C 22/01), Official Journal of the European Communities, 24 January 2002.

————. Resolution of 17 November 2003, on the use by Member States of bans on access to venues of football matches with an international dimension, (2003/C 281/01), Official Journal of the European Union, 22 November 2003.

European Parliament. Written declaration on tackling racism in football, 14 March 2006.

————. Session document. "Countering racism and xenophobia in the European Union." Committee on Citizens' Freedoms and Rights, Justice and Home Affairs, 28 February 2000.

————. Session document. "The situation as regards fundamental rights in the European Union." Committee on Citizens' Freedoms and Rights, Justice and Home Affairs, 21 August 2003.

————. Session document. "The situation as regards fundamental rights in the European Union." Committee on Citizens' Freedoms and Rights, Justice and Home Affairs, 22 March 2004.

————. Session document. "Commission report to the European Council with a view to safeguarding current sports structures and maintaining the social function of sport within the Community framework—The Helsinki Report on Sport." Committee on Culture, Youth, Education, the Media and Sport, 18 July 2000.

Evans, A. J. Jocelyn (University of Salford)., and Gilles Ivaldi (CIDSP-IEP, Grenoble). "Electoral dynamics of the European extreme right." Translation of "Les dynamiques électorales de l'extrême-droite européenne," in Revue Politique et Parlementaire (Juillet-Août 2002). Extreme Right Electorates and Party Success <http://www.politik.uni-mainz.de/ereps/> (30 August 2006).

Fax from Cyprus Football Association, "Request to carry out anti-racism campaign denied" November 2006.

Fédération Internationale de Football Association. "The colourful history of a fascinating game, More than 2000 Years of Football." by Gerhardt, Wilfried (Officer for the German Football Asoociation), Frankfurrt/Main, Germany. <http://www.fifa.com> (13 September 2006)

————. "The cradle of football." by Brinker, Helmut <http://www.fifa.com> (19 October 2004).

————. "100 years of debates over player nationality and status." <http://www.fifa.com> (13 September 2006).

————. "From Paris to Zurich, 30 years of trials and tribulations." <http://www.fifa.com> (13 September 2006).

————. "History of FIFA." <http://www.fifa.com> (13 September 2006).

————. "International Football Association Board. Ten dates that changed the game." <http://www.fifa.com> (13 September 2006).

————. "FIFA against Racism." <http://www.fifa.com> (13 September 2006).

————. "Amendment to article 55 of the FIFA Disciplinary Code." <http://www.fifa.com> (13 September 2006).

————. "Racism in Football: Kicking racism out—once and for all." <http://www.fifa.com> (13 September 2006).

————. "FIFA'S Anti-Racism Campaign. Talking Racism in Hitler's Stadium." Spiegel Online 2006, by Kaiser, Mario <http://www.fifa.com> (4 July 2006).

————. "FIFA Endeavours." <http://www.fifa.com> (13 September 2006).

————. "FIFA extraordinary congress Buenos Aires Resolution. Football Unites, Racism Divides." <http://www.fifa.com> (7 July 2001).

Finn, Gerry and Richard Giulianotti, eds. Football Culture: Local Conflicts, Global Visions, London and Portland: Frank Cass Publishers, 2000.

Fishwick, Nicholas and Donald F. Bittner. (Review author). "English Football and Society, 1910–1950." The American Historical Review Vol. 96, No. 1. (February 1991):172-173.

Fisher, Stephen. "The Vlaams Blok in Flanders. An overview." Extreme Right Electorates and Party Success <http://www.politik.uni-mainz.de/ereps/> (2 August 2006).

Flutlicht. "A useful passing game." <http://www.flutlicht.org> (1 November 2006).

————. "Are you Yurdum, or what?" <http://www.flutlicht.org> (1 November 2006).

————. "Clubs with a conscience." <http://www.flutlicht.org> (1 November 2006).

————. "Football Against Racism in Europe." <http://www.flutlicht.org> (1 November 2006).

————. "Football alone is not enough." by Lanfranchi, Pierre <http://www.flutlicht.org> (1 November 2006).

————. "Human trafficking and plunder?" <http://www.flutlicht.org> (1 November 2006).

————. "Kicking Racism out of Football." <http://www.flutlicht.org> (1 November 2006).

————. "Prevention or stopping the match." <http://www.flutlicht.org> (1 November 2006).

————. "Racism in a new guise." <http://www.flutlicht.org> (1 November 2006).

————. "The ball as a migrant." <http://www.flutlicht.org> (1 November 2006).

————. "The Mondiali—festival and protest." <http://www.flutlicht.org> (1 November 2006).

————. "The scapegoat." <http://www.flutlicht.org> (1 November 2006).

————. "Different Roots—One Game." <http://www.flutlicht.org> (1 November 2006).

Foer, Franklin. *How Soccer Explains the World: An Unlikely Theory of Globalization*, New York: Harper Perennial, 2005.

Foot, John. *Calcio, A History of Italian Football*, London: Fourth Estate, 2006.

Football Against Racism in Europe. "World Cup Summary. No. 1." <http://www.farenet.org> (June 12th 2006).

————. "European Parliament team up against racism." <http://www.farenet.org> (15 March 2006).

————. "Finals in Cup of Friendship and Tolerance in Slovakia." <http://www.farenet.org> (22 September 2006).

————. "Team captains speak out against racism." <http://www.farenet.org> (22 June 2006).

————. "Media Information, FARE Action Week launched by Champions." (Vienna/London, 17 October 2006) <http://www.farenet.org> (18 October 2006).

————. "Broad support from Venice fans for 2006 Action Week, 17 October 2006." <http://www.farenet.org> (29 October 2006).

————. "European Football fights Racism and Celebrates the Beautiful Game, 20 October 2006." <http://www.farenet.org> (29 October 2006).

————. "Media Information, European Football get ready for Action Week against Racism, (Vienna/London, 11 October 2006)." <http://www.farenet.org> (12 October 2006).

————. "Media Information, "Make racism a thing of the past"—European Football is fighting racism and celebrating the beautiful game." <http://www.farenet.org> (20 October 2006).

————. "German Week of Action off to a great start." <http://www.farenet.org> (23 October 2006).

————. "Media Information, Cologne, Anti-racism network sees positive start to World Cup." <http://www.farenet.org> (20 June 2006).

————. "Media information, Vienna, Balkans' youngsters unite through football." <http://www.farenet.org> (2 August 2006).

————. "Media Information, Croatian fans form human swastika in Italy." <http://www.farenet.org> (17 August 2006).

———. "Polish fans displayed Nazi banner in Vienna." <http://www.farenet.org> (3 October 2006).

———. "Racist incident at Borac Cacak in Serbia." <http://www.farenet.org> (17 October 2006).

———. "World Cup summary No. 1." <http://www.farenet.org> (12 June 2006).

———. "Partnership with the European Commission." <http://www.farenct.org> (22 December 2005).

———. "FARE pushes the campaign in Eastern Europe." <http://www.farenet.org> (22 December 2005).

———. "MEPs call for tougher action on racism." <http://www.farenet.org> (11 March 2006).

———. "Di Canio repeats fascist salute." <http://www.farenet.org> (14 December 2005).

———. "Partnership with UEFA." <http://www.farenet.org> (22 December 2005).

———. "Joint Media Release of FIFA, LOC and FARE, Football against racism at the 2006 FIFA World Cup—alliance between FIFA, LOC and FARE." <http://www.farenet.org> (9 June 2006).

———. "Media information—Mandela backs anti-racism initiatives." <http://www.farenet.org> (30 June 2006).

———. "Media information—World Cup finalists back." <http://www.farenet.org> (7 July 2006).

———. "Media information—Cup summary, Number 3. World Cup Quarter Finals to highlight football's drive against racism" <http://www.farenet.org> (29 June 2006).

———. "Media Information—FARE and FIFA joint World Cup programme announced." <http://www.farenet.org> (9 June 2006).

———. "Media Information—Mondiali Antirazzisti celebrates 10th birthday." <http://www.farenet.org> (13 July 2006).

———. "Ball work. Scenes from football and migration. New exhibition on football and migration opens in Hamburg." <http://www.farenet.org> (15 November 2006).

———. "Media information—Polish national team send out a clear message." <http://www.farenet.org> (14 June 2006).

———. "Campaigning for a football without discrimination."<http://www.farenet.org> (22 December 2005).

———. "Cadiz Action Week. Conference, artistic and sportive events." <http://www.farenet.org> (3 November 2006).

———. "Racism Breaks the Game." <http://www.farenet.org> (7 November 2006).

———. "Death of fan at PSG in atmosphere of racism and anti-Semitism." <http://www.farenet.org> (24 November 2006).

———. "Tension remains between Zoro and Inter fans." <http://www.farenet.org> (18 December 2006).

———. "Action Week Against Racism 2006." <http://www.farenet.org> (2 October 2006).

"Football and football hooliganism." Fact sheet 1. *Sir Norman Chester Centre for Football Research, University of Leicester, UK.* (January 2001).

Football Foundation. *Annual Report 2000/2001*, (2001).

Football Governance Research Centre, Birkbeck. *Building Sustainable Supporters, Trusts in the West Midlands.* Interim Report April 2003, University of London & the Cooperative College, Manchester, Research Paper, No. 3. (2003).

Football Task Force. *Eliminating Racism from Football,* Submitted to the Minister for Sport (30 March 1998).

————. *Investing in the community,* Submitted to the Minister for Sport (January 1999).

Football Unites Racism Divides. *Review 2003* (2004).

————. *Reducing Racial Harassment*

————. *The first 10 years 1995–2005* (2006).

————. *Annual Report 2000–2001* (2001).

————. "Anti-racist education, Why education and football?" <http://www.furd.org> (7 July 2006).

————. "Racist incidents." <http://www.furd.org> (7 July 2006).

————. "The European dimension." <http://www.furd.org> (7 July 2006).

————. "Racism Divides, Where are the Asian players?" <http://www.furd.org> (7 July 2006).

Garland, Jon and Michael Rowe. (Scarman Centre, University of Leicester). "Antiracism in Football: Has the Bubble Burst?" in *Football Review 2000–01 Season,* Singer & Friedlander. Produced in association with and hosted by The Centre for Research into Sport and Society at the University of Leicester.

Garland, Jon and Michael Rowe. *Racism and Anti-Racism in Football,* Basingstoke and New York: Palgrave, 2001.

Giulianotti, Richard and John Williams, eds. *Game Without Frontiers: Football, Identity and Modernity,* Aldershot: Arena, 1994.

Giulianotti, Richard, Norman Bonney and Mike Hepworth, eds. *Football, Violence and Social Identity,* London and New York: Routledge, 1999.

Giulianotti, Richard. *Football: A Sociology of the Global Game,* Polity Press, 1999.

Goldblatt, David. *The Ball is Round: A Global History of Football,* Viking (an imprint of Penguin Books), 2002.

Hamil, Sean, Jonathan Michie and Christine Oughton. "A Game of Two Halves? The Business of Football." *Football Governance Research Centre, Birkbeck, University of London,* 1999.

Hare, Geoff. *Football in France: A Cultural History,* Berg: Oxford and New York, 2003.

Harris, Nick. *England, their England: The definitive story of foreign footballers in the English game since 1888,* East Sussex: Pitch Publishing, 2003.

Hesse-Lichtenberger Ulrich. *Tor! The Story of German Football,* London: WSC Books, 2003.

Home Office. *Statistics on football-related arrests & banning orders. Season 2001–2002,* 7 August 2002.

————. *Statistics on football-related arrests & banning orders. Season 2002–2003,* 18 August 2003.

————. *Statistics on football-related arrests & banning orders. Season 2003–2004,* 23 October 2004.

————. *Statistics on football-related arrests & banning orders. Season 2004–05,* 4 November 2005.

————. *Statistics on football-related arrests & banning orders. Season 2005–2006,* 21 October 2006.

————. *Impact of measures introduced by the Football (Disorder) Act 2000. Report to Parliament."* November 2005.

————. *Home Office guidance on football-related legislation.*

————. *Statutory Instruments 2004 Nos. 2409 and 2410: The Football Spectators, (Prescription) Order 2004 & The Football (Offences) (Designation of Football Matches)*, Updated July 2005.

Irish Football Association. *Football For All*, by Robin Wilson, December 2005.

Justin, Mathieu. "Background analysis; Football World cup: Risk at racist and fascist violence." *European Strategic Intelligence and Security Center*, (June 2006).

Karagiannis, Voris. Selected articles from Cyprus daily 'Haravgi,' October–November 2005.

Kick It Out. "German FA tries to purge NAZI past before World Cup." by Kirschbaum, Erik (Reuters) <http://www.kickitout.org> (11 April 2006).

————. German police urge NAZI march ban." <http://www.kickitout.org> (4 May 2006).

————. "Pardew seeks end to 'war of words' with Wenger." <http://www.kickitout.org> (16 March 2006).

————. "Countdown begins to the largest series of anti-racism activities in Europe." <http://www.kickitout.org> (October 2005).

————. "Media information. Football building bridges for the displaced." <http://www.kickitout.org> (29 June 2005).

————. "New FIFA rules." <http://www.kickitout.org> (30 March 2006).

————. "Pioneers, past masters and future challenges." <http://www.kickitout.org> (30 September 2004).

————. "About us." <http://www.kickitout.org> (19 March 2006).

————. "Asians in Football." <http://www.kickitout.org> (30 March 2006).

————. "Banning orders issued for racist chanting." <http://www.kickitout.org> (1 May 2006).

————. "Blatter backtracks on points deduction for racism." <http://www.kickitout.org> (27 April 2006).

————. "British embassy host anti-racism event." <http://www.kickitout.org> (5 May 2006).

————. "Bulgarian side fined for racist abuse." <http://www.kickitout.org> (26 April 2006).

————. "Croatia stadium abuse condemned." <http://www.kickitout.org> (14 February 2006).

————. "Cut sound or colour from racist football matches, TV firms urged." <http://www.kickitout.org> (11 March 2006).

————. "England and Israel join for anti-racism football campaign." <http://www.kickitout.org> (8 March 2006).

————. "Eto'o makes anti-racism protest." <http://www.kickitout.org> (27 February 2006).

————. "Eto'o subjected to racist chants at Racing Santander." <http://www.kickitout.org> (9 April 2006).

————. "EURO MP'S join call for action to tackle racism." <http://www.kickitout.org> (13, 16 March 2006).

————. "European Declaration." <http://www.kickitout.org> (19 March 2006).

————."FIFA beef up rules." <http://www.kickitout.org> (16 March 2006).

————. "FIFA investigates Zidane red card." <http://www.kickitout.org> (11 July 2006).

————. "FIFA ready to make show of opposition to racism." <http://www.kickitout.org> (7 June 2006).

————. "France adjusts to racially diverse team." <http://www.kickitout.org> (9 July 2006).

————. "Glasgow United." <http://www.kickitout.org> (22 April 2006).

————. "Gyan subjected to racial abuse." <http://www.kickitout.org> (16 March 2006).

————. "Iranians seeking politics-free sport." <http://www.kickitout.org> (23 June 2006).

————. "Italian FA adopts FIFA anti-racism measures." <http://www.kickitout.org> (31 March 2006).

————. "German neo NAZI group banned for World Cup racism." <http://www.kickitout.org> (5 July 2006).

————. "Nuremberg protest over Iran visit." <http://www.kickitout.org> (11 June 2006).

————. "Racism in European Football." <http://www.kickitout.org> (30 March 2006).

————. "Religions unite through football to promote understanding." <http://www.kickitout.org> (4 May 2006).

————. "Russian League clamps down on racism." <http://www.kickitout.org> (28 March 2006).

————. "Spanish fans reignite racism row." <http://www.kickitout.org> (29 June 2006).

————. "Stop racist neo-NAZIS at World Cup says Asamoah." <http://www.kickitout.org> (30 May 2006).

————. "Swastika fan given 25-month match ban." <http://www.kickitout.org> (14 June 2006).

————. "Top Romanian clubs punished over racist behaviour." <http://www.kickitout.org> (26 May 2006).

————. "Zoro calls for sanctions after fresh abuse." <http://www.kickitout.org> (3 April 2006).

————. "Sign of the cross by Celtic goalkeeper 'was not an offence.'" <http://www.kickitout.org> (29 August 2006).

————. "Africans lead charts in Europe." <http://www.kickitout.org> (3 November 2006).

————. "Agbonlahor warned over England." <http://www.kickitout.org> (12 October 2006).

————. "Anti-racism success of World Cup 2006 should spur action at EU level." <http://www.kickitout.org> (5 July 2006).

————. "Aragonés will not say sorry." <http://www.kickitout.org> (27 June 2006).

————. "Asamoah targeted by racist taunts." <http://www.kickitout.org> (12 September 2006).

————. "Cameroon International tells of the dangerous situation in Russia." <http://www.kickitout.org> (8 August 2006).

————. "Croatian fans form human swastika in Italy." <http://www.kickitout.org> (18 August 2006).

————. "Croatian racists a 'National disgrace.'" <http://www.kickitout.org> (18 August 2006).

————. "German DFB fine Rostock for racist chants." <http://www.kickitout.org> (15 September 2006).

————. "Germany under 21 striker hunt handed two-match ban." <http://www.kickitout.org> (10 November 2006).

————. "Kick It Out welcome ban." <http://www.kickitout.org> (26 October 2006).

————. "Racism blights Zaragoza again." <http://www.kickitout.org> (3 October 2006).

————. "Racism sanctions reduced." <http://www.kickitout.org> (6 September 2006).

————. "Rangers revive traditional songs." <http://www.kickitout.org> (4 August 2006).

————. "Ref praised for handling of racist chants." <http://www.kickitout.org> (18 September 2006).

————. "Reports of sectarian chanting at Celtic." <http://www.kickitout.org> (15 November 2006).

————. "Roberts—I was racially abused." <http://www.kickitout.org> (31 October 2006).

————. "Pioneers, past masters and future challenges." <http://www.kickitout.org> (30 September 2004).

————. "Fan banned for three years." by Traynor, Luke (Liverpool Echo) <http://www.kickitout.org> (11 December 2006).

————. "Henry launches charity." by Huggins, Trevor (Reuters) <http://www.kickitout.org> (7 December 2006).

————. "Paris Mayor warns PSG." <http://www.kickitout.org> (11 December 2006).

————. "Scottish FA announce new measures against sectarianism." <http://www.kickitout.org> (12 December 2006).

————. "UEFA fine Levski for racist chants." <http://www.kickitout.org> (2 May 2006).

————. "Asian football network set for launch." <http://www.kickitout.org> (1 January 2007).

————. "Barnes: black bosses don't get a fair chance." by McGrath, Mike (PA Sport) <http://www.kickitout.org> (4 January 2007).

————. "FA investigate claims of racist abuse." by Ducker, James (The Times) <http://www.kickitout.org> (3 January 2007).

————. "Ince says age of most chairmen is bar to black managers." by Fifield, Dominic (The Guardian) <http://www.kickitout.org> (5 January 2007).

————. "Paul Ince manager." <http://www.kickitout.org> (2 January 2007).

————. "Fans receive bans for racism." <http://www.kickitout.org> (9 January 2007).

————. "Atletico fined and threatened with stadium closure." <http://www.kickitout.org> (23 January 2007).

————. "Getafe fans chant racist abuse at Valencia's Miguel." <http://www.kickitout.org> (12 January 2007).

————. "Posh part company with Alexander." <http://www.kickitout.org> (15 January 2007).

————. Smith, Faith. "Study reports: Chinese fans prefer three Lions." <http://www.kickitout.org> (18 January 2007).

————. "Aragones fine for racist comments overturned." <http://www.kickitout.org> (February 2007)

————. "Life ban for racist fan in Germany." <http://www.kickitout.org> (5 February 2007).

————. "Football fans charged over racist chanting." <http://www.kickitout.org> (20 March 2006).

————. "Football fan banned for racial abuse." <http://www.kickitout.org> (13 September 2006).

————. "Spectacular night in Manchester." <http://www.kickitout.org> (14 March 2007).

————. *Racial Equality Standard for Professional Clubs*. Awarded by Kick It Out.

King, Andy. *The European Ritual: Football in the New Europe*, Aldershot: Ashgate, 2003.

King, Colin. *Offside Racism: Playing the White Man*, Oxford and New York: Berg, 2004.

Kissinger, Henry. "World Cup According to Character," *The Los Angeles Times*, 29 June 1986.

Kuper, Simon. *Soccer Against the Enemy: How the World's Most Popular Sport Starts and Stops Wars, Fuels Revolution, and Keeps Dictators in Power*, New York: Nation Books, 2006.

———. *Football Against the Enemy*, London: Orion, 1996.

Long, Jonathan, Kevin Hylton, Mel Welsch and Jon Dart. *"Part of the Game? An examination of the levels of Racism in Amateur Football."* School of Leisure & Sports Studies, Leeds Metropolitan University, Published September 2000.

Lowrey, James, Sam Neatrour and John Williams. "The Bosman Ruling, Football Transfers and Foreign Footballers." Fact sheet 16. *Sir Norman Chester Centre for Football Research, University of Leicester, UK.* (August 2002).

Malcolm, Dominic and Oliver Last. "A Game of Two Halves?: The Experiences of Black Footballers" in *Football Review 1998–99 Season*, Singer & Friedlander. Produced in association with and hosted by The Centre for Research into Sport and Society at the University of Leicester.

Marschik, Matthias. "Between Manipulation and Resistance: Viennese Football in the Nazi Era." *Journal of Contemporary History*, Vol. 34, No. 2 (April. 1999): 215–229.

Martin, Simon. *Football and Fascism: The National Game Under Mussolini*, Oxford and New York: Berg Publishers, 2005.

May, Pete. *Football and Its Followers*, London and Sydney: Franklin Watts, 2004.

Merkel, Udo., and Walter Tokorski, eds. *Racism and Xenophobia in European Football*, Aachen: Meyer & Meyer, 1996.

Missiroli, Antonio. "Playing the European Game." *Center for European Reform Bulletin*, Issue 24 (June/July 2002).

Murphy, Patrick and Ivan Waddington, eds. *Soccer Review 2003*. Facilitated by the Professional Footballers Association, Published by Patrick Murphy & Ivan Waddington, Produced by Anchor Print. 2003.

Murray, Bill. *The Old Firm in the New Age: Celtic and Rangers since the Souness revolution*, Edinburgh: Mainstream Publishing, 1998.

Murray, Bill. *The World's Game: A History of Soccer*, Urbana and Chicago, University of Illinois Press, 1998.

Never Again Association. "Let's kick racism out of the stadiums" <http://www.nigdywiecej.prh> (1 November 2006).

———. "Let's kick racism out of football." <http://www.nigdywiecej.prh.> (1 November 2006).

Parks, Tim. *A Season with Verona*, London: Vintage, 2003.

Pearson, Geoff. "The Bosman case, EU Law and the transfer system." Fact sheet 1. *Football Industry Group, University of Liverpool*. This fact sheet has been put together with the kind cooperation of Liverpool FC.

Perryman, Mark. *Hooligan Wars: Causes and Effects of Football Violence*, Edinburgh and London: Mainstream Publishing, 2002.

Poli, Raffaele., and Loic Ravenel. "Annual Review of the European Football Player's Labour Market." *International Center for Sport Studies*. (2006).

Premier League. *Annual charter reports, season 2001/2002*, (2002).

———. *Annual charter reports, season 2003/04*, (2004).

———. *Annual charter reports, season 2004/05*, (2005).

———. *National Fan Survey 2001*, (2001).

———. *National Fan Survey—Research Report. Season 2002/03*, (2003).

———. *National Fan Survey Report, Season 2003/04*, (2004).

————. *National Fan Survey Report. Season 2004/05*, (2005).

————. *National Fan Survey Report. Season 2005–2006*, (2006).

————. *Football For All*, 2004.

————. *Annual Report 2003/04*, (2004).

————. *Annual Report 2004/05*, (2005).

————. *Annual report 2005/06*, (2006).

————. *Community Report 2003/04*, (2004).

————. *Community Report 2004/05. Young people matter*, (2005).

————. *Community Report 2005/06*, (2006).

————. *Customer Charter Report 2003–2004*, (2004).

————. *Annual Review 2002–03*, (2003).

————. *Annual Review 2004–05*, (2005).

Progetto Ultra. "About us" <http://www.progettoultra.it> (1 November 2006).

Redhead, Steve. *The Passion and the Fashion: Football fandom in the New Europe*, Aldershot: Avebury, 1993.

Rufino, Filipe. "EU kicks off 50th birthday with football match," <http://www.eupolitix.com> (12 March 2007).

Schalker Fan-Initiative. "An Introduction." <http://www.fan-ini> (1 November 2006).

Sharma, Aj. "Promoting racial equality through sport, a standard for local authority sport and leisure services." Commission for Racial Equality. October 2004.

Show Racism the Red Card. *Annual Review 2004*, (2005)

Sibbitt, Rae. *The perpetrators of racial harassment and racial violence.* Home Office Research Study 176. Research and Statistics Directorate. London: Home Office, Crown copyright. First published 1997.

Sir Norman Chester Centre for Football Research. University of Leicester, UK, *New Findings in FA Premier League 2001 National Fan Survey*, (2002).

————. University of Leicester, UK *Racism and Football*, Fact Sheet 6 (June 2002).

————. University of Leicester, UK *Black Footballers in Britain*. Fact Sheet 4. (June 2002).

————. University of Leicester, UK. *A Profile of FA Premier League Club Supporters in 2000*. Fact Sheet 13. (2000).

Sport England Research. Rowe, Nick and Ross Champion. "Sports Participation and Ethnicity in England. National Survey 1999/2000." <http://www.sportengland.org> October 2000.

————. *Making English sport inclusive: Equity guidelines for governing bodies*, London, Governing Body Resource Pack, Planning for sport, Factfiles: Sports equity, June 2000.

————. Rowe, Nick and Ross Champion. "Sports Participation and Ethnicity in England, National Survey 1999/2000. Headline Findings." Sport England Research. <http://www.sportengland.org> October 2000.

Stephen, Herbert. *Stamping out racism in football*, This briefing provides background to the issue of racism in Scottish football and on the role of the 'Show Racism the Red Card' campaign, for a Member's debate in the Chamber on Tuesday 18 May 2004, on motion S2M-1214 in the name of Bill Butler MSP, Scottish Parliament Information Centre (SPICe)

Tacon, Richard. "Football and Social Inclusion: Evaluating Social Policy." *Football Governance Research Centre, Birkbeck, University of London*, Research Paper, No. 1. (2005).

The BME Sports Network East. *Increasing BME Participation in Sport & Physical Activity by Black and Minority Ethnic Communities*, A Report by Ploszajski Lynch Consulting Ltd. January 2005.

The Football Association. *The FA Annual Review 2003/04. Putting Football First*, (2004).

———. "Combating racism." <http://www.thefa.com> (19 November 2004).

———. "England the example." <http://www.thefa.com> (14 December 2005).

———. "Equality work recognized." <http://www.thefa.com> (16 May 2006).

———. "FA acts on Euro racism." <http://www.thefa.com> (30 March 2000).

———. "FA backs UEFA race probe." <http://www.thefa.com> (25 September 2002).

———. "FA reports racism." <http://www.thefa.com> (18 November 2004).

———. "FA spells out racist language." <http://www.thefa.com> (25 April 2004).

———. "Funding Fair for All." <http://www.thefa.com> (8 December 2005).

———. "Get on the ladder." By Stone, Alex <http://www.thefa.com> (22 November 2005).

———. "Palios on racism." <http://www.thefa.com> (10 February 2004).

———. "Response to FIFA verdict." <http://www.thefa.com> (21 December 2004).

———. "UEFA investigate racist abuse." <http://www.thefa.com> (13 October 2002).

The Independent Football Commission, "Independent Football Commission Annual Report 2004" <http:www.theifc.co.uk> 2005.

Tomlinson, Alan and Christopher Young, eds. *German Football: History, Culture, Society*, London and New York: Routledge, 2005.

Union of European Football Associations. *We care about football. UEFA Executive Committee Report 2005, XXX Ordinary UEFA Congress*, Budapest, Hungary.

———. "Unite against racism in European football, UEFA guide to good practice." Produced by UEFA & FARE, Printed and published by UEFA Communications and Public Affairs Division. <http://www.uefa.com> (June 2003).

———. "Anti-racism week ends on high." <http://www.uefa.com> (31 October 2006).

———. "European football's modern democracy." <http://www.uefa.com> (31 March 2006).

———. "Balkan sides battle bigots." <http://www.uefa.com> (4 August 2006).

———. "Bringing cultures together." <http://www.uefa.com> (13 July 2006).

———. "Clubs given anti-racism backing." <http://www.uefa.com> (25 August 2006).

———. "DFB launches racism inquiry." <http://www.uefa.com> (19 September 2006).

———. "Eto'o defiance earns respect." <http://www.uefa.com> (28 February 2006).

———. "History helped rangers." by Roberts, Chris <http://www.uefa.com> (14 April 2006).

———. "Italy opens doors to world." by Menicucci, Paolo <http://www.uefa.com> 19 July 2006

———. "UEFA, Protecting football's image." <http://www.uefa.com> (28 July 2006).

———. "Rewarded for uniting fans." <http://www.uefa.com> (24 August 2006).

———. "Blot on German landscape." by Honigstein, Raphael <http://www.uefa.com> (21 April 2006).

———. "Cannavaro and Zidane speak out." <http://www.uefa.com> (7 July 2006).

———. "Ceo says Euro2008 can help ant-racism drive." <http://www.uefa.com> (18 May 2006).

———. "EC support for homegrown plan." by Szreter, Adam <http://www.uefa.com> (4 May 2006).

———. "FARE at the World Cup." <http://www.uefa.com> (13 June 2006).

———. "FARE learns for 2008." <http://www.uefa.com> (20 June 2006).

————. "FARE play in Nyon." <http://www.uefa.com> (24 October 2006).

————. "High profile for Action Week." <http://www.uefa.com> (10 October 2006).

————. "Last eight lend their weight." <http://www.uefa.com> (30 June 2006).

————. "Preserving the local identity." by Harrold, Michael and Adam Szreter <http://www.uefa.com> (21 April 2006).

————. "Racism sanctions for World Cup." <http://www.uefa.com> (6 April 2006).

————. "The week in UEFA." <http://www.uefa.com> (12 October 2006).

————. "UEFA to clamp down on racism." <http://www.uefa.com> (12 April 2006).

————. "Top clubs take Action." <http://www.uefa.com> (20 October 2006).

————. "Anti-racism initiative unveiled." <http://www.uefa.com> (17 February 2006).

————. "Barcelona of crucial importance." by Harrold, Michael <http://www.uefa.com> (1 February 2006).

————. "Call for players to join fight." by Chaplin, Mark <http://www.uefa.com> (2 February 2006).

————. "Club guide in the pipeline." by Chaplin, Mark <http://www.uefa.com> (14 February 2006).

————. "Delegates await Camp Nou talks." by Chaplin, Mark <http://www.uefa.com> (31 January 2006).

————. "Denmark boosts grassroots." <http://www.uefa.com> (3 February 2006).

————. "EXCO emphasises the positives." <http://www.uefa.com> (23 March 2006).

————. "Kerr states his case, Wednesday." by Farrelly, David <http://www.uefa.com> (1 February 2006).

————. "Leeds show the way, Tuesday." by Harrold, Michael <http://www.uefa.com> (24 January 2006).

————. "Olsson urges anti-racism action." <http://www.uefa.com> (13 May 2005).

————. "Pope backs anti-racism fight." <http://www.uefa.com> (2 March 2006).

————. "Seminal moment in Barcelona." by Chaplin, Mark and Adam Szreter <http://www.uefa.com> (31 January 2006).

————. "Showing the example." <http://www.uefa.com> (20 January 2006).

————. "Spain's battle against racism." by Chaplin, Mark <http://www.uefa.com> (10 January 2006).

————. "UEFA's raison d'être." by Szreter, Adam <http://www.uefa.com> (10 March 2006).

————. "United against the racists." <http://www.uefa.com> (17 January 2006).

————. "Uniting to eliminate racism." by Chaplin, Mark <http://www.uefa.com> (1 February 2006.

————. "You're not going to hurt me." by Brown, Lucas <http://www.uefa.com> (21 February 2006).

————. "Eyes of Europe on Bucharest." <http://www.uefa.com> (28 March 2006).

————. "Cup events to close FARE Action Week." <http://www.uefa.com> (1 November 2006).

————. "Belgrade's red to racism." <http://www.uefa.com> (3 November 2006).

————. "Tackling racism in club football, A guide for clubs." Second Unite Against Racism Conference. Produced by FARE for UEFA. 2006.

————. *Vision Europe*, Nyon (April 2005).

————. "Many stars join the Europe XI squad at Old Trafford." Media Release No. 36, UEFA. <http://www.uefa.com> (11 March 2007).

————. "Chronology of selected measures and projects taken by the DFB (German football association) since 2003" <http://www.uefa.com> (20 September 2006).

van Sterkenburg, Jacco, Jan W. Janssens and Bas Rijnen, eds. *Football and Racism: An inventory of the problems and solutions in eight West European countries in the framework of the Stand Up Speak Up campaign*, Nieuwegein: Arko Sports Media, 2005.

Vasili, Phil. *Colouring over the White Line: The History of Black Footballers in Britain*, Edinburgh and London: Mainstream Publishing, 2000.

Vialli, Gianluca and Gabriele Marcotti. *The Italian Job: A Journey to the heart of two great footballing cultures*, London, Toronto, Sydney, Auckland and Johannesburg: Bantam Press, 2006.

Wagg, Stephen, ed. *Giving the Game Away: Football, Politics and Culture on Five Continents*, London and New York: Leicester University Press, 1995.

Welch, Mel., Karl Spracklen and Amanda Pilcher. National Sports Development Centre at Leeds Metropolitan University, "Racial Equality in Football." No. 2004/1, Commission for Racial Equality (CRE), Published October 2004.

White, Amanda, ed. *Social Focus in Brief: Ethnicity 2002*. A National Statistics Publication. Published with the permission of the Controller of Her Majesty's Stationery Office (HMSO). London: Office for National Statistics, Crown copyright 2002.

Wilson, Jonathan. *Behind the Curtain: Travels in Eastern European Football*, London: Orion Books, 2006.

Winner, David. *Those Feet: An Intimate History of English Football*, London: Bloomsbury, 2006.

———. Brilliant Orange: The neurotic genius of Dutch football, London: Bloomsbury, 2001.

Working Group on Football Disorder, Chaired by Lord Bassam, Report and Recommendations, March 2001.

ZARA—Zivilcourage und Anti-Rassismus—Arbeit. *Racism Report 2002, Case Report on Racist Incidents and Structures in Austria, Focus: civil courage*, published by ZARA Fair Play, Fibel, Forum gegen Antisemitismus, Integrationshaus, Initiative muslimischer ÖsterreicherInnen, Peregrina, Romano Centro, WITAF—Arbeitsassistenz für Gehörlose.

Index

About the Author

Christos Kassimeris is assistant professor in political science and heads the Department of Social and Behavioral Sciences at Cyprus College in Nicosia. He is also coordinator of the European Studies (BA) and International Relations (MA) programs. Before joining Cyprus College, he was teaching European Integration Politics (BA) and International Relations of the Mediterranean (MA) for three years at the University of Reading. He has published in journals such as *Democracy and Security* and the *Journal of Comparative Policy Analysis*. He holds a PhD in political science, an MA in international security studies and a BA in sociology from the University of Reading. His research interests concern the process of European Union integration, Euro-Mediterranean relations and the external dimension of the European Union.

5002388R00153

Printed in Great Britain
by Amazon.co.uk, Ltd.,
Marston Gate.